School for Young Children

Second Edition

School for Young Children

*Developmentally
Appropriate Practices*

Charles H. Wolfgang
Florida State University

Mary E. Wolfgang
Tallahassee Community College

Allyn and Bacon

Boston • London • Toronto • Sydney • Tokyo • Singapore

Series editor: Frances Helland
Series editorial assistant: Bridget Keane
Manufacturing buyer: Suzanne Lareau
Director of education programs: Ellen Mann Dolberg
Marketing manager: Brad Parkins

Library of Congress Cataloging-in-Publication Data

Wolfgang, Charles H.
    School for young children : developmentally appropriate practices
 / Charles H. Wolfgang, Mary E. Wolfgang. -- 2nd ed.
    p.   cm.
    Includes bibliographical references and index.
    ISBN 0-205-28258-X
    1. Early childhood education--United States--Handbooks, manuals,
etc.   I. Wolfgang, Mary E.   II. Title.
LB1139.25.W65   1998
372.21--dc21   98-20686
                                      CIP

Printed in the United States of America
10 9 8 7 6 5 4 3 2 1   02 01 00 99 98

Contents

Preface

An overwhelming amount of research and a plethora of theories have been produced relating to the developmentally and educationally appropriate needs of young children—so much that the teacher trainer wonders where to begin in instructing potential teachers of young children. What must they know and what may be left out?

To give order to one's thinking about what beginning teachers of young children should know, one may view teaching as a process having different levels. The first level is survival—how to get through Monday morning with a group of 15 to 20 4-year-olds and give them worthwhile experiences. Only after this survival level has been mastered can teachers "keep their heads above water" long enough to ask questions related to more advanced concepts—to higher levels of performance. This book is designed to help the beginning teacher get past the survival level.

The School for Young Children (SYC), for ages 3, 4, and 5, was started in 1986 by the authors. Classrooms needed to be set up, teachers needed to be grounded in SYC philosophy, and problems related to day-in and day-out practice with children and parents needed to be solved. There was little time to spend on theory and research because the children "appeared" each morning, needing to be taught.

Gradually, however, in weekend training sessions and at weekly faculty meetings, such issues as teachers' needs for guidance in organizing classrooms and materials, methods of teaching, discipline, working with parents, and more, were met with practical ideas and constructs supported by theory and research. The chapters that follow contain syntheses of these practical methods and constructs, as well as some basic survival theory. Each chapter was written with this question in mind: What is absolutely necessary for the teacher to know related to this chapter topic? For example, an entire book could be written on playgrounds, and hundreds have been; what we have done is said simply, "Here is how we would design a playground for young children; here are constructs so that you, the reader, can design your own."

In this second edition, we have responded to feedback from readers of the first edition. We address antibias issues and have expanded the chapter related to families, offering several ideas for proactive steps teachers may take in dealing with parents. This edition also includes a chapter on direct instruction. The SYC position is not to enter the heated debate over whether direct instruction should be used or how much it should be used with young children, but simply to take the position that an informed beginning teacher needs to understand the basic concepts regarding direct instruction. With this knowledge, the new teacher will be empowered to make meaningful and enlightened decisions regarding what is "developmentally appropriate" for young children.

What follows, then, is a practical guide for what to do on Monday morning when 15 or 20 young children enthusiastically troop into your classroom. We hope it will help you survive—and more.

Acknowledgments

Heartfelt thanks are due to many people who helped us make this book a reality. We gratefully acknowledge the teachers at SYC; Jamileh Mikati, a master teacher; and Pam Phelps from Creative Preschool, Tallahassee, Florida, a student who taught us as much as we taught her. For reading the manuscript and giving useful feedback, we thank Mark Koorland and Adrienne Herrell. Also, we are grateful to Sara Smilansky for her important research and ideas on sociodramatic play that form the basis for the play curriculum, and to Nancy Curry from the University of Pittsburgh, who taught us a great deal about young children. Our appreciation goes to the following reviewers for their comments on the manuscript: Julie K. Biddle, University of Dayton; Mary-Margaret Harrington, Southern Illinois University; and Nancy F. Sayre, Clarion University. Our gratitude is also extended to our children, Ellen, Ann, and Kate, who give us so much joy and outstanding examples of developmental behavior. And, finally, a special thanks to Dr. Vivian Fueyo and Dr. Beth Quick for helping us develop new chapters and content for this second edition.

1

Models of Teaching
Young Children

What should we teach—and how should we teach—young children ages 3 to 7? With the birth of Head Start programs for young children in the mid-1960s, the federal government sought to answer this same question: What and how should young children ages 3 to 7 be taught? The federal government encouraged a number of colleges and universities to develop a wide variety of educational models for young children. These models, called *planned variations,* represented the best creative thinking on programs for young children, but they differed dramatically in philosophy. These historical planned variation models may be viewed along a continuum from child-centered, activity-based learning models to those that are teacher directed, with a narrow curriculum of skill development related to pre-reading and math readiness.

Historical Early Childhood Models

The historical early childhood education models (Figure 1.1) may be viewed as our legacy of pedagogical practices, setting the foundations or basis for today's practices. Beginning with the most child-centered models, we have the Bank Street Model (Biber, Shapiro, & Wickens, 1977), named for a College of Education in New York City. The College based its practices on the philosophical thinking of Dewey (1915), and then later drew on the psychological concepts of psychoanalyst Erikson (1963), which produced a knowledge base regarding social-emotional development. Later still, the College used the words of Piaget (Piaget & Inhelder, 1969) and Vygotsky (1978) on how young children under-

FIGURE 1.1   Historical and Current Early Childhood Models

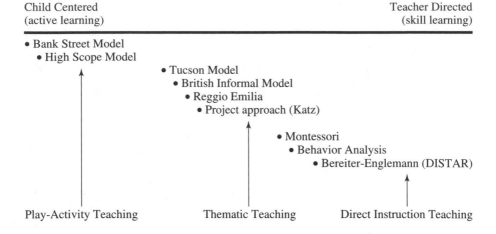

Child Centered   Teacher Directed
(active learning)   (skill learning)

- Bank Street Model
  - High Scope Model
        - Tucson Model
           - British Informal Model
             - Reggio Emilia
               - Project approach (Katz)
                    - Montessori
                       - Behavior Analysis
                          - Bereiter-Englemann (DISTAR)

Play-Activity Teaching   Thematic Teaching   Direct Instruction Teaching

stand and think about their world. In the Bank Street early childhood classroom, we would find young children actively playing with blocks and similar manipulatives; using expressive materials by painting, modeling with clay, and drawing; and engaging in fantasy play in the "dress-up" center or with miniature toys of animals, people, and furniture. We also would find a library, as well as areas for music, science, and large movement activities.

Also on the child-centered side of the continuum we would find the High Scope Model, conceived by David Weikart (Weikart et al., 1970), which attempted to apply Piagetian constructs to a generally play-centered classroom. The High Scope Model is still actively disseminated through nationally available training sessions. It is modeled in schools and centers today, and is also widely utilized in prekindergarten programs in public schools.

Moving along the continuum toward slightly more structured programs, we come to the thematic and project approach. The best example of the thematic approach in the United States is the Tucson Model, first started in Tucson, Arizona, for Latino children as a way to help them learn through thematic projects. For example, the children go to the market to purchase vegetables and ingredients, using money and especially using language, and then return to make soup. Out of these activities or projects related to a theme (making soup), concepts of language development and traditional subjects such as math are actively used rather then simply taught through direct instruction. The British Informal Model (Katz & Chard, 1989) approach also follows a theme construct to carry out real-life situations through which children work and gain skills inductively.

At the midpoint of the continuum between total child autonomy and total teacher control is the new popular approach begun in Italy and called the Reggio

Emilia approach (Malaguzzi, 1987). Reggio Emilia's curriculum is based on (1) the teacher's belief that children learn best when they actively explore problems; (2) use of the art medium, as a natural form of expression and exploration, to provide the vehicle by which children can express themselves and their learning; (3) involvement of the entire community—parents, local experts, senior citizens, and such community resources as museums and observatories; (4) the teacher's role in coconstructing activities and learning with the children. This project approach has also been made popular by the educators Katz and Chard (1989), who describe in their book, *Engaging Children's Minds: The Project Approach,* how to go beyond themes and units for an in-depth study of a particular topic by one or more children.

Toward the more structured end of our hypothetical models continuum, we reach the Montessori Model (Montessori, 1912), where we shift from the use of the word *play* (as in Bank Street Model) to that of *work.* Play sees the child self-initiating ideas and activities using prepared materials in the classroom, whereas work is defined as the child's ability to carry out arbitrary tasks typically designed or assigned by adults (Montessori, 1912). Generally, the Montessori apparatus is designed by adults to be used in one way or in an arbitrary manner. The child working with these didactic materials is actively using engineered apparatus to build in a specific manner; when used correctly, the equipment teaches the child a special cognitive concept such as classification, seriation, time, or a similar concept. The teacher using these materials in the Montessori classroom would direct, encourage, and facilitate the child's work-learning, at times using small groups to teach students in the use of the Montessori apparatus and materials. The direct teaching related to the use of the equipment follows the direct instruction "three-period lesson" technique of *Say, Show, and Do* (also used in behavioral models that follow).

A central focus in the Montessori Model is the *control of error*—that is, the use of equipment, room arrangement, and even "soft" teacher interventions to prevent the student from making errors and thus mislearning certain behaviors. Although direct instruction on the use of equipment is used in Montessori programs, the primary goal is to give the child maximum autonomy to follow his or her own interests. The child's interests are narrowed by the available equipment displayed on the shelves for his or her use. This control of error principle is also used in behavioral models of direct instruction.

At the teacher-centered end of the continuum, we may now place the Behavioral Analysis Model and the Bereiter-Englemann Model, two direct instruction models based on the behavioral analysis instructional theories of Pavlov (1927), Watson (1916), and Skinner (1968). These models seat groups of children before the teacher, who uses scripted lessons organized around instructional design principles to teach children language skills, prereading and reading, and math concepts. A variety of direct instruction kits may be purchased, but the programs known as DISTAR, originally designed by Englemann and Carnine (1975), is the most popular. DISTAR lessons follow a *Say* (This is a _____!), *Show* (Hold up a _____ for all to see), and *Do* (Pick out the _____ among these three) approach. Generally, in the direct instruction model, activities that are not teacher directed, such as art and music, are used to practice the skills being taught, and free-play activities, if they exist, are for the narrow purpose of a reward (called *preferred activity time* or *PAT*) for doing well on the academic activity.

To be fair, in real-world practice, there often are not "pure" models. In other words, many programs in practice might label themselves as Montessori but also contain centers, as seen in the play-activity classroom such as a block area or a dress-up center, while those using play may at times use some forms of direct teaching. The preceding descriptions characterize the traditional view of those models, even though they are routinely modified in everyday use.

With this broad view of past educational models, let us now return to our original question: What and how should young children ages 3 to 7 be taught? Which of these models, on our continuum from child centered to teacher directed, is correct? If we bring a group of educators, parents, or administrators together to come to a consensus answer to this question, a very heated debate is likely to break out. Each orientation, model, and philosophy has its strong advocates as well as its equally strong critics.

Developmentally Appropriate Practices (DAP)

Although most of these early childhood models became popular in the mid-1960s with the birth of Head Start, we may also add a new historical development to this debate. Beginning in the 1980s, public schools began to "find" early childhood. That is, public schools began opening educational programs for young children ages 3 and 4, as well as full-day kindergarten for 5-year-olds—programs that previously were nonexistent or operated on a half-day basis. Until that time, most early childhood programs were located in private or government-supported Head Start or day-care facilities in church centers, or in a host of "mom-and-pop" preschools throughout the country. Generally, such programs were not housed in public schools. Many states have now begun to channel money—sometimes from newly established state lotteries—to school districts for prekindergarten programs, and even some programs for 3-year-olds. The creation of programs for young children age 4 or younger was an alarming occurrence for members of the established early childhood community because their "territory" was now being threatened. They realized that they stood to lose their enrollment of children to a wealthier and better established competitor: the public schools. In addition, public schools historically "shifted down" to the kindergarten level to the direct instructional curriculum of basal reader workbook/phonetic analysis, and now the question for the early childhood community became: If the public schools begin serving pre-K children, will they force a direct instruction/workbook-oriented curriculum on that age group—and on us—as well?

In an attempt to speak for good programs and to hold the line for relevant curriculum for young children, the National Association for the Education of Young Children (NAEYC), the largest and most powerful professional association of educators of young children, published a position paper called *Developmentally Appropriate Practices in Early Childhood Programs,* or *DAP* (Bredekamp & Cople, 1997). The desired goal of DAP, along with other popular writings such as David Elkind's (1987) *Miseducation: Preschoolers at Risk,* was to stop "curriculum creep"—that is, the movement of curriculum that may be appropriate for elementary school-age children but that is allowed to "creep" down into programs for 3-, 4-, and 5-year-olds for whom it clearly is not appropriate. The DAP position paper was widely accepted by such powerful educational leadership groups as the Elementary School Principals Association and a host of other eminent curriculum associations. The DAP document began to educate public school principals, administrators, and teachers who previously had been uninformed about the needs of very young children.

At first, the early reading of the DAP document—or at least the public's interpretation of it—appeared to suggest that direct instruction, as seen in such models as Behavior Analysis and Bereiter-Englemann (DISTAR), was clearly inappropriate for young children. However, later rewrites of this document began to make the case that some direct instruction under certain conditions in early childhood classrooms, and especially for certain children with special needs, may be quite developmentally appropriate. The direct instruction models have generally offered the most preferred approach for special education educators, who have generally been outside the NAEYC professional sphere. While the debate rages on, this book, *School for Young Children,* will take the position that a teacher of young children ages 3, 4, 5, and 6 should know, understand, and be able to teach using the legacy and traditions across the entire continuum of models, including that of direct instruction.

The continuum of early historical models suggests three clear traditions regarding curriculum, teaching, or instruction: (1) a play-activity-based curriculum, (2) a thematic-project curriculum, and (3) direct instruction (see Figure 1.1). These three approaches vary significantly in terms of child initiative, shared teacher/child planning, and teacher initiative and control regarding (1) the concept of how learning occurs; (2) the methodology for teaching or instruction; (3) the role of the teacher; (4) the instructional framework; (5) individual versus group activities; and (6) the use of time, space, and materials (Table 1.1).

It is the position of this book that a full understanding of all three traditions will empower the teacher of young children to make informed decisions as to how much of each of these three approaches is appropriate for that teacher's particular children at their particular developmental age.

TABLE 1.1   Characteristics of Teaching and Curriculum Orientations

Play-Activity	Thematic Project	Direct Instruction
Child initiated	Shared planning and carried out by teacher and child	Teacher Initiated
• **Concept of Learning**		
Self-initiated activities based on the internal motivation of the child	Direct experience with real functional tasks associated with content; projects demonstrate the child's understanding; motivation is embedded in the task	Hear, make discriminations, drill, and practice, with motivation centered on external rewards
• **Methodology**		
Maximum freedom to use teacher's intuition, feelings, and judgment	Teacher must use knowledge of real-world events to bring new experiences to the classroom, and then, through questions and guidance, lead the child to explore and express his or her understandings	Scripts normally designed by the model or by the teacher
• **Teacher's Role**		
Follow the child's lead and interests; clarify experiences and serve as an aid or resource to the child	Design and bring to the student experiences related to theme	Request the child's response, evaluate, and reevaluate the child's performance
• **Instructional Framework**		
Facilitation of the child's free expressive needs	Activity oriented; experiments, explores, and questions	Step-by-step sequence based on preplanned goals
• **Individual vs. Group**		
Focus on individual child's interest and needs	Groups, led by the teacher, are used for planning and discussion, but the child is able to accomplish projects based on skill level or interest group	As a whole, group needs ability grouping
• **Time, Space, and Materials**		
Child is free to use, with limited demands	Teacher arranges initially, with changes made by group decisions through discussion	Teacher determines, based on the need for direct instruction

Summary

Considerable debate exists today over appropriate curriculum and teaching methods for the very young child. The historical development of early childhood education models gives us a tradition and knowledge based on past—and in many cases, current—practices for the early childhood models we find today in our centers and schools. An understanding of "how to teach" within the broad models related to play, thematic curriculum, and direct instruction provides the teacher with an in-depth understanding that will work—and, in fact, already *is* working—with young children in today's classrooms.

Before moving on to the next chapter, complete the Beliefs about Teaching Inventory (pages 8 to 10). It will help you assess how you feel and identify your own personal values about the nature of teaching young children. Later, after you have completed this book, take the inventory again to see if your values changed or stayed the same.

References

Biber, B., E. Shapiro, and D. Wickens, *Promoting Cognitive Growth: A Developmental Interaction Point of View* (2nd ed.). Washington, D.C.: NAEYC, 1977.

Bredekamp, S., and C. Cople, eds., *Developmentally Appropriate Practices in Childhood Programs*. Washington, D.C.: NAEYC, 1997.

Dewey, J., *Schools of Tomorrow*. New York: Dutton, 1915.

Elkind, D., *Miseducation: Preschoolers at Risk*. New York: Knopf, 1987.

Engelmann, S., and D. Carnine, *DISTAR*. Chicago: SRA-Macmillan/McGraw-Hill, 1985.

Erikson, E., *Childhood and Society*. New York: Norton, 1963.

Katz, L. G., and S. C. Chard, *Engaging Children's Minds: The Project Approach*. Norwood, N.J.: Ablex, 1989.

Malaguzzi, L., *The Hundred Languages of Children*. Reggio Emilia, Italy: Department of Education, 1987.

Montessori, M., *The Montessori Method*. New York: Stokes, 1912.

Montessori, M., *Dr. Montessori's Own Handbook*. New York: Schocken, 1965.

Pavlov, I., *Conditioned Reflexes: An Investigation of Physiological Activity of the Cerebal Cortex* (trans. G.V. Anrep). London and New York: Oxford University Press, 1927.

Piaget, J., and B. Inhelder, *The Psychology of the Child*. New York: Basic, 1969.

Skinner, B. F., *The Technology of Teaching*. Englewood Cliffs, N.J.: Prentice Hall, 1968.

Vygotsky, L., *Mind in Society: The Development of Higher Psychological Processes*. Cambridge Mass.: Harvard University Press, 1978.

Watson, J. B., "The Place of Conditioned Reflex in Psychology," *Psychological Review*, 23 (1916), 89–116.

Weikart, D., et al., *The Cognitively Oriented Curriculum: A Framework for Preschool Teachers*. Washington, D.C.: NAEYC, 1970.

Beliefs about Teaching Inventory

After you have answered the following questions, which force you to choose between two competing values or practice statements, this inventory will identify your preference toward differing philosophies regarding the teaching of young children. In each of the 12 questions that follow, you should choose between the two statements. With some questions, you will definitely like one statement and dislike the other, making it easy for you to choose. With others, you will like or dislike both options; this likely will be frustrating to you, but you must choose the opinion that most closely represents your view.

Instructions: Select the statement you value more and circle the corresponding letter, *a* or *b*. You must choose between the two statements for each item.

1. a. The role of the teacher in the fantasy play of young children, such as dress-up play, is to support and facilitate themes that are initiated by the children.

   b. The role of the teacher in the fantasy play of young children, such as dress-up play, is to supply props and facilitation that encourages children to play themes that are related to the topic being studied.

2. a. Art activities, such as painting, should permit children to express their own ideas and symbol-drawing ability.

   b. Art and music activities can be used for learning letter identification and math numerals.

3. a. Children should be given real activities that involve active participation and exploration, with the teacher asking questions to expand and extend their learning.

   b. Teacher questions should be used to test the child's understanding of the concept being taught.

4. a. Children's art products displayed on the wall and on shelves should clearly communicate to the visitor the topic studied.

   b. Children's art production primarily allows children to express their emotional concerns and develop symbolic representation.

5. a. Dress-up play is an activity center that should be available to all children every day and for extended periods of time.

   b. Time and privilege to play in the dress-up corner is a reward as a preferred activity for doing well on an assignment or task assigned by the teacher.

6. a. Concepts should be presented to children in such a manner that children name and label correctly without any error or possible mistakes, because once learned, incorrect habits are hard to change.

   b. When actively exploring materials (such as fluids), spills, accidents, or similar problems arise, and these incidents should be viewed as "teachable moments" for learning with children.

7. a. A wide variety of activity centers should be available in the classroom, and children should be permitted to choose their own centers of interest and move among them as they wish.

   b. A wide variety of activity centers should be designed and available, but children should start the day by participating in a planning period with the teacher and commit themselves to one center and the completion of a child-chosen task.

8. a. If a child cries when the mother departs from the center or classroom, the teacher should encourage and permit the parent to stay, perhaps even for a day or two until the child can separate without stress.

   b. If a child cries when the mother departs from the center or classroom, the parent should be told, "Everything will be OK," and asked to leave. The child should be ignored while crying, but should receive teacher attention when exhibiting mature behaviors.

9. a. Children should occasionally be brought together in groups and presented with a motivational activity, such as a presentation of a new classroom pet, which will serve to focus interest in pets and set the direction for future leaning activities.

   b. Children can be effectively brought together in groups and presented one concept, such as making letter sounds or counting numbers. Teachers can asses if children grasped the concept by observing their actions.

10. a. One of the best math learning activities for young children (ages 3 and 4) is measuring liquids for baking a cake.

    b. One of the best math learning activities for young children (ages 3 and 4) is building and playing with large wooden unit blocks.

11. a. One of the best prereading activities for young children is to have the children learn as they wipe the table, or with similar physical activities that require them to wipe moving from left to right across a surface, as one does when reading.

b. One of the best prereading activities for young children is dramatizing symbolic or fantasy roles in dress-up play, or with construction activities using clay or paints.

12. a. Children should learn letter sounds, and then be given a task to combine the sounds into words they can read.

   b. Children should dictate stories that the teacher will transcribe. Later, the children may trace the teacher's writing, draw pictures, and then finally write the words themselves.

Scoring Key and Interpretation: Circle your responses, using the *a* and *b* items above, on the table below.

Table 1		Table 2		Table 3	
1a	2a	1b	3a	2b	3b
4b	5a	4a	6b	5b	6a
7a	8a	7b	9a	8b	9b
11b	10b	10a	12b	11a	12a

Total number of responses in Table 1 _____
Total number of responses in Table 2 _____
Total number of responses in Table 3 _____

The table in which your total number of responses was the highest is the one where your values are clustered. Table 1 is the play-activity approach to teaching, Table 2 is thematic-project teaching, and Table 3 is direct instruction. The table with the next highest score would be your second choice, and the table with the least number may be the philosophy you value least. If your responses are equally distributed across all tables, you may be an eclectic teacher who picks and chooses from all philosophies. In the coming chapters, you will place these three philosophies on a continuum between a child-centered curriculum and that of teacher-controlled and directed instruction.

2

Understanding the Young Child's Play

Play-activity learning is basically a child-initiated play curriculum, permitting the young child to select from a well-chosen variety of play materials. These would include clay, paint, drawing materials, blocks, puzzles, and make-believe or socio-dramatic play materials. The role of the teacher is to design a well-balanced play area, evaluate each child's level of play, and use methods and techniques to promote the play to more advanced levels. Following is a case for the value of children's play, a thorough description of young children's development, and instruction on how to apply theory to real life.

"Wait just a minute! Play? What's this play stuff? I'm interested in being a *teacher* of 3- to 6-year-olds, not in letting these kids waste their time by playing all day. They can do that at home...." Often, parents and elementary teachers express similar thoughts: "You're cheating those children. All they are doing is playing all day! When are they going to learn something?"

In a competitive, upwardly mobile society, all parents expect the best for their children (and the best is often interpreted as "My child must be first... competitive... able to do better than others"). There is the expectant father who reads to his unborn prodigy so that the newborn will be ready to read sooner than any of his peers on the block, and there are the parents objecting to the preschool teacher's recommendation that the slow-to-develop child stay another year in the 4-year-old class before entering public school kindergarten ("But she will be late in taking the qualifying exams for med school!").

In such a society, play is held by most of the public and many educators as the most useless of activities—as almost sinful. The myth that "idle hands do the devil's work" is a hard one to slay. Perhaps the public will never understand the value of play, but what about you? Do you yourself question its value?

The direct instruction model is probably familiar to you; this is the way you were most likely taught during most of your schooling. People tend to teach the way they were taught, and if we put you in a classroom for young children tomorrow, you most likely would put on the familiar, teacher-directed shoes and proceed in the manner in which you were taught.

I had taught for many years in an elementary school, junior high school, and boarding high school, and had been an elementary principal, when I decided to return to graduate school to study early childhood education and child development. The very first day, my professor sent me out to the playground to observe, and I found five 3-year-olds "playing." Having just come from working with older students, I wondered how I would even be able to talk to these small creatures. I soon found out, when one rode his tricycle up to me and inquired with a smile, "What's your name, Mister?"

"Ha!" I thought, "This is not going to be so hard after all!" I announced in a clear voice, "My name is Mr. Wolfgang," bending over to be sure he heard me, and returned his smile. But suddenly his face went blank and his body froze— and then, like a bat-out-of-heck, he jumped from the tricycle, screaming, "Wolf! Wolf!" and ran to the other four children to tell them that Little Red Riding Hood's assailant had abandoned the woods for their playground. Quickly, they found a branch lying nearby and, using it as a woodcutter's axe, advanced courageously upon the evil wolf, driving him from their sanctuary.

Thus, I quickly learned that the child under age 6 is a very different "breed of cat" from the elementary school student. The assumptions about learning in the elementary school (where I had been using a teacher-centered model) did not necessarily hold for the preschooler.

Now, you can imagine how the "big bad wolf" felt when assured by his professor that it was safe to come out of the storage shed and join not just the "woodcutters" but 15 of their compatriots—in their classroom. What was really terrifying was that I did not find them all safely deposited in chairs or desks, but rather moving about uncontrolled, some in a housekeeping corner playing mommies and daddies, some painting at easels, some building with blocks, and some doing apparently nothing. Good grief, I thought, what if the woodcutters tell the other 15 that the wolf is among them? I might be set upon, my stomach cut open, filled with rocks, and sewed shut!

Joking aside, the experience was disturbing. In a teacher-centered classroom, I had been comfortable because I was "the boss" or king in my kingdom. The children were seated and moved only with permission. In this new setting, children were moving about at will, and I was afraid that chaos would erupt at any moment. However, after about 40 minutes, I began to realize that no one was in imminent danger, especially me; my heartbeat began to return to normal and I made it through the morning intact!

The Basics of the Play-Activity Curriculum

In the direct instruction classroom, what is to be learned is clearly defined: a system for teaching is clear, which materials to use and when are specified, and criterion testing is used to indicate what learning has occurred. Historically, this degree of specificity has not been true for play-oriented curricula. *Play* had been difficult to define, and a system for teaching through play was nonexistent; in fact, there were those who believed that adults did not belong in children's self-initiated play.

As play-oriented curricula began to emerge, beginning teachers were trained by working or "apprenticing" with an expert who knew from experience what to do and could ignite others' enthusiasm for similar methods of teaching. However, the limitation of this apprenticeship system was that very few people could be trained at one time. Today, there are some publications available that describe this type of teaching, and we hope that what follows will be a complete and useful summary of this method. In the following sections, we will (1) define play, (2) demonstrate how play changes as the child develops, and (3) explain the value of play as a process for facilitating the child's emotional, social, intellectual, and physical development.

Play: How Do You Know It When You See It?

Developmental observers have noted four large categories of play: (1) sensorimotor play, (2) symbolic play, (3) construction play, and (4) games with rules. Let's look at each of these forms to learn the subcategories and developmental sequences of each.

Sensorimotor Play

Sensory Play.   From the moment of birth, the infant learns about the world through sensory play—tasting, touching, smelling, and hearing. Later, any new play item given to a child age 3 or older is first explored through sensory activities, sometimes called *tooling-up.* For example, when children get fingerpaint for the first time, they enjoy smearing it (touch), smelling it, and even sneaking a small taste of it before they begin to make markings or "pictures" with the paint.

Motor Play.   Fine-motor activity, the use of fingers and hands to manipulate objects and materials, begins formally with the 8-month-old infant's pincer grasp (use of thumb and forefinger to pick up small objects) and continues to develop into such finger activities as cutting with scissors and holding a crayon or pencil. Plastic manipulative materials such as interlocking blocks are first used in a motoric way and later in more advanced forms of play. Gross-motor play (walking, climbing) and the use of the large muscle and skeletal systems begins formally between 10 and 15 months, when children generally learn to stand upright and walk.

A child climbing up and over a climbing frame is deliberately moving his center of gravity and using the muscle system to maintain balance and movement. Simply put, motor play is practicing body skills in a gravitational field (Gerhardt, 1973). With increased abilities, the child will learn such physical skills as balance, climbing, and throwing.

It is generally agreed that six fundamental motor patterns develop during the early ages and reach maturity and coordination by age 5: walking, running, jumping, kicking, throwing, and catching. Table 2.1 summarizes the initial attempts at these skills, as well as their mature levels.

TABLE 2.1   Fundamental Motor Patterns

Initial	Mature
Walking	
Short steps.	
Flat-foot contact; knee bent as foot touches ground, then quick knee straightening. Relatively no ankle movement; leg bent excessively.	Increased step length. Heel contacts ground with the knee straight; weight rolls forward so toe pushes, then knee bends as it is lifted off the ground.
Toes point out.	Toes generally point straight ahead.
Feet spread apart wide.	Feet are placed closer together, narrowing the base of support.
Feet spread slightly apart.	Feet are placed closer together, narrowing the base of support.
No hip rotation.	Hip rotates back to the support leg, then forward to the side of the moving leg.
Arms held up with elbows bent for protection against falls (high-guard position).	Arms held straight, swing easily at sides of body.
Running	
Arms held straight, very little movement—mainly to help maintain balance.	Arms bent and swing in diagonal pattern in opposition to the leg action—that is, right arm forward when left leg is forward. Elbow brought up parallel with shoulder.
Short stride.	Increase in stride length.
Slow running speed.	Increase in running speed.
Support leg (back leg) straightens slowly as child takes off.	Support leg pushes off forcefully by straightening behind the buttocks.
No trunk lean.	Slight forward trunk lean.

TABLE 2.1   *(Continued)*

Initial	Mature
Leg is bent at low level as it comes forward. Motion of knee is out to the side and then forward.	Knee lifted high as leg comes forward, and the heel of the foot is brought close to the buttocks.
Toes point out.	Toes point forward.

Jumping (vertical)

Very minimal crouch.	Knees, hips, and ankles bend in crouch in preparation for jumping.
Arms are raised to side as jump starts. Arms may swing out to back if not given target to reach for.	Arms forcefully lift body.
Hips and knees bend in air on takeoff.	Hips, knees, and ankles straighten forcefully as body goes up.
Slight forward lean during pushoff.	Body remains straight until landing, then hips, knees, and ankles bend to absorb the shock.
Stepping or one-foot landing.	Two-foot landing.

Throwing

Stage 1
1. Feet are stationary.
2. Ball is held near ear. Child pushes ball straight down.
3. No rotation of body or step forward.

Stage 2
1. Some body rotation to side opposite throwing arm.
2. Hand holds ball cocked behind the head.
3. No foot movement.

Stage 3
1. Arm and trunk movements are the same as in Stage 2.
2. Child steps forward on foot that is on **same** side of body as throwing arm.

Stage 4
1. As movement is begun, body weight shifts to side with ball.
2. *Arm* is brought up and back behind head.
3. Weight is transferred by a step to foot that is on the **opposite** side of body from throwing arm.
4. Trunk rotates to opposite side.
5. Ball is released as elbow is straightened with a whipping motion.

Catching

Stage 1
1. Arms are held out straight in front of the body, with palms up.
2. When ball makes contact with arms, elbows bend. Child tries to trap ball against chest. May clap at ball or use hands like vise if ball is small.
3. May turn head to side and lean back.

(Continued)

TABLE 2.1   *(Continued)*

Stage 2
1. Arms are in front, with elbows slightly bent.
2. As ball approaches, arms encircle it at chest.
3. Robotlike performance.
Stage 3
1. Arms are bent.
2. Ball bounces on chest, then is controlled with arms.
3. Child tries to catch with hands but may resort to using chest.
Stage 4
1. Hands are positioned to intercept ball.
2. Grasps and controls ball.
3. Gives way to force of ball by bending at hips and knees.
4. Absorbs force by continuing to move and give way in direction ball came from.

Kicking

Stage 1
1. Kicking leg is straight, moved up, and forward.
2. No accompanying body movement.
Stage 2
1. Lower part of kicking leg is lifted up and behind body to prepare for kick.
Stage 3
1. Upper leg is brought back, with knee bent.
2. Leg swings through greater arc than in stage 2.
3. Some body adjustments.
4. Leg may be overcocked resulting in loss of mechanical advantage.
Stage 4
1. Hip and knee are cocked effectively.
2. Trunk leans backward.
3. Leg moves through greater range of motion.
4. Knee straightens as leg swings through to contact ball.
5. Arm and body adjustments are made during follow-through.
6. Child starts farther behind ball and moves total body into it.

Source: Reprinted by permission of the publisher from Curtis, Sandra, *The Joy of Movement in Early Childhood* (New York: Teachers College Press, © 1982 by Teachers College, Columbia University. All rights reserved.)

Symbolic Play

Symbolic play (Millar, 1973; Piaget, 1962; Weikart et al., 1970) is fantasy play, whereby the child expresses or represents her ideas with gestures (stirs the batter of a pretend cake) or with objects (uses a block for a walkie-talkie). When this pretending becomes well developed, the child will play out "stories" with themes, characters, and beginnings and endings. We call this *dramatic play* when it contains these three criteria:

1. The child imitates a role.
2. The child must sustain the theme for 10 minutes or more.

3. The child uses gestures and objects or represents imaginary objects or people.

Later, the child develops the ability to play with other children in theater-like make-believe dramas, an advanced form of dramatic play called *sociodramatic play* (Smilansky, 1968; Smilansky & Shefatya, 1990). In addition to meeting the three criteria of dramatic play, sociodramatic play must also include these elements:

4. The child must interact with others.
5. The child must use verbal exchange.

Let's look at an example of sociodramatic play.

Medical World.   The playhouse has been moved into the center of the room and arranged so that it can be entered from all four sides. On one side of the playhouse is an imaginary ambulance, complete with a steering-wheel toy, walkie-talkies, and a blanket for a stretcher. On the opposite side is what looks like an operating table. In another part of the room is a combination doctor's office/hospital room with a bathroom scale, a yardstick for measuring height, and a bed with a tray. The play store in the classroom has become a pharmacy. In each of these areas is a doctor's kit and a few pieces of specialized equipment.

Doctor's Kit

Stethoscope
Shot "needles" (made from construction toy sticks)
Flashlight
Cotton balls and masking tape (for bandages)
Tongue depressors
Medicine bottles

Specialized Equipment

Rubber knives and large plastic needles (for operations)

Black box with two tin cans attached to the sides by electrical wire (for starting a heartbeat)

White jackets, masks, and rubber gloves

Blankets and towels

Ace bandages and slings

Plastic medicine bottles and spoons

Prescription pads

Plastic catsup bottle with a hose attached (for giving blood transfusions)

The children fan out quickly across the room and soon are playing in pairs and trios.* One child stands on the scale, while a second child administers a shot and dabs the immunized spot with a cotton ball. Another pair is involved in a makeshift operation. The patient lies on the operating table while the doctor pretends to amputate an arm. The doctor presses a flashlight against the arm, makes a buzzing noise and says, "Now I'll make you a bionic arm." Still another pair is sitting at the steering-wheel toy, pretending to drive somewhere, making siren noises and talking excitedly into their walkie-talkies. The play episodes are short and disjointed.

Two girls approach the doctor's office: "My daughter is sick," the older girl says to the doctor. "I guess she'll have to go to the hospital," the doctor replies, motioning with his arm toward the nearby cot. The mother helps cover up her daughter with a blanket and then watches as the doctor puts his stethoscope on the girl's forehead "She has lots of germs," he advises. "She will have to stay here three weeks." The "sick" girl giggles quietly to herself. In a matter of minutes, the three weeks pass, and the mother takes her daughter home. In just a few more minutes, she is back with another family member who needs to be hospitalized.

As the family members take turns going to the hospital, a boy rushes into the playhouse, announces loudly that he is dying, and then collapses dramatically on the floor. The teacher directs the attention of the driving pair to this catastrophe: "Hey, ambulance drivers, someone just died over there. Better get him to the doctor." In due course, the victim is carried and dragged to the operating table. Several doctors converge on the scene. "What happened to him?" the teacher asks. After some discussion, the doctors agree that the boy was shot. "Looks pretty serious," the teacher agrees, as she picks up the empty catsup bottle. "Maybe he needs some more blood." She inverts the bottle and touches the attached tube to the patient's arm. The doctors poke and probe the patient with their operating tools. "I think he's alive now," one of them finally says. "No, I'm still dead," the patient insists. "What do you do with dead people?" the teacher wonders. "Let's throw him in the river," suggests a doctor. Unable to cure the patient, the doctors and ambulance drivers haul him away to the river. But as they struggle to dispose of the corpse, it scrambles back to life and runs away laughing, "I'm OK, I'm OK."

Construction Play

The third form of play is construction. Construction has historically been referred to as "arts and crafts," which includes, among other activities, painting, clay modeling, coloring, and building with blocks and interlocking blocks. Construction play occurs when a child has an idea and represents it through some media (such as paints or clay) to produce a product—for example, Carol paints a "doggie" at her easel or Jim sculpts an elephant out of clay. The child has produced

---

*The remainder of this section is from *Play Together/Grow Together* (page17) by Don Adcock and Marilyn Segal, 1983, White Plains, NY: Mailman Family Press. Reprinted by permission.

symbols to represent these animals (Kellogg 1970; Millar, 1973; Piaget, 1962); that is, one thing (the child's marks on the paper) stands for another (the real object). These symbols go through a number of developmental stages as the child's intellectual capacity grows. For example, in drawing and painting, the symbols generally develop in the manner shown in Figure 2.1.

The human figure, which evolves into the face-like house, is given as an example in Figure 2.1, and does appear in the symbolic development of many

FIGURE 2.1 Developmental Stages of Children's Symbols (Ages 1–7 Years)

 1–2 years: random scribbling. The child uses random scribble marks simply as a sensorimotor activity.

 2–2½ years: controlled scribbling. The child begins to develop some control of his fine motor abilities, and the scribbles gain some direction and control. After some experience with controlled scribbling, you may hear a child name his picture a "motor cycle" or a "big wheel," although there appears to be no resemblance. This is an intellectual accomplishment for the child, an indication that he is taking his first step toward being able to do representation.

 2½–3 years: the face. The next major development is for the circle to become a face.

 3½–4 years: arms and legs. The circle "person" develops stick arms and legs, which protrude from the circle, or the head; there is no body as yet.

 4 years: the body appears. The human figure begins to acquire a body. Gradually, more body parts are added (hands, feet, hair, ears, etc.).

 5 years: floating house. First "house" drawings usually resemble a face, with windows placed like eyes and the door like a mouth. These first houses are usually somewhere in the middle of the paper and seem to be floating in space.

 5½–6 years: house on bottom line. The bottom of the paper is used as a baseline and the house rests on it.

 5½–6 years: baseline supports house in drawing. A baseline appears within the drawing and the house rests on it.

6–7 years: two-dimensional drawing. The baseline begins to take on the quality of a horizon, which indicates the child's awareness of two-dimensional space.

Source: Reprinted by permission of the publisher from Curtis, Sandra, *The Joy of Movement in Early Childhood* (New York: Teachers College Press, © 1982 by Teachers College, Columbia University. All rights reserved.)

children. However, each child will express the symbolic objects that are most meaningful for him, and some might not draw the human figure or the house. What is important to understand is that no matter which symbols children draw, they will progress through very similar stages. Therefore, when you, as a teacher, keep a record of symbolic development in construction (artwork), you can evaluate each child's progress in representational skill, and you can better facilitate the child's further progress (Goodnow, 1977; Kellogg, 1970).

It is important to save samples of the child's artwork over a period of many weeks. Marked with the date and placed in sequence, they form a record of the child's progress in symbolic representation.

Three-dimensional materials, such as clay, are the objects of a similar line of development (Smilansky, Hagan, & Lewis, 1988). When children work with clay, you can expect to see (1) random pounding (sensorimotor play), (2) controlled pounding (sensorimotor), (3) rolling clay into snake-like rolls and later into circles, (4) adding pieces to the rolls and circles (facial features and body parts), and (5) combining products, such as people in cars or a person on a horse. Development in this three-dimensional artwork could also be shown in the child's chart or in photographs of the three-dimensional products.

Using the preceding three categories of play (sensorimotor, symbolic, and construction), we can outline the types of materials used with these forms of play.*

Form	*Materials*
Sensorimotor Play	Slides, tricycles, balls, and similar items.
Symbolic Play Microsymbolic Play	Miniature toys (replicas of furniture, people, animals, etc.) and puppets.
Macrosymbolic Play	Child-sized furniture, toy eating utensils and food, dolls, toy telephones, and similar items.
Construction Play Construction—Fluid	Clay, easel paints, drawing tools. (Fluid materials have a high sensorimotor quality and easily transform their shape and generally have little or no form [Wolfgang, 1977, 1981].)
Construction—Structured	Carpentry materials, interlocking blocks, and puzzles. (These structured materials maintain their shape and have a more work-like quality.)

Note: The two common forms of symbolic play materials include toys used for microsymbolic play and macrosymbolic play (Erikson, 1950). Looking at a storybook or reading a book could be viewed as a related form of passive-symbolic play.

Games with Rules

Games with rules include baseball, softball, and such board games as Chutes and Ladders, Candyland, Monopoly, and checkers. It will be at age 6 or 7, or even later, that the child will be able intellectually to grasp the point of view of others. Therefore, games with rules should usually not be included as play activities until elementary school (Piaget, 1962; Smilansky & Shefatya, 1990).

The Value of Play

As mother is taking the groceries from the car to the kitchen, the 3-year-old sees the ice cream on top of the grocery bag.

"Mommy, I want some ice cream!" she says.

"No, not now, dear," answers mother. "You will spoil your appetite for dinner. You may have some for dessert, after dinner!"

"No, Mommy, I want it now!" demands the child.

"After dinner, dear!" mother replies.

The child screams, "No, now, Mommy" and begins a major temper tantrum. Mother scoots the young child outside to her sandbox to play and begins to prepare dinner. At first, the child crosses her arms and pouts. Then, in one last rage, she kicks the sand bucket. She then begins to pick up handfuls of sand and let it slip through her fingers—until she appears to have an idea. She begins lining up small cups that she has found, carefully forms wet sand into well-shaped balls, and positions a ball on top of each cup (construction play).

Finally, after exhausting her supply of cups and making 15 to 20 sand balls, she carefully leans back to admire her creations. With a giggle (and a sideways glance toward the kitchen window where mother is working) she carefully picks up one of the cups with a sand ball on top and pretends to lick the ball. Right under the eyes of her unsuspecting mother, she pretends to devour, in a beginning form of dramatic play, all the ice cream she wants, without concern for ruining her appetite! Later, she will set the table for each of her baby dolls and act out the serving of a three-course imaginary dinner (a fully developed form of dramatic play).

Emotional Development

Just what does this anecdote illustrate? Because of young children's limited language and intellectual abilities, it is difficult for them to deal with frustrating, scary, or stressful experiences—such as "no ice cream until after dinner," or being frightened, or being given an injection by a doctor. It is through symbolic or representational play, including construction, that the child can digest, a little bit at a time, larger emotional experiences that are too hard to digest all in "one bite" (Erikson, 1950; Moustakas, 1974; Peller, 1959).

A clear illustration of the emotional value of play can be seen in the experience of a child who visits the doctor's office and gets "shots" from a scary man in white clothing. When the child returns home, she retreats to her toys, dresses one of her dolls in white, uses a pencil as a hypodermic needle, and gives the doll-doctor a "shot" with full vengeance. The child might continue playing doctor for the next few weeks until the scary incident becomes emotionally "digested."

In symbolic or fantasy play, the child can change from a helpless victim to an aggressor (and get revenge), or she may obtain what she wants in fantasy when she cannot get it in reality (ice cream cones). And, after all, don't we do this as adults? Remember, perhaps, the ride home after work, on the day the boss reprimanded you unfairly, when you mentally tongue-lashed him, setting him straight in no uncertain terms? We adults do this emotional self-healing by fantasizing in our daydreams, while preschool children "play out" what is bothering them (Peller, 1959). Some parents or other adults who see these sometimes violent themes in the child's play worry that their offspring might be emotionally disturbed. Generally, the opposite is true. Symbolic-fantasy play is nature's built-in method of self-healing and it is more likely that the child who *cannot* fantasize or play is not emotionally healthy (Singer, 1973).

Social Development

Children are not born with the ability to be "social." How is sociability acquired? Some teachers define "being social" as waiting in line to take a turn, or saying "please" and "thank you." Actually, these are only narrow customs; true social competence involves the ability to "play" a social role.

Let's imagine a 3-year-old coming down the preschool hallway wearing a man's hat and a woman's skirt and carrying a baby bottle. This image symbolizes the pivotal developmental stage of the 3-year-old. He is experimenting with the role that he "is not," learning the role that he will accept and become, and still clinging to the role of infancy that he must give up.

Being social requires that one have a repertoire of roles to move into and out of daily. At one moment, an adult is a driver of a car; next, he or she is a patron in a restaurant; next, a teacher, and so on. This role changing is constant and ongoing. In fact, many people institutionalized as social misfits are those who cannot understand roles or who have defined for themselves nonsocial roles.

It is through sociodramatic play that young children learn to be role players enabling them to become socially adaptive as adults. It is this roleplaying that will permit children, at age 6 or 7, to play the game of formal schooling in first grade (Smilansky, 1968; Smilansky & Shefatya, 1990); it is those who do not roleplay who are found by teachers as "not ready for school" or "still immature for his age." Thus, sociodramatic play helps a child develop social readiness for formal schooling—to become a cooperative worker with others (Smilansky, 1968; Freud, 1968).

A number of social skills must be mastered before sociodramatic play is acquired. The following are stages of increased social ability: unoccupied behavior, solitary play, onlooker behavior, parallel play, associative play, and cooperative or organized supplementary play.

Unoccupied Behavior: The child apparently is not playing, but occupies himself with watching anything that happens to be of momentary interest. When there is nothing exciting taking place, he plays with his own body, gets on and off chairs, just stands around, follows the teacher, or sits in one spot glancing around the room.

Solitary Play: The child plays alone and independently with toys that are different from those used by the children within speaking distance, and makes no effort to get close to other children. He pursues his own activity without reference to what others are doing.

Onlooker Behavior: The child spends most of his time watching the other children play. He often talks to the children he is observing, asks questions or gives suggestions, but does not overtly enter into the play himself. This type differs from the unoccupied in that the onlooker is definitely observing particular groups of children rather than just anything that happens to be exciting. The child stands or sits within speaking distance of the group so that he can see and hear everything that takes place.

Parallel Play: The child plays independently, but the activity he chooses naturally brings him among other children. He plays with toys that are like those that the children around him are using, but he plays with the toy as he sees fit, and does not try to influence or modify the activity of the children near him. He plays beside rather than with the other children. There is no attempt to control the coming or going of children in the group.

Associative Play: The child plays with other children. The conversation concerns the common activity; he borrows and loans play materials; he follows and is followed when playing with trains or wagons; and he exhibits mild attempts to control which children may or may not play in the group. All the members engage in similar if not identical activity; there is no division of labor and no organization of the activity of several individuals around any material goal or product. The children do not subordinate their individual interest to that of the group; instead, each child acts as he wishes. By his conversation with the other children one can tell that his interest is primarily in his associations, not in activity. Occasionally, two or three children are engaged in no activity of any duration, but are merely doing whatever happens to draw the attention of any of them.

Cooperative or Organized Supplementary Play: The child plays in a group that is organized for the purpose of making some material product (construction), or of striving to attain some competitive goal, or of dramatizing situations of adults and group life (sociodramatic play), or of playing formal games (games with rules). There is a marked sense of belonging or of not belonging to the group. The control of the group situation is in the hands of one or two of the members who direct the activity of the others. The goal as well as the method of attaining it necessitates a division of labor, taking of different roles by the various group members and the organization of activity so that the efforts of one child are supplemented by those of another.

These stages help establish criteria for determining where children are in their social development, so that the teacher can intervene and help each child move to more advanced stages of development, and finally to sociodramatic play.

Cognitive Development

The direct instruction models of early education are based on the idea that learning is an input-output process based on words and language (Bereiter, 1966; Engelmann, 1980) ("Children, this is the numeral 3. Show me the numeral 3"). But the play-based play-activity models reject that position and purport that children must first have direct physical experiences with objects and people in their world (Biber, 1977; Piaget, 1962; Weikart et al., 1970). During these experiences, problems will occur, and solving these problems will entail getting, using, and assimilating (or digesting) information.

Play, especially high levels of sociodramatic play, has been demonstrated to be related to a host of other developmental growth aspects such as language development (Marshall & Hahn, 1967; Smilansky, 1968), imaginativeness or creativity (Freyberg, 1973; Feitelson & Ross, 1973; Dansky, 1980; Udwin, 1983), group prospective taking and social skills (Rosen, 1974; Burns & Brainerd, 1979), and various cognitive tasks (Saltz & Brody, 1982).

Developmental Play Capacities of Young Children

The play forms—sensorimotor, symbolic, construction, and, later, games with rules—will change in complexity and duration as the child matures. In the elementary school years, sensorimotor play becomes absorbed in games with rules, symbolic play is replaced by the fantasy images evoked in reading (Smilansky & Shefatya, 1990), and construction play develops into hobbies and projects for school (Hurlock, 1972). The bars running from left to right in Figure 2.2 suggest the prevalence of the play abilities (Engstrom, 1971) from birth to age 7.

Figure 2.2 gives an approximation of the amount of time and space you, as a teacher, would give to a classroom of children of various ages. For example, the

FIGURE 2.2 Developmental Play Abilities of Children

Age	Percentage of Time in Play Form
	0 10 20 30 40 50 60 70 80 90 100%

```
Age    0    10    20    30    40    50    60    70    80    90   100%
0–1 |------------------------ Sensorimotor --------------------
1–2 |---------------------- Sensorimotor -------------|Symbolic
2–3 |------------------ Sensorimotor --+-- Symbolic -----|Construction
3–4 |--------------- Sensorimotor --+--- Symbolic --+-- Construction -------
4–5 |------------ Sensorimotor --+-- Symbolic --+--- Construction ---------
5–7 |-------- Sensorimotor ---+-- Symbolic --+-- Construction ------------
7+  |----- Sensorimotor ---+-- Symbolic ------+- Construction ----------
         to GWR            to Reading
```

3-year-old will have some success with construction by using media such as crayons or paints, but will find working with clay or three-dimensional media difficult. This will change as the child matures and gains experience with these materials.

The figure suggests that large amounts of time and space should be given to 3- to 4-year-old sensorimotor play (approximately 40%), a lesser amount to symbolic play (30%), and a similar amount to construction (30%). The 4- to 5-year-old would have sensorimotor play (approximately 30%) and continued large amounts of time and space (40%) for symbolic play, while construction play would increase (30%). This trend would continue for the 5- to 7-year-old child, with sensorimotor play (20%) dropping, continued large amounts of time for symbolic play (40%), and construction play (40%) increasing.

At age 7, the child enters a new stage of development called *middle childhood;* she becomes a "school-age" child. During this period, the energies once directed toward sensorimotor play are now directed toward games with rules (which, if we look closely, are sensorimotor play held together by socially agreed-upon rules). Symbolic play tends to dissipate, but its mechanisms are seen in reading and in the shared fantasy of books. Construction continues to grow in importance, with the school-age children making clubhouses, models, collections of rocks, and generally doing "craft" activities. Children in middle childhood are project oriented.

Summary

Let's go to a play-activity classroom, where we do not find a front or back to the classroom, and at first cannot find the teacher. The room may look confusing to us, but if we understand the play concepts, we can make sense out of the activities going on. We see a "store" play area (sociodramatic play). We see a child painting at the easel and another making an "alligator" with clay (fluid construction). We watch the children painting and sculpting to see where they are developmentally, and we know how to begin to chart their progress in symbol development in construction. We see two boys in the block area, each making a castle (structured construction), and (from Parten's stages) we recognize parallel play.

In the play-activity environment, the "lessons" are created by the child-initiated play activities. Child-centered learning is guided by the teachers' (1) understanding of play forms, categories, and developmental stages; (2) knowledge of the classification of materials and equipment; (3) diagnosis of the child's play abilities (see Chapter 12); and (4) appropriate intervention (see Chapter 4).

Before moving on to the next chapter, complete the Materials Preference Inventory (MPI) (page 29) to better understand your own preference or lack of preference for certain materials. In organizing a classroom full of materials this may lead to a profusion or a dearth of materials preferred or not preferred. We suggest a balance of all appropriate materials; in Chapter 3, you will find out how to do just that.

Activities

1. Visit a well-designed play-oriented school for children ages 3 to 5, and seat yourself passively either in a corner in an indoor classroom or an outdoor playground. Observe three children for a 30-minute period. From your observation, determine what percentage of their time was spent in sensorimotor play, symbolic play, or construction. In your judgment, what facilitated these forms of play? Note the abundance of materials that support each particular play form, including the teacher's control, intervention or nonintervention, and the arrangement of space.

2. Observe two 3-year-old, two 4-year-old, and two 5-year-old children of the same sex in active physical play on the playground. Using Table 2.1, Fundamental Motor Patterns, analyze each of these six children's fundamental motor abilities with regard to walking, running, jumping, throwing, catching, and kicking. If they did not demonstrate these actions, try to encourage each child by supplying objects to throw, catch, or kick. Did you see an increase in the maturity of the child's action based on age?

3. For the same children you observed in activity 2, take a sample of the children's drawings or paintings and use the developmental sequence of symbolic development analysis to describe where each child is in his or her construction from random scribbling to two-dimensional drawing. How would you facilitate the next stage in symbolic development for each child?

4. Observe two or more children in the sociodramatic play corner and analyze their play based on the five criteria on pages 16 and 17. Which of the five elements of the sociodramatic play were missing? How would you facilitate the missing elements in each child's play?

5. Select three 4-year-old children and introduce (without coercion on your part) a simple game with rules, such as the board game Candyland. Were they able to grasp the rules and play the game? Interview them as to what "winning" means, and what is a "rule" as it relates to this game. Are games with rules appropriate for the age of the children you teach?

6. Ask an experienced early childhood teacher, an elementary teacher, and a parent with a child in an early childhood setting to fill out a Materials Preference Inventory. What might each person's score indicate regarding their view of play regarding academics (number and letter teaching)? Interview the adults about their first and last choice and have them explain why they chose as they did. What aspect of their answers related their philosophy of how young children learn?

7. Using the Materials Preference Inventory, cut pictures of these toy materials from supply catalogues and place them in sets of two on sheets of cardboard. Now present these 20 cardboard-mounted dichotomous pictures to children ages 3, 4, and 5, and ask them to indicate which materials they like best from the two choices. Score their preferences. What materials do young children prefer and not prefer? Are there differences between boys' and girls' preferences? Are there differences based on age?

References

Adcock, Don, and Marilyn Segal, *Play Together/Grow Together.* White Plains, N.Y.: Mailman Family Press, 1983.

Bereiter, Carl, *Teaching Disadvantaged Children in the Preschool.* Englewood Cliffs, N.J.: Prentice-Hall, 1966.

Burns, S. M., and C. J. Brainerd, "Effects of Constructive and Dramatic Play on Perspective Taking in Very Young Children," *Developmental Psychology,* 15 (1979), 512–521.

Curtis, Sandra, *The Joy of Movement in Early Childhood.* New York: Teachers College Press, 1982.

Dansky, J. L., "Make Believe: A Mediator of the Relationship between Play and Associative Fluency," *Child Development,* 51 (1980), 576–579.

Engelmann, Siegfried, *Direct Instruction.* Engelwood Cliffs, N.J.: Prentice Hall, 1980.

Engstrom, Georgianna, ed., *Play: The Child Strives Toward Self-Realization.* Washington, D.C.: NAEYC Publications, 1971.

Erikson, Erik H., *Childhood and Society.* New York: Norton, 1950.

Feitelson, D., and G. S. Ross, "The Neglected Factor—Play," *Human Development,* 16 (1973), 202–223.

Freud, Anna, *Normality and Pathology in Childhood: Assessments of Development.* New York: International Universities Press, 1968.

Freyberg, J. T., "Increasing the Imaginative Play of Urban Disadvantaged Children through Systematic Training," in *The Child's World of Make-Believe,* L. S. Singer, ed. New York: Academic Press, 1973.

Gerhardt, Lydia A., *Moving and Knowing: The Young Child Orients Himself in Space.* Englewood Cliffs, N.J.: Prentice-Hall, 1973.

Goodnow, Jacqueline, *Children Drawing.* Cambridge, Mass.: Harvard University Press, 1977.

Griffing, Penelope, "Sociodramatic Play among Young Black Children," *Theory Into Practice,* 13, no. 4 (October 1974), 257–266.

Hurlock, Elizabeth B., *Child Development.* New York; McGraw-Hill, 1972.

Kellogg, Rhoda, *Analyzing Children's Art.* Palo Alto, Cal.: Mayfield, 1970.

Krown, Sylvia. *Threes and Fours Go to School.* Englewood Cliffs, N.J.: NAEYC Publications, 1974.

Marshall, H. R., and S. Hahn, "Experimental Modification of Dramatic Play," *Journal of Personality and Social Psychology,* 5 (1967), pp. 119–22.

Millar, Susanna, *The Psychology of Play.* London: Penguin Books, 1973.

Moustakas, Clark, *Psychotherapy with Children: The Living Relationship.* New York: Ballantine, 1974.

Parten, Mildred B., "Social Play among Preschool Children," in *Child's Play,* R. E. Herron and Brian Sutton-Smith, eds. New York: John Wiley and Sons, 1971, pp. 83–95.

Peller, Lili E., "Libidinal Phases, Ego Development and Play," in *Psychoanalytic Study of the* Child, no. 9. New York: International Universities Press, 1959.

Piaget, Jean, *Play, Dreams, and Imitation in Childhood.* New York: Norton, 1962.

Rosen, C. E., "The Effects of Sociodramatic Play on Problem-Solving Behavior among Culturally Disadvantaged Preschool Children," *Child Development,* 45 (1974), 920–27.

Saltz, E., and J. Brody, "Pretend Play Training in Childhood: A Review and Critique," in *The Play of Children: Current Theory and Research,* D. J. Pepler and K. Rubin, eds. Basel, Switzerland: Karger, 1982.

Singer, Jerome L., *The Child's World of Make-Believe.* New York: Academic Press, 1973.

Smilansky, Sara, *The Effects of Sociodramatic Play on Disadvantaged Preschool Children.* New York: John Wiley & Sons, 1968.

Smilansky, Sara, Judith Hagan, and Helen Lewis, *Clay in the Classroom: Helping Children Develop Cognitive and Affective Skills for Learning.* New York: Peter Lang, 1988.

Smilansky, Sara, and Leah Shefatya, *Facilitating Play: A Medium for Promoting Cognitive, Socio-Emotional and Academic Development in Young Children.* Gaithersburg, Md.: Psychosocial & Educational Publications, 1990.

Udwin, O., "Imaginative Play Training as an Intervention Method with Institutionalized Pre-school Children," *British Journal of Educational Psychology,* 53 (1983), 32–39.

Weikart, David, et al., *The Cognitively Oriented Curriculum: A Framework for Preschool Teachers.* Washington, D.C.: NAEYC Publications, 1970.

Wolfgang, Charles H., *Helping Aggressive and Passive Preschoolers through Play.* Columbus, Ohio: Charles E. Merrill, 1977.

Wolfgang, Charles H., Bea Mackender, and Mary E. Wolfgang, *Growing and Learning through Play.* Paoli, Penn.: Instructo/McGraw-Hill, 1981.

Materials Preference Inventory (MPI)

The following is a preference inventory requiring you to make forced choices between two competing play materials. Once completed, you will know more about your own feelings and preferences for various types of play and play materials. Complete the instrument below without more explanation.

Part I. Forced Choice

Instruction: For each item below, there are two types of play materials, A and B. Choose the materials you feel a 3-, 4-, or 5-year-old would gain most from using. You might like or not like either choice, but you must choose one. Circle either A (left example) or B (right example), but not both. Please be sure to answer all 20 items. Circle the letter following the number of each item, based on your choice between two play materials.

(1) A. Toy farm animals vs. B. Water play
(2) A. Legos vs. B. Balance beam
(3) A. Puppets vs. B. Number steps
(4) A. Playhouse/furniture vs. B. Carpentry table
(5) A. Large playhouse vs. B. Climbing and sliding
(6) A. Clay modeling vs. B. Number puzzles
(7) A. Finger-painting vs. B. Unit blocks
(8) A. Sand play vs. B. Climbing structure
(9) A. Puzzles vs. B. Letter game
(10) A. Rocking boats vs. B. Letter stencils

(11) A. Easel painting vs. B. Dress-up costume play
(12) A. Tricycle vs. B. Color shape matching board
(13) A. Number cards vs. B. Child-sized toy kitchen
(14) A. Color pegboard vs. B. Doll with furniture
(15) A. Swings vs. B. Miniature toy people/furniture
(16) A. Number matching vs. B. Play dough
(17) A. Cardboard blocks vs. B. Crayons/construction paper
(18) A. Climbing structure vs. B. Easel painting
(19) A. Color puzzles vs. B. Large wooden blocks
(20) A. Magnetic board/nos. & letters vs. B. Climbing hoops

Part II. Scoring

Step 1. Circle your responses, from above, on the following tables and add to get a total for each table:

No. 1	No. 2	No. 3	No. 4	No. 5
1A 3A 4A	1B 6A 7A	2A 4B 7B	2B 5B 8B	3B 6B 9B
5A 11B 13B	8A 11A 16B	9A 12B 14A	10A 12A 15A	10B 13A 16A
14B 15B	17B 18B	17A 19B	18A 20B	19A 20A

Step 2. Place the totals from the above tables on the following blanks and divide.

Total responses in Table 1 _____ divide by 8= _____%
Total responses in Table 2 _____ divide by 8= _____%
Total responses in Table 3 _____ divide by 8= _____%
Total responses in Table 4 _____ divide by 8= _____%
Total responses in Table 5 _____ divide by 8= _____%

Each of the tables above has clustered together similar types of materials to do specific types of play: Table 1—Make Believe Toys for Symbolic Play, Table 2—Fluid Materials for Construction, Table 3—Structured Materials for Construction, Table 4—Equipment for Sensorimotor Activities, and Table 5—Academic Materials for Learning Numbers and Letters.

Questions to Consider: In understanding your results, it is important to see how you scored related to your extremes in likes or dislikes. What was your number-one choice of play and play materials? Would you include more of these materials in your classroom and encourage young children to spend more time playing and using these materials? What did you not prefer? Do you dislike these materials? Would you not put them into your classroom, and unknowingly discourage children from engaging in such play? Did you pick as your first choice Academic Materials? Would you design a classroom that is too academically oriented and not developmentally appropriate? In the chapters that follow, you will learn to design a classroom that will create a balance of all these types of play and play materials.

3

Organizing Classroom Space and Play Materials

Since young children spend most of their days actively involved in the play-activity curriculum, the basic classroom space should be organized around interest areas: fluid-construction (arts/crafts), structured-construction (manipulatives), dramatic play (macrosymbolic play), and restructuring-construction (carpentry). The classroom may appear to the uninitiated observer to be haphazard and disorderly, but in this apparent disorder are embedded the "structures" that facilitate learning through play. Studies indicate that the quality of a program is related to well-developed, organized, varied play materials. Poorly organized space results in low levels of play, increased aggression, and a very exhausted teacher at the end of the day.

At first sight, a large U.S. department store or grocery market might appear chaotic to a visitor from a foreign country, but quickly he would learn the structures: how the materials were classified and arranged for easy access. Similar structures and organization must be established to run an open-play classroom.

Classification of Play Materials

The three types of play activities that will go on in our play-activity curriculum are sensorimotor play, symbolic play, and construction. Let's look at the materials for each type of play.

Fluid-Construction and Structured-Construction

The materials used for construction play can be thought of as being on a continuum from fluids to structured (see Figure 3.1). The materials on the fluid side of the continuum are sensory materials; they lack an internal form and can be easily transformed. Children need to learn to control these materials, such as paints, before they can produce a symbolic product like a "doggie." Near the structured end of the continuum, the materials maintain their own internal form and have a narrower range of uses. Puzzles would be the most structured material, allowing only one predetermined product. As children move from the sensory-fluid materials to the more structured materials, their play becomes more work-like.

Fluid Materials and Children's Perceptions

Centeredness and Reversibility
Piaget has demonstrated that dynamic fluid materials (water play, fingerpainting, etc.) can present an intellectual challenge to the 3- to 5-year-old, who is in the stage of preoperational thinking. Young children's thinking is described as centered and irreversible, and they are incapable of comprehending movement between states.

In order to demonstrate the centeredness in children's thinking (see Figure 3.2), Piaget presented a child with equal quantities of clay in the form of two balls. After the child agreed that the two balls were equal, as the child watched, Piaget rolled one ball into a sausage shape. Piaget found that the preschool-age child would either declare that the sausage had more clay "because it is longer," or that the ball had more clay because "it is higher." A young child centers intuitively on the one dimension, either length or height. Unlike adults, young children cannot simply mentally reverse the sequence of events to realize that nothing was added or taken away and, therefore, that the two portions of clay are still equal. The irreversibility of thought limits a child's understanding of time, space, and causality in the use of fluid materials.

FIGURE 3.1   Construction Materials Continuum

Fluids		Structured
sand play	clay modeling	Legos
fingerpainting	drawing	Montessori materials
easel painting	blocks	puzzles

FIGURE 3.2   "Centering"

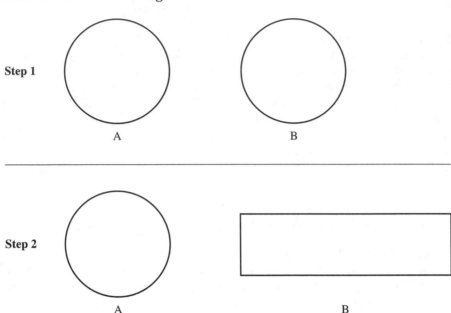

States versus Transformations

In order to explore children's ways of thinking related to transformation (see Figure 3.3), Piaget presented a child with a pencil held in a vertical position above a table top. The pencil was permitted to fall to rest on the table in a horizontal position. The children were then requested to draw a picture of the movement of the pencil. Of the many children tested, at various ages, the preschoolers represented the pencil in the static vertical state and the static horizontal state. It was not until the early elementary ages that children could understand the transformation between states and draw the pencil in various descending stages. This inability to comprehend transformation is a characteristic of the young child and becomes particularly apparent when he is required to understand any dramatic change in his world. For example, a child younger than age 6 would have difficulty understanding the children's story of *The Ugly Duckling,* in which the ugly duckling changes (transforms) into a beautiful swan (Brearley, 1969).

You can now see that the use of fluids—such as fingerpaints, water, or juice poured at snack time—by a young child presents a major intellectual challenge. For a child simply to pour water from a larger container to a smaller container would involve a classic example of a transformation (change in states). For the child to understand when to stop pouring would require decentering (taking into

FIGURE 3.3   **"States vs. Transformations"**

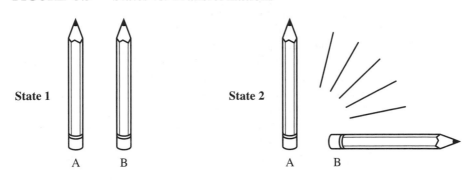

consideration at least two variables) and how to coordinate the two containers and the flow of water.

Providing a Structure for the Use of Fluids

Materials classified as fluids are constantly transforming, making both cognitive and (since young children are often disciplined harshly for spills) emotional demands that require the child to apply control. Structured materials, such as puzzles, foam-boards, Legos, and similar items are more manageable and predictable. This is well demonstrated in the excellent insights of Maria Montessori (1965), who had the responsibility of teaching many "street" children whose world lacked predictability and structure in relation to time, space, and objects. She therefore created a classroom where every object had to be used in a structured manner.

This brings us to two important Montessori concepts: *control of error* and *degree of freedom.* Montessori wanted to create open, activity-based classrooms where children were free to choose from all materials provided, but she realized that it was upsetting to children when things drop, break, and spill. So, she designed the environment, including the toys, to minimize these occurrences. The equipment is built to be introduced "one concept at a time." Let's consider graduated cylinders. This equipment involves a large block of wood 4 inches square and 14 inches long. Cut out of the block are nine cylinders, each 1½ inches thick, but from left to right the cylinders' depth increases gradually from ¼ inch to 3 inches deep. Once removed from the block, the cylinders can be put back only in one order, as with any puzzle; thus, the child cannot learn to do this task "wrong," and *control of error* is assured.

Let's examine water play to see a demonstration of "error" and "freedom." In the Montessori classroom, water-play would involve two 4-inch vinegar jars with handles, placed on an oval tray. One jar would be half full of colored water. Also on the tray would be a small sponge and paper towel. All of this is stored on a shelf at the child's height. The child takes the water-play equipment by grasping handles at either end of the tray and carries it to a child-sized table, where he practices pouring from the full jar to the empty jar and back again. Thus, there is little possibility that the child will drop, spill, or make an "error" and if a small mishap does occur, a sponge and paper towel are within easy reach.

The Montessori goal of controlling for error is in direct contrast to a pure play preschool such as the Bank Street or British models, which include a large table, 6 inches deep by 4 feet long by 2 feet wide filled with water and equipped with funnels, measuring cups, hoses for siphoning water, and small suction basters. Sometimes the teacher even adds liquid soap. This water-play table gives the greatest *degree of freedom* to the children in their play.

You may take any fluid material and arrange it for the amount of *freedom* it grants to the child. A small plastic tub for use by one child at a time (4 inches deep by 12 inches square) with 2 inches of water and liquid soap could be seen as a halfway point between the Montessori water-play and an open water table.

Play-curriculum purists would criticize the Montessori model as being too structured and stifling to children's creativity. However, the child-centered, play-based educator, with an understanding of control of error and degree of freedom, can deliberately use this type of structure to achieve certain purposes with certain children. For example, if you have a shy, overcontrolled child who is fearful of water-play, fingerpainting, or easel paint, you may first borrow from the Montessori method and give her the vinegar jars of water to pour. Once the child practices control with these, you can move her along the "structuring" continuum by introducing the plastic tub with 2 inches of water and then, finally, assist the child to meet the challenge of the large, open water-play table. Thus, "structuring" by controlling for error may be used as an important tool in the open environment.

Restructuring-Construction

Carpentry, cutting and pasting, paper collage, and similar forms of construction involve processes whereby children take materials that maintain their shapes and forms and, by cutting or sawing, restructure them to create unique products. This restructuring-construction requires a child to have well-developed mental or object permanency in order to keep a mental image of a symbol that she would like to make, while at the same time solving the problems in restructuring (cutting, sawing, pasting, etc.) to produce a desired product.

Symbolic Toys

Another class of play materials is *symbolic objects,* or *toys.* This category includes the miniature (microsymbolic) toys designed to replicate people, animals, furniture, and other everyday items that children use in isolated dramatic play. It also includes macrosymbolic toys such as child-sized furniture, eating utensils, clothing, and role-play items. Both microsymbolic and macrosymbolic toys help young children carry out highly social, cooperative make-believe play.

Figure 3.4 asks some questions that will help you think about the diversity of objects and materials that you will want to select for your classroom.

Steps and Procedures for Organizing Space

The teacher who has developed an understanding of the fluid-to-structure continuum, restructuring of materials, and symbolic toys is prepared to design a well-balanced environment to support play. One cannot overstate the importance of the room arrangement; just as a well-organized airport provides for efficient movement of many people, so the organization of the classroom is a prerequisite for successful play.

FIGURE 3.4   Anti-Bias Environments

Objects and materials that you choose and place in your environment or classroom "speak" to children. Posters, books, music, dolls, and a host of other materials may reflect a narrow all-White, stereotypic culture, race, or sex that may prevent the child of color, the child of different abilities, or the child who is poor from gaining a feeling of identity that values and expresses his or her uniqueness. Therefore, it is critical to gain a sensitivity of the materials that you place in your classroom.

Do the materials in your classroom:

- Reflect diversity in gender roles, racial and cultural backgrounds, and special needs and abilities?
- Deal with a range of occupations and ages?
- Accurately present images and information, or are they stereotypical?
- Show family and children within groups?
- Depict various life-styles, income, and family patterns?
- Overly depict the dominant religious or cultural group's dramatic play?
- Include tools of people with special needs, such as wheelchairs, crutches, braces, canes, heavy glasses, and hearing aids?
- Support roleplay of a wide variety of occupations to both boys and girls?
- Include dolls that represent a balance of all major groups in the United States—Black, Latino, Asian-Pacific, Native American, and White?
- Provide language signs and labels reflective of other cultures; languages, as well as Braille or sign language?
- Provide experiences with music and sound reflective of a wide variety or regions and backgrounds, including dance?

The Floor Plan

Begin by actually drawing a plan or sketch of your classroom on a piece of graph or grid paper. Measure the classroom length and width, and draw it to scale, making one square equal one foot in the actual classroom. Better still, write to Childcraft Education Corp., 20 Kilmer Road, Edison, New Jersey, 08818, and request the *Early Childhood Planning Guide.* The guide provides grid paper and pieces of silhouetted furniture, in scale, that can be arranged on the grid paper to represent your classroom—as in Figure 3.5.

Permanent Structures and Features

On your clean grid paper, first mark windows, doorways, poles, partitions, and other permanent fixtures such as coatracks, storage cupboards, water fountains, and sinks in your classroom. At this point, it is important to include these permanent items in the floor plan drawing in order to work around them. With a crayon, lightly color the "floor" area, giving different colors for *permanent* rugs, wood floors, and/or linoleum. Do this to scale.

Coatracks and Children's Storage

Now, decide which door the children and parents will enter through each morning. Do they exit through this same door when going to the playground or is there a second door for this? If there is only one door, the coat lockers and children's storage bins (sometimes called *cubbies*) must be placed inside this door for easy access. Depending on classroom space and the size of storage bins, children may have to share these spaces.

If there is a second door to exit for the playground, it might be best to place the cubbies along the wall near this door. In the morning, there is usually one parent to one child, helping the child to dress or undress, but when one or two teachers have all the "helping" to do, having an exit door near to the playground will create less commotion for the teachers. Another advantage of having a second exit door is that it requires parents to cross the classroom to get out, which means parents and teachers are more likely to see and greet each other.

Scaled Furniture

Cut rectangles from black construction paper scaled to the cubbies, and place the cubbie cutouts against the wall at whatever door you decide to use. (*Note:* The Childcraft guide provides all the furniture shapes you will need from this point on.) Do not permanently glue any of the cutout forms suggested!

You will need shapes representing your tables, nonpermanent shelves or partitions, and movable rugs. Shelving and partitions will be used to section off special play areas in the classroom.

Example Classroom Map

In the Sample Classroom Map (Figure 3.5), we have divided the classroom into zones Al, A2, B1, B2, C1, and C2. Note that zones Al and A2 have floors of permanent linoleum. The fluid-construction area (two easels, sand/water table, two circular tables with six chairs each, and a hideaway storage area containing scissors, construction paper, glue, and similar items) and a nearby sink make up zone Al. Keep in mind that in this area, activities of restructuring-construction (paper towel roll cutting, paper cutting, etc.) also will take place.

Zone A2 contains the entrance door, parent message book with sign in/out form, parent bulletin board, mirror mounted on the wall near the door, and science table with fish tank, gerbils, plants, and so on, as well as two chairs (this is generally an "onlooker" activity, and the chairs delineate the number of children who can be at the table at once). Also, between the Al and A2 zones is a long shelf containing adult storage underneath, and above, a water fountain and sink.

A variety of materials are found in zone B2—structured-construction pieces (puzzles, Legos, etc.); fine-motor objects (dressing pads, lacing pads, etc.), and sensory materials (smelling bottles, sound boxes, color bars, etc.)—as well as two rectangular tables with chairs, two storage shelves, a nature table, a display bookshelf, and a soft couch on which children may relax and "read." A tape-listening station (tape recorder with headphones) might be added near the couch. It would be ideal if a window were located behind the couch to give natural light to book reading.

We consider the computer to be a structured-construction item. Since research indicates that children learn best by working in pairs, two chairs are placed in front of the computer.

Notice that zones Al, A2, and B2 contain all of the seated activities and 30 child-sized chairs. We recommend that all structured-construction be done on tabletops, not the floor, because items with many pieces get lost on the floor and at times trampled and broken. The tables help "control of error."

Zone B-1 is for structured-construction. It contains a microsymbolic play area and the circle area with an adult-sized rocker, piano, and audio center (tape and CD player). Rhythm instruments are mounted on a display board above the piano, with the VCR-TV unit at shoulder height, either on the piano or mounted on the wall. Blocks are stored on all three shelves. On top are placed four fruit baskets with handles, containing aggressive toy animals (lions, tigers, etc.), passive domestic animals (cows, chickens, etc.), miniature-life rubber people, and miniature-life furniture pieces.

The block and toy storage shelf nearest zone C1 would have wheels to enable it to be pushed back along the movable divider to increase the space for story/circle time, or for putting cots down for rest time. A half-round table could also be pushed against the divider or the wall to create a potential unit space. The blocks and miniature toys are used on the floor, which is covered by a rug to cut

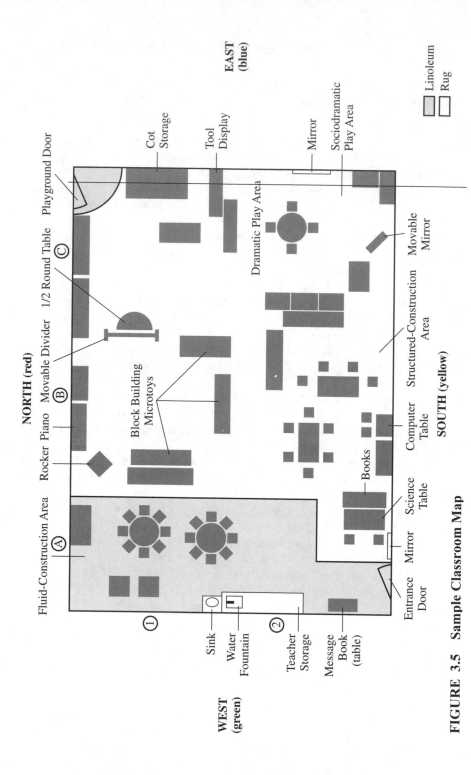

FIGURE 3.5 Sample Classroom Map

NORTH (red)

EAST (blue)

SOUTH (yellow)

WEST (green)

Fluid-Construction Area

Rocker Piano Movable Divider 1/2 Round Table Playground Door

Block Building

Microtoys

Cot Storage

Tool Display

Dramatic Play Area

Mirror

Sociodramatic Play Area

Structured-Construction Area

Movable Mirror

Computer Table

Books

Science Table

Mirror

Entrance Door

Message Book (table)

Teacher Storage

Water Fountain

Sink

Linoleum

Rug

38

down the noise when blocks fall; rug surfaces are also better for sitting on during circle time. A rug would be better used in this area than in any other.

In zone C1 are coat lockers, the playground exit door, cot storage, and the woodworking bench, along with a display board with the woodworking tools. Notice that much space is given to the carpentry table, allowing the children considerable elbow room; and, since it is sectioned off, fewer children will be wandering aimlessly through this area. On good outdoor days, the carpentry table could be moved outside, in view of the teachers, alleviating the sawdust problem.

All of zone C2 is devoted to sociodramatic play (macrosymbolic play), with its center being a child-sized table and four chairs. Also located here is a permanently mounted mirror (a movable mirror is available also). Notice, again, that zones B1, C1, and C2 have all the activities for which children will be standing and moving about during their play (with the exception of paint easels and the sand table).

Adequate Play Units

One of the most unique and interesting ways of determining good play space organization is found in the system proposed by Sybil Kritchevsky in her pamphlet *Planning Environments for Young Children.* In this system, each play area within the classroom is considered a "sponge" that can absorb children into productive play. The evaluation for each play area is based on how many children it can accommodate, which can be calculated using this scoring system: A *simple unit* refers to play items that can be used successfully only by one child. This would include such items as a puzzle or an easel with paints and paper. The simple unit receives a score of 1, and would thus have a "play potential" involving only one child.

A sand table with sand alone has limited play potential, but when miniature life toys and water are added, its complexity and capacity to accommodate children increases. When two or three materials are arranged together, you have a *complex play unit,* with a score of 4. The number refers to the approximate number of children who might be accommodated (absorbed) by the play space. When more than three types of materials are placed together, you have a *super-complex unit,* with a score of 8. Usually, the dress-up corner or the sociodramatic play corner—with items such as clothing, furniture, clay, and household items—is easily made into a super-complex unit.

Note that the simple unit has more "control of error," and, as the units become more complex, they begin to have maximum "degrees of freedom." The next time you visit a Montessori classroom, notice that the entire room is designed with mostly simple units and only a few complex units. Rarely if ever will you find a super-complex unit. If we use Parten's definition of the stages through which young children progress socially, we would find in the standard

Montessori classroom children performing socially in stages of unoccupied, onlooker behavior, with an abundance of solitary and parallel activity, and very limited associative play. True cooperative play would be very rare because of the lack of super-complex units. Therefore, your arrangement of space and objects can help determine whether the classroom might facilitate or hinder development.

The final play unit, the *potential unit,* is an open table or space where material can be changed daily. Though the potential unit does not receive a score, each classroom should contain one or two of these in order to add variety.

Once the classroom is organized, add the number of play units and divide by the number of children who will be using the area. Ideally, there will be 2½ potential play units for each child. You should balance the number of simple, complex, and super-complex units based on the amount and types of play expected from each age group of children (see Figure 2.2, Developmental Play Abilities of Children) and on the amount of time that the children will spend in the classroom. For all-day programs, many more simple units might be added to enable children to isolate themselves and find privacy occasionally during the day. It is unrealistic to require egocentric young children to spend large amounts of time in highly socialized activity with other children.

If we add up the play potentials (Table 3.1) of our sample classroom, we find that a score of 58 is obtained. When we divide that number by 2.5 play spaces desired for each child, we get a rating of 23+ children that the sample classroom could hold effectively.

TABLE 3.1   Play Spaces or Units for Sample Classroom Map

Play Potential	Score
Zone A1	
2 2-sided easels	
4 simple units	4
Sand/water table	
1 complex unit	4
2 tables with 6 chairs	
12 simple units	12
Zone A2	
2 seats at science table	
2 simple units	2
Zone B1	
Block/microsymbolic play	
1 super-complex unit	8

TABLE 3.1   *(Continued)*

Play Potential	Score
Zone B2	
12 chairs at structured-construction tables	
12 simple units	12
Couch for book reading	
2 simple units	2
Computer with 2 chairs	
2 simple units	2
Zone C1	
Carpentry table	
1 complex unit	4
Zone C2	
Sociodramatic play area	
1 super-complex unit	8
	58 divided by 2.5 per child = 23+

Table 3.2 provides a list of basic play materials and equipment needed in a classroom for 20 or more children.

Label Activity Areas

Let's return to our sample classroom map (Figure 3.5). The large "sponges" or interest play areas to be put on the map and into our play environment are:

> Fluid-Construction Area
> Structured-Construction Area
> Restructuring-Construction Area
> Sociodramatic Play Area
> Microsymbolic or Block and Miniature-Life Toy Area

Structured-Construction Organization

The structured-construction area is full of manipulatives such as interlocking blocks; child-sized shelves face rectangular tables (two or three) with chairs. The shelving should create a "walled-in" effect, with the third side partially blocked (making a natural "door") and the fourth side left completely open. Every zone that is sectioned off, such as the manipulative area, should have two entrances to permit an easy flow of children in and out of the area. Having only one entrance

Table 3.2   Basic Play Materials and Equipment

	Quantity	Description
Zone A1		
Fluid-Construction*		
	2	Sand and water table with cover
	2 sets	Water play kit
	2 sets	Sand tools—20 pieces
	1 set	Aluminum funnels and scoops
	2	Aluminum can and sifter
	1	Fancy molds
	2	Double adjustable easel
	3 sets	Nonspill paint storage pots
	2 sets	Plastic smock
	3 sets	Beginner paintbrushes
		Tempera paint
	2 gal	blue
	2 gal	green
	2 gal	orange
	2 gal	red
	2 gal	yellow
		Fingerpaint
	2 qt	blue
	2 qt	green
	2 qt	orange
	2 qt	red
	2 qt	yellow
	5 pkgs	Fingerpaint paper
	5 pkgs	Easel paper
	5 pkgs	Manila drawing paper
	1	Paper holder/cutter
	1 roll	White paper roll
	2 sets	Standard crayons
	2 sets	Finger crayons
	2 sets	Watercolor markers
	3	Marker stand
	2 gal	Glue
	2 doz	Roll-on glue
	2 boxes	Standard chalk
	2 boxes	Colored pencil-set
	3 sets	5-in. blunt scissors (right-handed)
	4	5-in. blunt scissors (left-handed)
	2	Teacher's scissors
	4	Beginner's scissors
	2	Scissor rack
	1 set	Yarn with dispenser box

*Note: Thumb tacks, desk pins and plastic push-pins are not recommended for an early childhood classroom—children swallow them.

Table 3.2 *(Continued)*

	Quantity	Description
	1	Pencil sharpener
	5 sets	Primary pencils
	2	Tape dispenser
	5 rolls	Tape
	10 rolls	Masking tape
	5	Beginner's ruler
	2	Stapler
	1 box	Staples
	5	Paperpunch
	1	Rotary paper trimmer
		Construction paper
	1 pkg	brown
	1 pkg	blue
	1 pkg	green
	1 pkg	orange
	1 pkg	black
	1 pkg	red
	1 pkg	violet
	1 pkg	white
	1 pkg	yellow
	2 pkgs	Air-drying clay (25 lbs)
	2 sets	Clay design kit
	2 sets	Clay hammers
	2	Airtight containers
Zone A2 **Science Equipment**		
	1	Easy-view magnifier
	1	Thermometer
	2	Classroom pet cage
	1	Giant ant farm
	2	Aquarium and kit
	1	Magnastiks
Zone B1 **Structured-Construction**		
		Blocks
	48	Half units
	192	Units
	96	Double units
	48	Quadruple units
	18	Pillars
	24	Large cylinders
	20	Small cylinders

(Continued)

Table 3.2 *(Continued)*

	Quantity	Description
	6	Circular curves
	8	Elliptical curves
		Triangles
	8	Large
	16	Small
	6	Floor boards—11"
	12	Ramps (double triangle)
	2	Y switches
	1	Hollow blocks (1/2 set)
Microsymbolic Toys		
	2 sets	Rubber zoo animals
	2 sets	Rubber animals (farm)
	1 set	Animal families
	1 set	Zoo play—22 pieces
	1 set	Police patrol (wheeled toys)
	1 set	Fire patrol (wheeled toys)
	1 set	Interstate road master (wheeled toys)
	2 sets	Pliable people—Black family
	2 sets	Pliable people—White family
	2 sets	Pliable people—Hispanic family
	1 set	Hardwood doll furniture—35 pieces
	1 set	Puppets (donkey, dolphin, rabbit, frog, pig, mouse, wolf, shark, elephant, alligator, hippo, giraffe)
	1	Puppet stand
Music		
	1	Cassette tape recorder
	15	Blank audio tapes
	1	Portable CD player
	1 set	Listening center
	1	VCR-TV combination
		Rhythm instruments
	1	Resonator bells
	2 sets	Maracas
	4	Tambourines
	5	Castanets on stick
	5	Cymbals
	10 sets	Rhythm sticks
	3	Triangle
	5	Handle bells

Table 3.2 *(Continued)*

	Quantity	Description
Zone B2		
Structured-Construction		
		Legos
	2 sets	Snap togethers
	2 sets	Interlocking cubes
	1 set	Frontier building blocks (300 pieces)
	1 set	Tinker toys (224 pieces)
	2 sets	Ring-a-majigs
	3 sets	Octons
	1	Jumbo Hundred pegboard
	1	Patterns for Jumbo Hundred pegboard
	4	Stick pegboards
	1	Box of 1,000 pegs
	3	Parquetry
	1	Parquetry pattern cards
	2	Colorama
	1	Tactile domino blocks
	1	Double puzzle—numbers
	4	Color quantity math board
	2	Number pegboards (him)
	1	Fruit count
	1	Set and sequences—numbers
	1	Beg. tape-measuring
	1	Jumbo domino set
	1	Jumbo animal dominoes
	1	Judy clock
	1	Computer
	1	Printer
		Software
	1	Printshop
	1	Stickiebears
Sensorimotor		
		Fine motor
	1 set	Dressing pads
	1	Lacing pads
	1	Lock board
	2	Etch-a-sketch
	1	Smelling bottles
	1	Sound boxes
	1	Color bars
	1	Mystery sensori-box

(Continued)

Table 3.2   *(Continued)*

	Quantity	Description
	1	Bag of feelies
	1	Pictures and objects matching game
	1	Jumbo touch and match
	1	Hide and seek memory board
	1	Memory shapes
	1	Listen lotto 1
	1	Listen lotto 2

Zone C1
Restructuring-Construction

	Quantity	Description
	1	Carpentry table
	1 set	Tool set (2 7-oz. claw hammer, 12" back-type saw, 3" screwdriver, 4" screwdriver, pliers)

Zone C2
Sociodramatic Play

	Quantity	Description
	1 set	Kitchen furniture—complete set (refrigerator, sink, stove, dutch cabinet)
	2 sets	Miniature play food
	1 set	Aluminum cooking set (tea kettle with lid, 1 covered and 1 uncovered saucepan, frying pan, strainer and ladle)
	1 set	Aluminum luncheon (teapot, 4 cups and saucers, plates, covered sugar bowl and creamer)
	1 set	Kitchen utensils
	1 set	Aluminum flatware
	1	Cash register
	1	Shopping cart
	2	Wood phone
	1	Housecleaning set and stand (straight broom, wet mop, dust brush, push broom and dustpan)
	1	Iron and board
	2 sets	"Cast of characters" plastic hats
	2 sets	Career costumes and accessories (police, fire chief, and doctors uniform)
	1	Trunk #1 of costumes (black cape, mustache, bowtie, loincloth, turkey quill, head-dress, magician's wand, sheriff's badge, monster-teeth and bandana)

Table 3.2 *(Continued)*

	Quantity	Description
	1	Trunk #2 of costumes (metallic flapper band, ostrich plume, necklace, satin ribbon, red cape, witch's hat, devil's horns and tail, plus a crown)
	1	Doll bed
	1	Doll cradle
	1	Mattress, pillow, and blanket for doll
	1	Baby doll—Hispanic
	2	Baby doll—Black
	3	Baby doll—White
	1	Brentwood baby carriage
	1	Baby doll highchair
	4	2-position plexi-mirror (36 inches by 12 inches)
	1 set	8 nonsexist career puzzles
	1 set	8 nursery rhyme puzzles
	2	Wood puzzle rack
General Furniture*		
	1	Modular organizer shelves
	1	32-tray hideaway cabinet
	1	Classroom cubbies with 25 white trays
	6	Toy shelves
	1	Hideaway cabinet
	1	Book mobile
	4	Bulletin board screen
	20	See-all storage tray
	20	See-all storage lid
	3	48" round table
	2	48" half-round table
	4	Rectangle tables (24 inches by 26 inches)
	10	Chair (11½ inches) (dark colors only)
	10	Chair (13½ inches) (dark colors only)
	1	Adult rocker chair
	2	Rest cot
	1	Flannelboard
	2	4-drawer vertical file
	4	Large waste paper cans
Playground Gross Motor	5	Jumping balls
	3	Tricycles (12 inches)
	1	Wagon

* *Note:* An adult teacher's desk is not recommended.

(Continued)

Table 3.2   *(Continued)*

	Quantity	Description
	2	Twinwheeler wheel barrow
	10	Balls (2)
	1	Air pump and needles
	1	Bean bag toss game
	1	Playground tower center (tire swing, slide pole, 12-foot single slide, platform, enclosed step)
	1	Thornhill double tire ladder, plastic slide, platform, tire swing, fireman's pole, sandbox
	8	Suspension bridge
	16	Fireman's pole
	19	Chin-up bars (1 at 25 inches, 1 at 36 inches)
	21	18-inch wide plastic slide
	25	Hand-over-hand ladder
	27	Sandpulley, pail, sandchute
	30	Sandbox (8 feet by 8 feet) with canvas cover (use sand toys as suggested for indoor play)
		Oval sidewalk, 4 feet wide (for trikes)
		Large galvanized water trough for lambs (12 feet by 2 inches by 5 feet) (use water-play toys suggested for indoor play)
	4	Hang-on-the fence easel (include brushes, paints, cups)
	3	Balance beams (2 feet by 4 feet by 8 inches)
	1	Outdoor playhouse
Outdoors		
		Picnic table
	1	Adult porch swing
	3	Adult wooden bench
	1	Outdoor water fountain
	2	Large trash can with lid

forces children to enter and exit through the same narrow space, and this may lead to pushing and shoving.

Shelves and Containers

Well-constructed multipurpose shelves (three shelves divided into units) are sold by most good preschool supply catalogues. Manipulatives should be on the shelf in containers that permit the child to take large quantities of, for example, Legos to a table and back again with little chance of "error" (spills or accidents). We suggest placing the easiest manipulatives in a storage container on the top shelf, left corner; place the manipulatives next in difficulty in the container to the immediate right. Continue this easiest-to-more-difficult pattern across the first shelf until the shelf is full. Drop down to the second shelf and continue the pattern. The most difficult manipulatives would be found on the bottom shelf, right corner. Facing these shelves, you should be able to reach out and select the top left container and know that it contains the easiest manipulatives.

Color-coding shelves and containers helps children, teachers, and even strangers to the classroom to put everything in its place. Using colored plastic tape, ½ inch wide, let's suppose you assign red for north, blue for east, yellow for south, and green for west. Begin by declaring as "south" the classroom wall in which the morning entrance door is located. Mark the other walls on your classroom map as north, east, and west appropriately.

If the multipurpose shelves containing manipulatives in containers make up the west wall, use green tape for labeling, since green represents west. Starting with the top-shelf, far-left container, place on the front of the container one horizontal strip of tape and one vertical strip, each 1 inch long. Now, on the container to the right again make one horizontal strip, but this time two vertical strips. Continue moving to the right, using one horizontal strip and increasing by one the number of vertical strips on each successive container. Now, on the edge of the shelf *underneath* each of the containers make parallel markings to match those on each container.

With the first shelf completed, drop down to the middle shelf, working from left to right, but this time make two horizontal strips in green (to denote that this is the second shelf), and one vertical; then, moving right, two horizontal strips and two vertical strips, and continue across in this pattern, increasing the number of verticals as you move left to right. We hope you are ahead of us by now and realize that the third shelf will begin with the bottom left container having three horizontal strips and one vertical strip.

With the shelves thus organized, a 3-year-old can take a container from the shelf and, when it's time to return it, simply look on the end of the container, turn to the green wall, match the markings on the container with those on the shelf, and place the toys in the correct spot. This gives him self-sufficiency, brings order to the classroom, and teaches him about using symbols for problem solving, and about spatial relationships, numbering, and concepts of color—all without direct teaching.

The containers on the same shelf should be similar in size and, if possible, of a clear plastic so that the child can see inside. To further label the objects, we glue onto the container a picture of the toy from its package—or, if necessary, we take a picture of the material. Both the color-coding strips and the picture should be painted over with clear varnish, so that they will not soil or come off. We do not recommend writing the names of the manipulative on the outside or using a numeral system before ages 5 to 6.

Tables

The structured-construction manipulatives—such as octagons, blocks, or ring toys—tend to be simple units that children bring to a table and use in isolated play. Two rectangular tables in this zone are suggested because children need more personal tabletop space for manipulatives. Round tables may be used in the fluid area where children are coloring, making paper collages, and doing other activities where they need to draw from a central supply of equipment. Also, circular tables permit greater sharing, and thus support parallel and cooperative play.

With very large rectangular tables it may become necessary to tape off the tabletops to mark private spaces in front of each chair. Another solution often found in the Montessori classroom is to use four to six very small tables (24 by 24 inches) in the manipulatives area, each with two chairs facing each other from opposite sides.

Some teachers carry the color-coding scheme to the tables by painting them red, blue, yellow, and green, and training the children to take containers from a shelf with a green symbol to a green table. (This is an arbitrary decision which, we feel, further limits the child's "degrees of freedom.") As with structured construction, we do not recommend the use of manipulatives on the floor, because the playthings may get stepped on by children passing through.

Table 3.3 matches chair and table sizes and suggests sizes for various ages. If you have children "family grouped"—that is, with 3s and 4s, or 4s and 5s

TABLE 3.3   Match Chair and Table Size

Ages	Chair Height	Table Height
2–3	10 inches	18 inches
4–5	12 inches	20 inches
5–6	14 inches	22 inches
6–8	16 inches	24 inches to 30 inches

together—it would be wise to mix the sizes. But if you are doing homogeneous grouping, it is easier to use the correct table selected from the chart.

If you err in selecting sizes of chairs and tables, it would be better to err with smaller chairs and higher tables, thus being always assured of plenty of knee room. Kidney-shaped and trapezoidal tables look novel but are very hard to live with and are generally not recommended. The exception is the purchase of two to four half-round tables that can be pushed individually flat against a wall in a small open area, providing a space in which a child may work in privacy.

Puzzles

Puzzles are expensive, have pieces that are easy to lose, and require control of error. They would consume too much shelf space if you simply laid them out on shelves, so most puzzles of the same size are stacked in purchased puzzle racks. It is suggested that the puzzles be placed on the rack from top (easiest) to bottom (most difficult). Puzzles with small handles connected to pieces containing complete symbols (such as fruits or animals) are classified as simplest. You may need to watch the children for some time before determining how to order your collection of puzzles.

Here again, we use color coding. If the puzzles are stored on the top shelf of a "southern" shelf unit, we would use yellow tape, making one vertical strip on the top (or easiest) puzzle, and adding strips as we move down in difficulty. If more than five puzzles were on the rack, we might use horizontals and verticals, much like the Roman numeral system.

If the puzzle does not have a puzzle base, but comes completely apart (like an adult puzzle), it may be stored on a small plastic cafeteria tray, and stacked and coded according to the system described. The tray, of course, keeps all the pieces together and, if the tray is big enough, the puzzle can be assembled right on the tray at the table.

A word to the wise: For your own sanity, label the puzzle pieces. Before school starts, but after you have created the coding system, take every puzzle and turn each puzzle over, one at a time, on a table. With a magic marker of the same color as the front coding, make a similar coding on the back at the top-left corner. Number all the loose pieces while the puzzle is still together from left to right, top to bottom. Do this with each puzzle, not repeating your numbers (use the alphabet symbols if necessary or a combination of letters and numbers). Once this is done, when you find a loose puzzle piece after cleaning up, you will not have to spend an exhausting amount of time trying to find where the piece goes.

Fluid-Construction Area

The next play area to be placed on your classroom map is the fluid-construction area, which will be located according to the water supply and type of flooring. If the northwest corner of the room has a sink, that corner becomes the hub for the fluid materials. If a sink or water supply is not in the room and one must go out the door to another room for water, the area near that door becomes the fluid area. Ideally, the floor surface needs to be one that can take getting wet. If there is a rug in this zone, it might be wise to have a large section cut away and the floor recovered with linoleum. If this cannot be done, large sheets of heavy plastic need to be placed under the easels as well as the sand and water tables.

Scream, shout, and become stubbornly insistent (but professional) if the authorities for your building tell you that you may not put fluids in your classroom. Fluids are not a frivolity; they are essential equipment to a play-based program.

Water-Play and Sand-Play

A large (40 inches by 21 inches by 26 inches) sand or water table is basic equipment in the fluid zone. If space is limited and you cannot have two tables, it might be better to use the indoor table for dry sand, which still has a watery-pouring quality, and move large water-play tubs or wet sand-play to the playground. Caution: Wet sand kept indoors goes sour quickly, so it must be changed often. Otherwise, you may return to your classroom after a long weekend to be met by a horrible odor.

The indoor dry-sand table should sit on a piece of indoor-outdoor carpet (5 feet by 5 feet) to keep the sand from spreading throughout the classroom. A broom and dustpan should be mounted on the wall nearby. Also, trace the form of the broom and pan as they hang, to form a silhouette, and then paint the silhouette to correspond with the color-coded wall. Then, when the broom or pan "wanders off," both the teachers and children will know where its "home" is (another example of the use of the control-of-error concept).

Plastic smocks are recommended and may be mounted nearby in a similar fashion. Limit the number of smocks to the number of children you feel can play at the water table at one time. Since this is a complex play unit, four or even more children can usually be accommodated here. Controlling the number of smocks per play unit permits us in a child-centered environment to say, "You need to wait until a smock is free before you can paint," which is more understandable to the children than, "You can't water-play now because there are too many children there!"

Water and Sand Playthings

A host of items can be used in the water table (except glass or metal, which rusts). Plastic is preferred. Here are a few suggested props: castoff teapots or coffee percolators, funnels, tubes, strainers, pitchers, squirt bottles, spoons, and pieces of garden hose. A large liquid container may be cut in half to make a funnel and a water container. Punch holes in plastic cups or cans to create jets. Small boats, pieces of wood and cork, bubble pipes and straws, and liquid detergent are also items that might encourage microsymbolic play.

Sand-Play

Sand is a relatively inexpensive material available in abundance in most communities. Order the prewashed type, as close to the color white as possible. The sand with a reddish tint contains a high concentration of iron and will stain children's clothing. Props for dry sand are very similar to those suggested for water-play because of sand's pouring-flowing quality. Here are suggestions for wet-sand props: spades, shovels, spoons, rubber or plastic buckets of varying sizes, small pie pans, old aluminum kitchen pots and pans, and large gelatin-molds (animal shapes preferred).

Although the table is designated for sand- and water-play, smaller plastic wash tubs periodically can be allowed on the table for fluids that are "potential play units," but these will be more restrictive than the large water table.

Clay, Modeling Clay, and Dough

Potter's clay is quite cheap and available at neighborhood art supply stores in 25- to 50-pound boxes encased in thick plastic bags. Move the bag of clay into 5-gallon plastic buckets or containers with lids that can be sealed airtight (closed diaper pails are excellent). This will help keep the clay moist. If it does get dry, add water and rework it. As with sand, avoid clothing stains by getting clay that is not red.

To control for error, have "clay boards" made (pieces of wood, approximately 14 inches square by 1 inch thick) and teach the children to sculpt on the boards. This not only defines ownership of space and clay but it also facilitates clean-up.

Once the child is finished making a symbolic product in clay, the product can be kiln-fired. More likely, you will simply move this "treasure" to the windowsill, paint it with glue or spray it with clear varnish, and let it dry to harden. Children may, of course, paint their sculptures first, before a hardener is applied.

Homemade Dough

Made with flour and salt, sometimes with food coloring added, homemade dough provides a fun activity for most children. It has a more fluid quality than earthen pottery clay and is easier to squeeze and use for sensory play. The dough does not lend itself to three-dimensional products, but children produce two-dimensional figures by rolling, cutting, and shaping the material, much like adults make Christmas cookies. Some tools for dough and clay are rolling pins, small tin cans of various sizes, old butter knives, forks, and spoons, pie pans, plastic plates, lollipop sticks, wooden hammers, and gelatin or cookie cutters of various shapes. (Note, however, that by supplying molds or cookie cutters, creative possibilities are diminished, and rather than producing their own creative symbols, the children are limited to those shapes in the molds.)

Recipes

Simple Uncooked Dough

1cup salt
1 cup flour
1/2 cup water
Knead the mixture. Add flour to reduce stickiness. Store, covered, in the refrigerator.

Cooked Play Dough

1 cup salt
1/2 cup cornstarch
2/3 cup water
Mix and cook until thickened, stirring constantly. Cool, then add vegetable coloring. Store in refrigerator.

Generally, commercial play dough is far inferior to both the earthen potter's clay and homemade dough. Not only is it gummy, but it would have to be purchased in very large quantities before there would be enough to work with; also, it dries out quickly. The only attractive feature of purchased plastic play dough is that it is easier to clean up. Save money and make your own—or get some good potter's clay.

Suggestion: Periodically take a photo of each child's best products so you may assess their symbolic development in this medium, and show the photos to parents during conferences. Note the date and any dialogue or information that the child has given you about this sculpturing, and file it in an art folder (which you maintain for each child).

Painting

Flat paper painting can be done either at an easel (where the paint drips) or at a table (where the paint tends to "pool up" and make holes in the paper). A double easel is a must for any early childhood classroom, and two doubles side by side are even better, if there is space. Keep in mind that painting is generally a simple unit, and the surrounding space, approximately 3 feet, belongs to this unit. To avoid accidents, pathways should not cut through this unit's space. If space is a severe problem, two plywood boards (2 feet square) can be mounted directly to the wall with two large metal binder clips to hold the paper.

There are a few rules to remember in creating a painting center. The smaller the child, the bigger the brush and the thicker the paint needed. A 3-year-old could enjoy a 2-inch brush, while the small, finer water-coloring brushes are suitable for children in elementary school. The chubby 7-inch by ¾-inch preschool paintbrushes are best for both easel and table painting. Deep paint pots are stored in their holes in the commercially purchased easels and help keep the long brushes from tilting over the paint pots. Lacking these, the teacher must wedge the paint pots into a sturdy box or a cardboard six-pack container with a handle. It is also helpful if the pots have some form of lid so the paints can be covered and not dry out overnight. If lids are not available, cover each pot with plastic wrap. Remember, after three or four days, the water in the paints will spoil and give off a bad odor.

Purchase primary colors and black and white powder paints. A small quantity of Ivory soap may be added for easier removal of spills from clothing. Some early childhood teachers give young 3-year-olds only black or dark-color paints at first (true for crayons and magic markers, as well) because they give greater contrast on white paper, which they feel helps the children develop an earlier ability to produce recognizable symbols with their paints.

We hope that the preschooler would soon have three to five colors available daily, as we reject that old kindergarten idea that painting with only one color each week will help a child learn his or her colors. Quite the reverse: Children learn to classify colors by comparing one color with the colors that it is not.

Storage of paper, in containers just slightly larger than the paper size and accessible to the child, is critical for control of error. Newspaper, butcher paper (ask a butcher to purchase an extra roll of butcher paper with the next order), and recycled computer paper are fine media for beginners.

Another critical need is to cover windowsills or shelf tops with newspaper or plastic for laying paintings out to dry. Make sure you place the child's name and date on the top left corner of the back side before he or she begins to paint so you will know who it belongs to afterwards. Drill a hole through a large primary school pencil and tie it onto a string (or tape the string to the pencil) and attach it to the side of the easel for ready access.

Also, it is advisable to create a form on small pieces of paper (about 2½ inches by 2 inches) with space for the child's name, date of painting, and any explanation the child has given of his product. Some of the most advanced symbol paintings should be kept every two to three weeks so you may assess the child's development and discuss it with parents in upcoming conferences.

Pencils, Crayons, Chalk, and Permanent Markers

In selecting sizes, the same principle applies for pencils and crayons as for paint-brushes: The smaller the child, the larger the marking tool. All of these media have very high interest for children, who will need space at child-sized tables with plenty of inexpensive paper within reach. Pencils, crayons, and similar media permit the child to do elaborate symbol drawings. These, too, should be labeled with name, date, and any description given by the child. In the thematic-project curriculum, discussed in another chapter, we see the teacher using these drawings for writing children's stories and making books. Again, samples of this work should be collected and stored in the child's artwork folder.

Paper Constructions and Junk Creations

Paper, as well as paints and crayons, can be a source of color and texture. A child might make a "picture," using green paper as the grass, cardboard as the tree trunk, a "forest" background from a wallpaper design, and aluminum foil as an ice-cov-ered pond. Added to this picture could be junk materials such as straws for tele-phone poles and old buttons for the wheels of a car. The child might glue, staple, or tape many other fasteners, and they should all be available in the fluid area.

Great care and creativity will be needed when the teacher arranges and stores these paper goods and junk materials if they are to be used by the children cre-atively and with a limited amount of "error." For example, after a group of chil-dren has used three balls of knitting yarn for a morning at the construction tables, the yarn will be a tangle of snags and knots, useless for further projects. To avoid this, put the yarn in a small, heavy cardboard box with a lid that folds tightly, put a hole in the lid the size of a nickel, and bring the end of the yarn out through the hole. Now when the children pull out a quantity of yarn, the "ball" will not be bouncing off the table and rolling across the floor with three young children in pursuit.

In a child-centered play environment, all of these materials—paper, yarn, junk, and so on—should be at the children's fingertips, permitting them to make their own creations. If the teacher announces, "Today we are going to make valentines," and sets up goals and objectives for the children, she or he has moved to method 2 (the project-centered curriculum), which we explore in another chapter.

Other Fluids

There are a host of other types of play using fluids—such as fingerpainting, mak-ing stencil prints with different shapes, sand painting, string painting, and so on—that can provide valuable experiences. However many of these require a great deal of teacher help and supervision.

Macrosymbolic Play or Sociodramatic Play Area

If you have chosen the northwest corner of your classroom for fluids, place the sociodramatic play area (also known as the macrosymbolic play area) in the directly opposite end of the classroom, the southeast corner. These are favored activities by children, and locating the fluid play and the sociodramatic play at opposite ends of the room will tend to distribute the children evenly over all the classroom space. Also, this maximum distance away from the wet play area will more likely keep the dress-up clothing and similar materials dry and paint-free. Small alcoves are especially nice for sociodramatic play; if available, you may choose to use an alcove, even though it is not opposite the fluids.

Traditionally, the sociodramatic play area includes a "domestic" play area with a child-sized stove, refrigerator, sink, table, and chairs. There also may be a toy ironing board, washer and dryer, or microwave oven. Many similar items may be included—for example:

Shopping/push carts or baskets

Miniature play food for each meal

A variety of kitchen utensils

Aluminum luncheon sets

Baking set and cookware

Plastic table setting with plates, cups, glasses, and "silverware"

Play toaster

Telephone

Housekeeping cleaning stand with a real mop, broom, dustpan, and hand broom

Hats of various occupations

Dress-up clothing, high-heeled shoes, and jewelry

A nurse and doctor set with uniform and kit

Cash register and play money

Any other castoffs that might support roleplay of young children

The key to making the sociodramatic play area effective is storing and organizing the materials so that the children know exactly where things belong. If you simply have boxes with any material thrown into them, children will not find what they want when they need it, and a low level of play will occur with a high likelihood of conflict and aggression. The color-coding system explained earlier may be used in the sociodramatic play area, as well.

Miniature food and miniature pots and pans, for example, may be stored in separate containers. If there are a dozen miniature plastic fruits, and a similar number of vegetables, two separate containers can be used and each labeled with a picture of the food group. The children can be taught the difference as the miniatures are put away. The containers should be marked with matching symbols. For things that will hang, such as large serving spoons and spatulas, mount a sheet of plywood on the wall, tacking headless nails on which the items will be hung. Draw around these items in silhouette form and paint them the appropriate color.

Finally, dress-up clothing can be organized on a plywood wallboard with standard hooks, or in child-sized cupboards, or in drawers. Sew the same color-coded pieces of ribbon inside the neck of shirts and jackets or inside the waistband of skirts or pants. Then, above the hooks in the wallboard, on the door of the cupboards, or on the outside of drawers, a parallel ribbon sequence can be glued and then painted with varnish. When dress-up clothing needs to be put away, children match the color ribbon sequences, first to the correct wall, before turning to the correct hook, cupboard door, or drawer.

In the sociodramatic play area, a large, permanent full-length mirror is suggested and, when possible, a movable mirror that can help define the "housekeeping" area. Also, small movable partitions (2 feet by 3 feet) effectively section off the macrosymbolic play area, as well as the block area, as suggested next.

Microsymbolic Play and the Block Area

Microplay with miniature life toys in combination with large unit blocks is most easily done on the floor. This is the easiest area to organize: Simply box it in by using shelving or the classroom walls on three sides, with the fourth side left open. One of the three sides might use a short shelf, creating a passageway for children to enter, since all play zones should have two openings to enter and exit.

Unit blocks will be stored together on multipurpose unit shelves. To indicate where each type of block goes, draw silhouettes of each type, color appropriately, and paste the silhouettes on the back of the appropriate shelves. If large wooden, wheeled toys such as tractors or trailer trucks are used, place silhouettes of them on the back of the shelves where they belong (or, if the shelves are backless, directly on the shelves). Generally, we place containers for the microtoys on top of the shelves: a container for rubber people figures, one for tame animals, one for wild animals, one for miniature furniture, and so on. A large (6 inches by 1 foot) woven wood fruitbasket with a large oval handle makes an excellent container for such items, as do plastic containers. As in the manipulative area, these containers and shelves will be marked with the horizontal-vertical colored symbols system, with a picture of the items glued to the front.

Blocks are another of the most valuable play materials. Don't skimp! You will need plenty of blocks so children can play associatively and cooperatively as they build castles, forts, houses, and other structures. Before putting out a new set of blocks, wax them with a hardwood floor paste wax, and periodically have the children wash them with a mild soap and rewax them. Never permit blocks to be taken from this play zone, especially to the carpentry table area, as you can guess what will occur. The following list (Hirsch, 1974) shows the seven stages in block building:

Stage 1. Blocks are carried around, not used for construction.

Stage 2. Building begins. Children make mostly rows, either horizontal (on the floor) or vertical (stacking). There is much repetition in this early building pattern.

Stage 3. Bridging: two blocks with a space between, connected by a third block.

Stage 4. Enclosures: blocks placed in such a way that they enclose a space.

Stage 5. When facility with blocks is acquired, decorative patterns appear. Much symmetry can be observed. Buildings generally are not named.

Stage 6. Naming of structures for dramatic play begins. Before that, children may also have named their structures, but the names were not necessarily related to the function of the building.

Stage 7. Children's buildings often reproduce or symbolize actual structures they know, and there is a strong impulse toward dramatic play around the block structures.

Usually, the children begin by building a structure and then bring out miniature life props that enable them to represent elaborate dramatic play sequences. Blocks with microprops are conducive to play that leads to development of the highest social stages; therefore, this area may be called a super-complex unit.

Interest Centers for Onlooker and Isolated Activities

Interest areas that require less active involvement by the child but are nonetheless highly educational and entertaining, such as the following, have traditionally been included in the play environment:

Listening centers with music and story tapes
Nature tables with plants and animals
Book displays
Computers

Room Planning

After you plan and arrange the play environment, you must "live" in the space to see if, in fact, the plan is working as desired. (The furniture pieces cut out for the classroom plan should be only taped or put down with "blue-tack" so they can be easily shifted around.) At the end of each school day, you should make some mark on the classroom map to indicate where there were accidents, spills, or social conflicts between children. At the end of a week or two, you may begin to see that these marks are all clustered in the same area, showing that this zone is not working and needs to be reorganized. Unfortunately, when spills, accidents, or social conflicts occur, teachers react many times by "laying on the rules" with young children, when a simple rearrangement of materials and equipment will very often eliminate the problems.

If excessive rules are needed regarding a certain piece of equipment, it might be best simply to remove it from the classroom. Possibly, it might be used on the playground, porch, or hallway more successfully. Each time teachers' rules are added, the child-centeredness of the classroom diminishes. Therefore, many teachers make lists of all teacher-imposed rules and decide as a staff what actions can be taken in the form of reorganization so that these rules are not needed. Because teachers have authority in their classrooms, slowly and without realizing it, they can make their classrooms so overregulated that the children lose their freedom. Use a faculty meeting with all staff, after a long holiday or at the beginning of a new semester, to list all teacher-imposed rules and decide as a staff on any reorganizing actions that might obviate these rules.

Let's take a concrete example (or, more accurately, a brick example). One school playground backed onto a dangerously busy street, which was separated from the school by a brick wall 4 feet high and nearly 18 inches thick. The children loved to climb to the top of this brick wall and look out over the playground or watch the passing auto traffic. A rule for not climbing up on the fence was understandably imposed. The rule required a teacher enforcer to be stationed near the fence.

After a meeting to reevaluate the rules, the staff decided that the children seemed to have a need to be free to climb and look out. A father of a child in the classroom was a bricklayer and was invited to build, in the middle of the playground, a brick wall—4½ feet high, 18 inches wide, and 8 feet long. The children could now use this new "safe wall." Also installed was a permanently mounted periscope containing mirrors with which a child could stand at ground level, in front of the wall, and see the "traffic" on the other side.

This minimizing of rules is central in an open, play-oriented school. Always try to find a safe outlet for the intrinsic curiosity of the children, rather than tell them what they may not do. Even good rules can often be creatively eliminated.

Summary

Let's review what you've read about child-centered teaching methods. If you now step into an open-play environment, you can recognize the various forms of play going on: symbolic (micro or macro), fluid-construction, structured-construction, and restructuring-construction. You can now organize a classroom for such play using the fluid-to-structured materials continuum, degrees of freedom construct, and the simple, complex, and super-complex play units.

Activities

1. Go into two or three play-oriented classrooms and make a map of the space and equipment on grid paper. Determine the play potential for the classroom and divide by the number of children normally using this space. What did you find? See if all play forms are abundantly represented or, if not, what is missing?
2. Interview a teacher in an open play preschool/kindergarten and ask the teacher for 5 classroom rules she or he has. Try to use the rearrangement of space and the concept of control of error to see if you can eliminate all those rules.
3. Using Parten's social development scale, observe four 3-year-old children playing and determine what levels of social development you observed. Do the same with four 4-year-olds and, finally, four 5-year-olds. Are there gender differences? In what category of play or materials did they demonstrate each of Parten's stages?
4. Do one 45-minute observation in each of the four zones—fluids, structured-construction, sociodramatic play, and microsymbolic-blocks. Write what you saw, using the constructs in the first three chapters.

References

Brearley, Molly, *The Teaching of Young Children: Some Applications of Piaget's Learning Theory*. New York: Schocken Books, 1969.

Hirsch, E. S., ed., *The Block Book*. Washington, D.C.: NAEYC, 1974.

Kritchevsky, Sybil, et al., *Planning Environments for Young Children: Physical Space*. Washington, D.C.: NAEYC, 1969.

Matterson, E. M., *Play with a Purpose for Under-Sevens*. London: Penguin Books, 1970.

Montessori, Maria, *Dr. Montessori's Own Handbook*. New York: Schocken Books, 1965.

Wolfgang, C. H., M. E. Wolfgang, and B. Mackender, *Growing and Learning through Play*. Paoli, Penn.: Instructo-McGraw Hill, 1981.

4

Play-Activity Learning: Goals and Teaching Methods

The play-activity curriculum views developmental needs as unique to each child; thus, the child's self-initiated ideas and activities are most valued. The goals are related to developmental theory and are long term in nature. The play-activity curriculum aims to facilitate the growth of adaptive abilities.

One of the highly regarded play-activity models, also known as a developmental-interactionist model, is the *Bank Street model*. The general goals of the Bank Street model are to help children develop competence, interpersonal relatedness (to have affection for and get along with others), individuality (independence), and creativity (Biber, 1977). These are also the goals to which the School for Young Children's play-activity curriculum subscribes.

Specifically, the Bank Street model lists the following as its goals:

1. To serve the child's need to make an impact on the environment through direct physical contact and maneuver. (This suggests that the child must learn by being free to work and play in a well-designed classroom full of a rich variety of materials, with a teacher and same-age level peers.)

2. To support the play mode of incorporating experiences. (Learning from a play-activity curriculum is not an input-output process; rather, the sequence of learning is experiencing, playing through symbols or representation, new experience, and more elaborate play. Through play, the child can emotionally digest experiences such as separation, feelings of smallness, family conflicts and pressures, and similar age-appropriate concerns [Peller, 1959; Erikson, 1950].)

3. To help the child develop impulse control and acquire patterns of positive social interaction (A. Freud, 1971). The children will encounter clashes and conflict with other children and adults as a natural part of living with others, and can progress though the developmental phases of passivity, physical aggression, and verbal aggression, to the level of maturity where they can master their emotions, learning to play and work with others through language and cooperation.

For a more detailed explanation of developmental-interactive Bank Street goals, see Biber (1977).

A child-centered method of teaching would be most appropriate for all three of the preceding goals. To begin to use this method, recall the concepts developed in earlier chapters:

1. The categories of play: sensorimotor, symbolic play (micro-, macro-, socio-dramatic), and construction-fluids and construction-structured
2. The level of Parten's social stages: unoccupied, onlooker, solitary, parallel, associative, and cooperative
3. The level of symbolic activity (e.g., can they role enact, interact with others, produce meaningful representations in art)

Teaching through Play

The Teacher Behavior Continuum

Now that you (1) know the forms of play (sensimotor, construction, and symbolic play), (2) know how that play changes developmentally (e.g., from random scribbling to controlled scribbling in a child's drawing, or the criteria for sociodramatic play), and (3) have created a play classroom with well-organized space (simple, complex, and super-complex units) with a balance of play materials (fluid and structured constructional materials, micro- or macrosymbolic toys, etc.), the next question is: How do you actually teach in such a play classroom? In a direct instruction classroom, you will see the teacher in full control, giving commands, modeling, and questioning the child to evaluate whether he or she understands the concept being taught deductively through a Say, Show, and Do or Check procedure. (For example: "Class, this is a three!" [Say and Show and model the concept]. "These are not threes!" [Show cards with a 2, 4, 5, and 6]. "Now I will ask you to come up and point to the three!" [Do or Check].) In this directive, deductive teaching, the teacher determines what concept will be taught, and holds total power over the activity and the child's behavior by requiring the child to act and perform through highly controlling *commands* and *questioning* while the concept is being *modeled.*

Teaching in a play environment, or inductive teaching, gives the child maximum freedom to engage fully with the play activity, with the teacher closely observing the activity and making judgments as to the advisability of intervening. The teacher's role is to follow the lead of the child and to extend the child's use of the materials to more mature forms of play and concepts. To provide the teacher with an understanding of the teacher's behavior when doing inductive play teaching or in facilitating and intervening, we have created a Teacher Behavior Continuum (TBC) of general teacher actions, which we place on a continuum that moves from minimum teacher power and control, such as simply *looking* (see Table 4.1), to that of *naming* (labeling concepts), *questioning* (extending the child's reasoning), *commanding* (requesting the child to perform a motor action), and finally to teacher *actions* (modeling or making a prop or materials change), with each behavior involving an increase in teacher control.

With the use of this Teacher Behavior Continuum, or power continuum, the informed teacher will understand the degree and appropriateness of the actions or intrusion into the ongoing play activity of the child. While observing direct instruction teaching, we see the teacher performing most of the actions while the child or children are observing. Just the opposite is true for teaching through play. Mostly, the teacher is observing (looking) and appears physically inactive, but this is only true in the outward behaviors. While looking and observing the child's play activities, the teacher is very mentally active. He or she is asking three levels of questions while watching the child: (1) What type of play is occur-

TABLE 4.1   Teacher Behavior Continuum (TBC)

Minimum Teacher Control (inductive)				Maximum Teacher Control (deductive)
Looking	Naming	Questioning	Commanding	Acting
While observing the child's play, the teacher determines the answers to (1) What play form is the child attempting? (2) What social stage (Parten) is the child doing? and (3) What symbolic level is the child able or not able to perform? (See Table 4.2)	The teacher verbally labels the concept or activities that the child is performing.	The teacher extends the child's thinking by questioning the child at: Level 1: Facts Level 2: Convergent ("How does this work?") Level 3: Divergent (requires creative thinking, going beyond the facts given) Level 4: Evaluative ("What is the best decision on solving this problem?")	The teacher requests a motor action by the child to extend his or her activity. (Example: "Place this puzzle piece here" or "Select the one that is red."	The teacher physically intervenes into the ongoing activity to add new props for the purpose of extending the child's play activity, or to model the concept to the child.

ring? (sensorimotor, symbolic, construction-fluids, or construction-structured); (2) At what social level? (unoccupied, solitary, onlooker, parallel, associative, or cooperative); and (3) At what level of symbolic or representative activity? (symbolic play, imitate a role, sustain a theme, fluid or structured construction) (see Table 4.1).

From Table 4.2, you can see that the form of play that is occurring is sensorimotor, symbolic (dramatic or sociodramatic), fluid construction, or structured construction. The social level is perhaps "unoccupied" or "onlooker."

Goal setting would come in when the teacher decides that the child needs help in moving to an advanced level of activity. For example, if the child was beginning sociodramatic play and socially was doing parallel play, the goal would be to intervene (through the use of nondirective statements, questions, directive statements, modeling, or physical intervention) to have the child move to "associative" and finally "cooperative" play. The next question to address is: At what level is the child in symbolic or representative activity? Does he (1) imitate a role, (2) sustain a theme, (3) use gestures, (4) use objects, (5) interact with others, (6) have verbal exchanges? If, for example, you discover that the child is performing the first four activities but not the last two, you would use techniques to encourage interacting with others and verbal exchanges.

Let's consider an example of the "looking and evaluating" process:

TABLE 4.2   Decision Making While *Looking*

Level 1: Play Form?	Level 2: Social Stage?	Level 3: Symbolic Level?

Sensorimotor
Symbolic
Construction-fluids
Construction-structured
	1. Unoccupied
	2. Solitary
	3. Onlooker
	4. Parallel
	5. Associative
	6. Cooperative
		1. Symbolic play—dramatic play
		    (micro)
		    a. imitates role
		    b. sustains theme
		    c. uses objects, gestures, socio-
		       dramatic (macro)
		    d. interacts with others
		    e. verbal exchange
		2. Construction-fluids—stages in
		    fingerpainting
		    easel painting
		    clay modeling
		    drawing
		3. Construction-structured—stages in
		    block building
		    Legos
		    puzzles
		    Montessori materials
		    form boards

TEACHER BEHAVIOR CONTINUUM
Looking (question 1—decision: sociodramatic play)

EXPLANATION
The teacher considers question 1—"What type of play?"—and decides that Jane is doing symbolic play and attempting sociodramatic play.

TEACHING BEHAVIOR
The teacher is seated on a chair near the housekeeping area. The children have placed the toy cash register on top of the toy ironing board and are playing store.

TEACHER BEHAVIOR CONTINUUM
Looking (question 1—associative or cooperative play; question 2—developmental level: make-believe with others and verbal exchange)

EXPLANATION
Since two other shoppers are doing similar things nearby, the teacher answers question 2—"What social level?"—with *parallel play,* remembering that 3½-year-old Jane has been doing this parallel activity for nearly two months. The teacher's objective is to see if she can move Jane to associative or cooperative play, and concomitantly to social levels 5 and 6.

As to question 3—"What developmental level?"—the teacher has decided that what is missing in this child's sociodramatic play is make-believe with others and verbal exchange.

TEACHING BEHAVIOR
Jane is wearing a large straw woman's hat, a full-length purple skirt, high-heeled shoes, and a plethora of beaded necklaces. She pushes her shopping cart about, plunking toy vegetables and canned goods into it. She seems to repeat these actions over and over without any further elaboration of the shopping theme.

TEACHER BEHAVIOR CONTINUUM
Naming

EXPLANATION
The teacher's first strategy is to use naming.

TEACHING BEHAVIOR
Teacher: "Oh, I see that Jane is a shopper today! She's collecting vegetables and cans of soup! Carol and James are also shoppers, and Mark, I see that you are the check-out teller and have set up a cash register ready to take shoppers' money."

Jane, Carol, and James all stop for a moment, appear to be thinking, and move to Mark at the cash register, but their activity seems to stop there.

TEACHER BEHAVIOR CONTINUUM
Questioning

EXPLANATION
In the use of questions, the teacher wants the children to reflect on what they are doing and what make-believe actions they may take next.

TEACHING BEHAVIOR

Teacher: "Jane, what could you say to Mark? What happens next in your shopping trip?"

Jane does not respond, but Mark does.

Mark: "Pay me three dollars, Jane!"

Carol and James: "Hurry, up, Jane, pay Mark!"

Jane does not respond. She appears confused but interested.

TEACHER BEHAVIOR CONTINUUM

Commanding

EXPLANATION

In commanding, the teacher suggests verbal responses or physical action.

TEACHING BEHAVIOR

Teacher: "Jane, open your purse, take out three dollars, and pay Mark."

Jane opens her adult-sized purse, takes out a handful of play money, and spreads the money on the ironing board-counter. She hands Mark a one-dollar bill.

Mark (with great disgust): "Give me three, three. I said three dollars for your food."

Jane hands Mark a five-dollar bill.

Mark: "That's not right. You gave me five. Give me three."

Teacher: "Jane, what is on this dollar?" (The teacher has moved back to questioning.)

Jane: "One."

Teacher: "And this one?"

Jane: "One."

Teacher: "And this one?"

Jane: "One."

Teacher: "Now, count with me, Jane. One, two, three. Now you count and give Mark three dollars." (The teacher has moved back to naming.)

Jane: "One, two, three. Here, here. I am leaving."

Jane waltzes out of her "store," taking her groceries with her.

TEACHER BEHAVIOR CONTINUUM

Acting

EXPLANATION

In acting in sociodramatic play the teacher may become a "player." Seeing that the play is stalling, the teacher goes to the kitchen table, gets seated, and ...

TEACHER BEHAVIOR

Teacher: "I am hungry. Could I get something to eat, please?"

The teacher has now become a "player" and begins to model for the children.

They all giggle. Carol sets the table for the teacher with knife, fork, spoon, and soup bowl. Jane goes to the stove, puts the vegetables in the pot, and stirs the pot on the stove as it cooks.

The teacher's objectives, again, are to have Jane, along with a number of the other children, move through associative to cooperative social play and to use all elements of sociodramatic play. In the preceding example, the teacher moved from least directive to most directive on the TBC. The TBC behaviors are listed to help you understand how to "fit into" the ongoing activities of the children. The skilled teacher uses a minimal amount of directiveness to best facilitate the children's play development. Once the child is playing at the highest levels of play, such as sociodramatic play, the teacher's role is to move out of the play and maintain a "visual" stance. Following the Teacher Behavior Continuum, the teacher intervenes, first from outside the child's play, then moves inside by becoming a "player," and then moves outside again (Smilansky & Shefatya, 1990). It has also been demonstrated that "shared" experiences, like visits to the doctor's office, a trip to the bakery, and similar field trips, where children get the opportunity with the teacher to view and experience adults carrying out work roles, can aid in facilitating play development when the children return to the classroom (Smilansky & Shefatya, 1990). Table 4.3 shows another example of the use of the TBC to support sociodramatic play.

TABLE 4.3 The Teacher Behavior Continuum with Symbolic Play

Looking	Naming	Questioning	Commanding	Acting
The teacher does supportive looking to encourage children to play out a variety of fantasies that might potentially be frightening. The teacher stands by to assist those children who get overexcited or lost in a fantasy.	The teacher verbally mirrors the beginning play actions of the child. (Example: "I see you have the dishes and are ready to set the table.")	The teacher uses questions to encourage children to play out and further develop fantasy themes. (Example: "Now that the table is set, what's going to happen next?")	The teacher helps the children select, start, or further develop their play themes by directly assigning roles ("You're the mommy." "You're the doctor.") or by directly describing a new development in their play theme. (Example: "Now that you've finished setting the table, the doorbell rings and the mail carrier has an overnight letter.")	The teacher introduces a new prop to encourage further play or assumes a part and inserts himself or herself into the play. (Example: The teacher picks up the telephone and calls the doctor.)

Fluid-construction play can also be facilitated using the three questions and the TBC.

Fluid-Construction

While *looking,* if the answer to question 1 ("What type of play is occurring?") is construction-fluids, then intervention with the TBC is used as follows:

TEACHER BEHAVIOR CONTINUUM
Looking

EXPLANATION
Mike is standing before the easel, dipping a large brush into the paint pots, about to apply the paint to the white paper.

TEACHING BEHAVIOR
Question 1 is answered as *construction-fluids.* Question 2 (social stage) is answered as *solitary.* Because of the nature of fluid materials, teachers will generally find children in the *onlooker* and *solitary* modes while using them. Although double or triple paint easels will encourage parallel social play, fluid-construction (such as fingerpainting, clay modeling, and coloring) does not lend itself to associative play—with the exception of large mural paintings or similar art. Thus, because of easel painting's solitary nature, social facilitation will not be an immediate objective by Mike's teacher at this time.

Later, the teacher can answer question 3—"What symbolic level?—by observing Mike's painting to determine if it contains:

1. Random scribbling
2. Controlled scribbling
3. Face (or a recognized symbol)
4. Arms and legs (added detail to the symbol)
5. Body awareness (internal detail of the larger symbol)
6. Floating house (no base line)
7. House on bottom line (or paper)
8. House supported by baseline (symbol)
9. Two-dimensional drawing

TEACHER BEHAVIOR CONTINUUM
Looking (question 1—type of play: fluid-construction; question 2—social stage: isolated; question 3—body awareness)

EXPLANATION

Mike's symbolic level has progressed to 3–4 (face and arms/legs). Mike has been painting to help him move to level 5 (body awareness) with internal details of his "dog."

TEACHING BEHAVIOR

As the teacher observes, Mike paints a small circle on top of a larger one, and puts two eyes in the top circle and a tail on the bottom. He announces, "Dog, dog!"

TEACHING BEHAVIOR CONTINUUM
Naming

EXPLANATION

The teacher must be careful in describing what he or she thinks is seen in children's symbolic products, since this might be very different from what the child is trying to represent. It would be best to have the child tell what he has painted, with the teacher possibly recording it.

TEACHING BEHAVIOR

Teacher: "Oh, I see you have painted a dog. I see eyes, a face, a body, and a tail (verbal encoding of symbols). You have worked hard on this all morning!" (an encouragement statement; see Chapter 8 on the difference between encouragement and praise).

TEACHING BEHAVIOR CONTINUUM
Questioning

EXPLANATION

The teacher might decide to escalate on the TBC with the use of questions.

TEACHING BEHAVIOR

Teacher: "Could you tell me about your painting, Mike?"
  Mike: "Dog. My daddy's going to get me a dog for my birthday. Here is his tail."
  Teacher: "What other things in your painting can you show me?"

TEACHER BEHAVIOR CONTINUUM
Commanding

EXPLANATION

If Mike does not respond, the teacher may move to commanding.

TEACHING BEHAVIOR

Teacher: "Show me the tail. Show me the dog's head."

TEACHER BEHAVIOR CONTINUUM
Acting

EXPLANATION
From a play-activity viewpoint, the teacher would not directly model "how to draw a dog" for Mike, because it is the child's role to construct from his own ideas. The teacher may, though, model how to hold the brush, or crayon, or scissors more effectively. Also, the teacher may guide the child to gain new knowledge about his interests. For example, the teacher might bring a real dog to school or might read well-illustrated books about dogs to the child.

TEACHER BEHAVIOR CONTINUUM
Naming

EXPLANATION
The teacher verbally mirrors the actions of the child.

TEACHING BEHAVIOR
Teacher: "Mike, I see you pointing to the dog's collar" (or bone, bowl, etc.).

TEACHER BEHAVIOR CONTINUUM
Questioning (facts/labels, convergent, divergent, evaluative)

EXPLANATION
The teacher might progress up a question taxonomy of (1) fact questions—"What do you call this?" (2) convergent questions—"How does this work?" (3) divergent questions—"What do you think would have happen if . . . ?" and (4) evaluative questions—"Which do you think would be best? Why?" See the problem-solving section to follow for a fuller explanation of higher order questioning.

TEACHING BEHAVIOR
Teacher: "Show me where in the picture the dog lives. Point to the dog's collar" (bone, bowl, etc.).

TEACHER BEHAVIOR CONTINUUM
Acting

EXPLANATION
After the story, Mike is encouraged to return to his painting. The teacher's objective is to continue to give Mike encouragement with easel painting, and if the theme "dog" continues to appear, she or he would help him begin a 4-year-old version of a research project on dogs.

Other representative artwork (fluids, fingerpainting, clay sculpturing, drawing, etc.) can be facilitated by using the TBC in a manner similar to that just described. Table 4.4 shows another example of the use of the TBC to facilitate fluid-construction.

TABLE 4.4   The Teacher Behavior Continuum with Construction

Looking	Naming	Questioning	Commanding	Acting
The teacher provides the materials and supportively looks on to encourage the child to freely and creatively use the materials.	The teacher supports the child's efforts in using art media through such statements as, "You're working hard." The teacher verbally mirrors the concepts found in the child's construction. (Examples: "You're using blue." "You've made a circle." "You've added ears to your person.")	The teacher uses questions to have the child verbally describe the concepts in her product. (Examples: "Can you tell me about your drawing?" "Is there a story in your drawing?" "What have you made with your clay?")	The teacher helps the child control materials or equipment with which she is having difficulty by using directive statements such as: "Keep the paint on the paper." "Brushes are used this way."	The teacher helps the child develop her construction abilities by providing direct physical experiences, such as feeling a tree before drawing one, providing a model for the child's clay animal construction, bringing a pet to the classroom.

Fluid Materials

Young children often have accidents with spilling of fluids and are corrected by adults, often with admonitions that stress "wrong" behavior. Thus, for some children, fluid materials can be frightening, and so they refuse to become involved. The opposite may also be true: Fluids are magnets to some children—but when they use them, they become covered with them or use the fluids aggressively, ripping the fingerpaint paper or throwing water or paints at others. You will therefore need to use "control of error" and "degrees of freedom" to mitigate such problems.

Water-Play

When a child starts water-play, you will often see a "tooling up" period when she uses the materials in the form of sensorimotor play. Later, she might move to symbolic play as dramatic play (with floating pieces for "motorboats," for example). Later, the higher level of social play is seen and should be facilitated as symbolic play (described earlier).

Fingerpainting

Fingerpainting is another fluid activity that has a high sensorimotor feel. Again, children will spend much time "tooling up," becoming comfortable with the materials, before they begin recognizable symbols. For the child who uses finger-paint aggressively, you may use cafeteria trays that have raised edges (control of error); or you may start with very large sheets of paper, gradually reducing these as the child learns to control and confine her movements. Thus, you are "structuring" the child gradually toward control. The opposite could be done with a child who is overly inhibited and can't stand to put his fingers into the paint. At first, give him a piece of paper, say 4 inches square; gradually expand in size as he becomes freer and more expansive. Make an effort to save fingerpaintings that contain recognizable symbols and that are labeled by the child.

Some teachers permit and encourage children to fingerpaint with food, such as chocolate pudding, on the tops of clean tables, and to use cuts of potatoes, peppers, or carrots dipped into paint for stamping shapes onto paper. We, however, reject such frivolous use of food in view of the fact that many children of poor families go hungry. Also, we feel that young children should be learning social realities—that food is to eat, and toys and other materials are for playing. Also, permitting children to play with food may cause confusion, especially at home.

Clay and Modeling Dough

Clay and modeling dough are valuable fluids that lend themselves to producing three-dimensional products or symbols. Usually, like fluids, they are used in onlooker, solitary, or parallel social levels, rarely at the associative or cooperative levels. These three-dimensional materials will also pass through the symbolic stages of (1) push, pull, squeeze; (2) pat into pancake/roll into sausage; (3) squeeze pot as "bird" nest; (4) put eggs in bird nest; (5) construct elaborate symbol with two or three parts (such as a snowman with arms, eyes, mouth, and buttons); and (6) sculpt realistic symbols (which look like the real item with much detail). The teacher would facilitate this symbolic development with the use of the TBC in the painting example given earlier; but, again, he or she would not model the symbol product for the child.

Keep in mind also that if you add cookie cutters of Christmas trees and animals from a play-activity point of view you would be imposing an external limit and would be restricting the child's own symbolic representation.

Structured-Construction

We have discussed what teacher actions may be taken if the "play" is symbolic or with fluids. Now let's look at structured-construction.

With the more open structured-construction, such as play with unit blocks or Legos, the child will be able to create his own ideas in symbols (possibly a castle of blocks or a spaceship of Legos). Therefore, you would use the TBC as in the painting example previously mentioned. Unlike the fluid materials, unit blocks (and, to a lesser extent, Legos) support a high level of social play. Children in groups cooperatively create elaborate block castles, communities, forts, and so on. Also, with these two structured materials, children often add microtoys to their end products (castles or forts) and then "jump off" into dramatic and socio-dramatic play.

Puzzles, Form Boards, and Montessori Equipment

Puzzles, form boards, and Montessori equipment are true structured-construction materials; that is, they have built into their materials one symbol, form, or system that requires the child to complete it in a work-like manner in a limited way. Completing a four-piece puzzle of a dog requires the perceptual and fine motor skills of the child, but it doesn't permit the child creativity. Let's take puzzles and run through the use of the TBC (a process that would be nearly identical if we were using Montessori equipment or form boards).

TEACHER BEHAVIOR CONTINUUM
Looking (question 1—type of play: structured-construction; question 2—social stage; isolated; question 3—developmental level: symbolic [6-piece puzzle])

EXPLANATION
Ellen is doing structured-construction (question 1) in social isolation (question 2) and the level of play is symbolic (question 3).

TEACHING BEHAVIOR
Ellen is seated at a child-sized table with a six-piece puzzle she has selected. Pieces are scattered randomly on the tray. Ellen reaches out and places two pieces correctly together, but then her activity stalls.

TEACHER BEHAVIOR CONTINUUM
Naming

TEACHING BEHAVIOR
Teacher: "Oh, I see you have found two green pieces, one with a flat side, and put them together."
     The teacher retreats to "looking on" to give the child time to think.
     The child finds a third green piece and adds it to the other two, but then appears helpless to continue.

TEACHER BEHAVIOR CONTINUUM
Questioning

TEACHING BEHAVIOR
Teacher: "What is this piece a picture of?"
    Child "An eye."
    Teacher: "Which one has the second eye?"

TEACHER BEHAVIOR CONTINUUM
Commanding

TEACHING BEHAVIOR
The child quickly finds the piece with the second eye and now has four pieces together. But then tension seems to build up in the child. She again appears not to make progress.
    Teacher: "Show me the corner piece that might go here."
    The child complies.
    "Now, a piece with flat sides here!"
    If the child continues to make no progress, the teacher escalates up the TBC to modeling.

TEACHER BEHAVIOR CONTINUUM
Acting

EXPLANATION
In acting, the teacher physically takes over all or part of the puzzle and models (demonstrates) how to complete it. The teacher then encourages the child to take the puzzle apart again and try it herself. Montessori equipment requires modeling in this manner also.
    The teacher may also make the judgment (based on a level-3 decision of development) to take from the shelf a puzzle that the teacher knows is slightly easier than the one the child is attempting, and physically place it in front of the child, encouraging her to try it.

To summarize the teacher's facilitation of learning with structured play materials: The teacher needs to make judgments as to what play is going on (level 1), the child's social level (level 2), and the child's developmental level (level 3). Then, with the construct of the TBC, the teacher gradually escalates the intrusion from minimal intervention (looking on) to maximum (commanding/acting), if this is needed. The objective is to enable the child to engage freely in all forms of play: sensorimotor, symbolic, fluid-construction, and structured-construction. Table 4.5 shows another way of using the TBC to support sensorimotor play.

Problem-Solving Activity as Nonplay

When observing the free-play activities in a well-designed play classroom, your first decision is to determine what type of play is going on. But there are occasions when play stops or is actually disrupted by a problem the child must solve.

TABLE 4.5   The Teacher Behavior Continuum with Sensorimotor Play

Looking	Naming	Questioning	Commanding	Acting
The teacher engages in supportively looking on to encourage the child in the use of equipment and is ready to provide help if needed.	The teacher verbally mirrors the child's actions. (Examples: "You're walking with your hands out for balance." "You like to walk all the way to the end and then come back.") The teacher helps develop concepts by using such descriptive words as *fast, slow, long, short, over, under,* and *between.*	The teacher uses questions to challenge the child to explore new ideas and skills. (Examples: "How many different ways could you go across the beam?" "What could you carry across the beam?")	The teacher helps the child who is having some difficulty with a task by direct instruction. (Examples: "Place your foot here and your hand here." "You need to wait for Billy to finish before you begin.")	The teacher physically moves the child's body while modeling the proper action. (Example: The teacher physically helps the child who cannot walk backwards on the balance beam as another child demonstrates how to do it.)

Such problems result from interacting with things or objects, or with people such as peers or adults. Here are two examples.

Problem Solving with Objects

Tommy and Chip are playing at a large water table, drawing from a nearby "junk" box full of wood pieces, pieces of metal (nails and nuts), bottle caps, cardboard, styrofoam, and similar items. The two boys have taken junk pieces and made them into "boats." They are playing cooperatively, using a theme of tug boats, barges, and boats for transporting materials from one side of the water table to the other. Tommy needs one more "boat"; first, Chip passes him a nail from the box (which sinks), and then an old round piece of clay (which sinks). They have a problem! The free play stops as they attempt to find a solution. They leave the water table and begin running around the playground, collecting any item they see that might become a "floating boat." Returning, they begin testing each item to see if it will float. They are now real 3½-year-old scientists. But what if the boys were not such good problem solvers, or the teacher wanted to help the children fully exploit this "teachable moment"? Again, the teacher would use the TBC to do this.

TEACHER BEHAVIOR CONTINUUM
Looking (question 1—type of play: problem solving; question 2—social level: cooperative; question 3—cognitive process: classifying [sink-float])

TEACHER BEHAVIOR CONTINUUM
Naming

TEACHING BEHAVIOR
Teacher: "Oh, I see that the nail sank. The piece of board floats. The bottle cap floats sometimes and sinks sometimes" (verbally encoding the objects and actions).

TEACHER BEHAVIOR CONTINUUM
Questioning (facts/labels, convergent, divergent, evaluative)

TEACHING BEHAVIOR
Teacher: "What is it called when the styrofoam stays on top of the water? (facts/ labels). What is it called when things drop to the bottom? (facts/ labels). What is this one that floats made out of? (facts). What would happen if I took the bottle cap and put it upside down on the water—would it sink or float? (convergent). What would happen if I put the cap right-side up on the water? (convergent). The ball of clay sank; what could you do with it to make it float like a boat? (divergent; the children could squeeze clay into a boat shape, and place it gently on the water). If you were going to make a real boat, what would be the best material to make it out of?" (evaluative).

In the preceding example, the teacher progresses up a taxonomy of questions (see Figure 4.1) from a simple question of facts and labels, to a second level of a convergent question—How does this work?—to a third level of a divergent question (going beyond the facts available), and finally to an evaluative question (making critical judgment based on previously acquired knowledge).

What is the child learning from this problem solving? Most problem solving by young children involves the following aspects:

Causality: How does one action make another occur? For example, the child puts his wet jacket on the warm radiator and at the end of the morning it is dry. The child wants to know why.

FIGURE 4.1   Taxonomy of Questioning

4	Evaluative
3	Divergent
2	Convergent
1	Facts/labels

Time: Concepts related to before, after, next, later, what did we do or must we do first, then, next, and so on.

Space: Concepts of over, under, through, in/out, and so on.

Classification: How things are alike or different, things that belong together.

Seriation: How things are ordered, such as biggest to smallest.

Number: One-to-one correspondence, such as one paper plate for each child's snack; or grouping, such as knife, fork, spoon, plate, and glass are grouped to make one place setting.

During level-3 decision making, in problem solving, the teacher does not ask what developmental level the child is demonstrating, but rather what cognitive process or problem solving is occurring. Questions of facts/labels, convergence, divergence, and evaluation help children raise their thinking to the highest levels.

TEACHER BEHAVIOR CONTINUUM
Commanding

EXPLANATION
The teacher may feel that the boys are ready to fully explore the problem, and may use directive statements to carry their inquiry further.

TEACHING BEHAVIOR
Teacher: "Boys, take the clay from the bottom of the water table and squeeze it into a pancake, and see if it will float."
(Later.) Teacher: "Now, squeeze it into a cup, and see if it will float."
The teacher might go back to the TBC taxonomy of questions to help the boys think about the actions the teacher's directions have stimulated.

TEACHER BEHAVIOR CONTINUUM
Acting

EXPLANATION
In problem solving, the teacher has added a taxonomy of questioning (fact/labels, convergent, divergent, and evaluative). It takes a skilled and intuitive teacher to make a judgment as to just how much directive teaching is appropriate and necessary to sustain the children's learning activities. Generally, in the play-activity curriculum, minimal directiveness is provided, permitting the children to play, discover, and solve their own problems.

TEACHING BEHAVIOR
The teacher could take over the items and teach, through modeling, those concepts related to sink and float (space classification), or physically intervene by adding new props or even liquid soap, causing a totally new problem in the water play table.

Problem Solving with Peers and Others

The following would be an example of the teacher's use of the TBC as she would help the child problem solve with a peer.

TEACHER BEHAVIOR CONTINUUM
Looking (social disequilibrium)

TEACHING BEHAVIOR
Martha and Jill are playing doctor in the sociodramatic play area, using true cooperative play and all elements of sociodramatic play. Jill is using the stethoscope to listen to her doll's heart. She sets it down briefly to straighten her uniform; when she grabs for it again, Martha has it. Both girls pull on the stethoscope, shouting at each other, "I want it, it's mine!" The play has stopped; there is a disequilibrium, or a clash between peers. How does the teacher help the children solve the problem?

The teacher brings the children together so they are facing each other with the item in dispute between them. The teacher looks on, saying nothing, giving the children time to verbally mediate this themselves. After a reasonable period of time, the teacher escalates to nondirective statements.

TEACHER BEHAVIOR CONTINUUM
Naming

TEACHING BEHAVIOR
Teacher: (the target child is Jill, who has lost her stethoscope) "You have lost your stethoscope, Jill" (verbally encoding the situation). If Jill speaks up and negotiating conversation occurs, the teacher could stop with nondirective statements; if not, the teacher might escalate to questions.

TEACHER BEHAVIOR CONTINUUM
Questioning

TEACHING BEHAVIOR
Teacher: "Jill, what could you say to Martha?" Then, if necessary, the teacher moves to directive statements and modeling.

TEACHER BEHAVIOR CONTINUUM
Commanding/Acting

TEACHING BEHAVIOR
Teacher: "Tell Martha, 'No'(directive statement). 'I was using it and still need it'" (modeling).

TEACHER BEHAVIOR CONTINUUM
Naming

EXPLANATION
The focus can now move from Jill to Martha, and the same progression up the TBC may occur.

TEACHING BEHAVIOR
Teacher: "Martha, toys are hard to give up."

TEACHER BEHAVIOR CONTINUUM
Questioning

TEACHING BEHAVIOR
Teacher: "Are you listening to Jill? Do you need my help?"

TEACHER BEHAVIOR CONTINUUM
Commanding/Acting

TEACHING BEHAVIOR
Teacher: "Jill said 'No.' She had it and she still needs it. Give it back."

TEACHER BEHAVIOR CONTINUUM
Acting (physical intervention)

TEACHING BEHAVIOR
At this point, it might be necessary for the teacher to take the item back from Martha and return it to Jill, and then try to get the play started again. The teacher is trying to teach Jill that she can defend herself with language, and Martha is learning to respond to language. If this incident or problem degenerates into a behavior management situation, where verbal or physical aggression is involved, turn to Chapter 7, Discipline and Child Guidance, to see what further actions a teacher may take.

Summary

To summarize this process, the teacher needs to make a judgment as to what play is going on (level 1), at what social level the child is (level 2), and what developmental level the child is demonstrating (level 3). The teacher, using the construct of the TBC, then gradually escalates from minimum teacher intervention (looking on), to maximum intervention (commanding and acting). The object is to enable the child to engage freely in all forms of play: sensorimotor, symbolic, construction-fluids, and structured-construction. Also, with problem-solving incidents, the TBC may help the activity-based teacher to intervene with an awareness of the power being exerted or the amount of freedom the child is given to solve the problems herself.

Having read all previous chapters, you should now be able to (1) define play, (2) understand the value of play for all aspects of development, (3) organize a play classroom, (4) use specific techniques for facilitating play, and (5) formally assist the developmental levels of this play activity. With the exception of evaluation and assessment (covered in Chapter 11), you can now teach in a play-activity curriculum.

Activities

1. Pick one child from each age group (3, 4, and 5) in a play-activity-based classroom, and observe them over a period of days, until you are able to do a Child-Play Behavioral Rating Scale (to be found in Chapter 11) on them. What are their strong areas, based on the profile sheet? What goals would you set for them as a teacher, based on this scale?

2. Observe an experienced teacher facilitating play activities. On a checksheet with the behaviors on the TBC (looking, naming, etc.), put one tally mark each time the teacher demonstrates one of these general behaviors. In what play area did the teacher observation occur? What behavior was used most by this teacher? Was this directed toward one child or many children? Watch the teacher in a different play area. Did the behavior change? Why?

3. Observe an experienced teacher facilitating play activities using the Record of Teacher's Play Facilitation (at the end of this chapter, pages 83 to 85).

4. With the use of the Teacher Behavior Continuum (make a small one on a 3 × 5 card to keep in hand if need be), go to each of the interest areas (sociodramatic, fluids, structured, and sensorimotor play) and attempt to facilitate the activities of one child. What was the highest performance level demonstrated based on the three decisions needed to be made while "looking on" (Figure 4.1)? Have a friend observe you and create a tally score based on the TBC, and then you do one for your friend.

5. Find three children using the water table. Use the taxonomy of questions (Figure 4.1: facts, convergent, divergent, and evaluative) to help the children problem solve around concepts of time, space, causality, classification, seriation, or number.

Suggested Readings

The following readings are ranked as (***) every preschool teacher should read, (**) very highly recommended, (*) highly recommended, ( ) recommended. Also, where appropriate, the book is marked very difficult reading or very easy reading for an undergraduate-level student.

(***) Axeline, Virginia, *Play Therapy* (6th ed.). New York: Ballantine Books, 1971. Read for nondirective techniques of facilitating play.

( ) Joyce, Joyce, and Marsha Weil, *Models of Teaching.* Englewood Cliffs, N.J.: Prentice Hall, 1986. Textbook, theoretical; difficult.

(*) Segal, Marilyn, and Don Adcock, *Just Pretending: Ways to Help Children Grow through Imaginative Play.* Englewood Cliffs, NJ.: Prentice Hall, 1981.

(**) Smilansky, S., and Shefatya, L. *Facilitating Play.* Gaithersburg, Md.: Psychosocial & Educational Publications, 1990.

(**) Wolfgang, Charles, and others, *Growing and Learning through Play.* Poali, Penn.: Instructo-McGraw Hill, 1981. Easy-practical.

References

Biber, Barbara, and others, *Promoting Cognitive Growth: A Developmental Interactional Point of View.* Washington, D.C.: NAEYC, 1977.

Erikson, Erik H., *Childhood and Society.* New York: Norton, 1950.

Freud, Anna, *Normality and Pathology in Childhood: Assessments of Development.* New York: International University Press, 1968.

Lenski, Lois, *Fireman Small.* New York: Oxford University Press, 1946.

Peller, Lili F., "Libidinal Phases, Ego Development and Play," in *Psychoanalytic Study of the Child,* no. 9. New York: International Universities Press, 1959.

Peterson, Nancy L., *Early Intervention for Handicapped and At-Risk Children.* Denver: Love Publishing Co., 1987, P. 398.

Smilansky, S., and L. Shefatya, *Facilitating Play.* Gaithersburg, Md.: Psychosocial & Educational Publications, 1990.

Record of Teacher's Play Facilitation

Child's Name _____ Birthdate __/__/__

Observer's Name _____ Obs Date __/__/__

Observe a teacher in a play-activity classroom for a period of 15 minutes, and then complete as these actions occur.

Description of Observation Incident

_____

_____

_____

Check all appropriate boxes:
1. Play Form
    ( ) a. Sensorimotor
    ( ) b. Symbolic-micro
    ( ) c. Symbolic-macro (sociodramatic)
    ( ) d. Construction-Fluids
    ( ) e. Construction-Structured
    ( ) f. Problem solving (with objects) name _____

    ( ) g. Problem solving (with peers) name _____

2. Social Stage
    ( ) a. Unoccupied
    ( ) b. Onlooker
    ( ) c. Solitary
    ( ) d. Parallel
    ( ) e. Associative
    ( ) f. Cooperative

3. Symbolic Level
    ( ) a. Symbolic Play
        ( ) 1. imitates a role
        ( ) 2. sustains a theme
        ( ) 3. uses objects and gestures
        ( ) 4. interacts with others
        ( ) 5. verbal exchange
    ( ) b. Construction-Fluids (describe stage)

        ( ) fingerpainting _____

        ( ) easel painting _____

( ) clay _____

( ) drawing _____

( ) others _____

( ) c. Construction-Structured

( ) unit blocks _____

( ) Legos _____

( ) puzzles _____

( ) others _____

Record (write) the teacher's play facilitation (based on TBC):
Looking (What decision needed to be made?)

_____

_____

_____

Naming (list)

_____

_____

_____

Questioning (list)

_____

_____

_____

Commanding (list)

_____

_____

_____

Acting (list)

_____

_____

_____

Give objective for future facilitation

_____

_____

_____

_____

New Learning through Thematic-Project Experiences

When young children have new experiences—such as a trip to the zoo, the visit of a pet to the classroom, or hearing new stories read to them—the experience itself is usually not enough for the young children to gain new knowledge or information (Smilansky & Shefatya, 1990). For real learning to take place, these experiences require a teacher to focus the children's attention on certain aspects and details, to name and label new objects and processes, to supply details of how things work, and to ask and answer children's questions. Children can be helped to gain this new knowledge through the use of thematic units and projects. Let's see how this might happen at the beginning of the first lesson of a new learning unit.

The teacher is seated on the piano stool with a class of 4-year-olds seated at her feet. She holds a book, a box-shaped object covered with a cloth is beside her, and there is a flannelboard in front of her. The children quickly become quiet because they know from past experience that they are in for a surprise. The teacher reads *The Tale of Peter Rabbit* by Beatrix Potter.

TEACHER BEHAVIOR CONTINUUM
Naming

EXPLANATION
The teacher begins with a story that serves as a motivational experience *(nondirective statement),* giving the children new information. A three-step lesson strategy is

followed: Step 1—Say (read the story); Step 2—Show (show the illustrations); and Step 3—Check.

TEACHER BEHAVIOR
Step 1—Say (read the story)
"Once upon a time, there were four little Rabbits, and their names were Flopsy, Mopsy, Cotton-tail, and Peter. They lived with their mother in a sand-bank, underneath the root of a very big fir tree. . . . "
Step 2—Show
The teacher turns the book so the children can see the illustrations on each page as she reads the words.

TEACHER BEHAVIOR CONTINUUM
Questioning (level 1—facts/labels; level 2—convergent; level 3—divergent; level 4—evaluate)

EXPLANATION
The teacher uses a series of questions, progressing up a taxonomy, helping the children think through the story content.

TEACHER BEHAVIOR
The teacher finishes reading *The Tale of Peter Rabbit.*
    Step 3—Check
    "Which rabbits did not go to the garden?" (facts/labels) "Why?" (convergent) "Why did Mother tell her children not to go into Mr. McGregor's garden?" (convergent) "Why did Mr. McGregor want to catch Peter?" (convergent) "How did Peter feel about the cat?" (convergent) "Why was the cat looking into the pond?" (convergent) "What do you think might have happened if the cat saw Peter?" (divergent) "Where do you think would be the best place to hide in the garden?" (evaluative) "What are two reasons for Peter's becoming ill?" (convergent) "Why did Mother give him chamomile tea?" (convergent) "What would your mother do when you got home after doing something that she told you not to do?" (divergent) "Who did the right thing: Mopsy or Peter?" (evaluative)

Question Taxonomy

The thematic-project method of teaching follows a progression from (1) providing the child a learning experience either verbally (reading *The Tale of Peter Rabbit)* or motorically (petting and caring for a real rabbit or visiting a zoo); to (2) helping the child to process new information through questioning; to (3) having the child represent this knowledge through play (see Chapter 3), in symbols (painting pictures about rabbits or doing sociodramatic play), and in signs (written or spoken words). These experiences cluster around a theme of study that now becomes "shared realities" or content (Smilansky & Shefatya, 1990) for classroom play.

The lesson generally follows a three-step format; Step 1—Say (provide the new experience for example, by reading the story); Step 2—Show (show the illustrations or represent the concept visually); and Step 3—Check (ask questions to further the child's understanding).

The Step 3 questioning facilitates an intellectual processing of the new information by following a taxonomy of four levels of increasing abstraction. The teacher generally begins with level 1, fact/label questions, which simply require factual recall: "What were the rabbits' names in this story?" (facts/labels) "Who went to Mr. McGregor's garden when he was told not to do so?" (facts/labels)

Then the teacher moves to level 2, convergent questions, which require that the child apply the facts and make simple deductions. "Why did Mother tell her children not to go into Mr. McGregor's garden?" (convergent) "Why did Mr. McGregor want to catch Peter?" (convergent) "How did Peter feel about the cat?" (convergent)

Level 3, divergent questions, require that the child go beyond the facts given and speculate creatively about hypothetical events: "What do you think would have happened to Peter if Mr. McGregor had caught him?" (divergent) "How do you think Peter could get his coat and shoes back?" (divergent)

At level 4, evaluative questioning, the child must make a value judgment among a number of competing choices. "Do you feel that Peter has learned a lesson from this, and will he be naughty again?" (evaluative) "Do you think it would be good for Peter to go back to the garden at night when Mr. McGregor is sleeping, to get his coat and shoes from the scarecrow? Why?" (evaluative)

To summarize, the child has an experience (hearing the tale of Peter Rabbit and seeing the story illustration), and then the teacher helps her process the new information by asking questions that progress from facts/labels to evaluative. Just what is the teacher trying to accomplish? Let's break down the lesson to answer that question.

TEACHER BEHAVIOR CONTINUUM
Questioning (level 1—facts/labels; level 2—convergent; level 3—divergent; level 4—evaluative) (Cognitive Content Area—classification/causality)

EXPLANATION
The teacher uses the Cognitive Content Area of classification/causality, and checks (3-step lesson) by asking questions from facts/labels, to convergent, to divergent, to evaluative.

TEACHER BEHAVIOR
Step 3—Check
"Who were the friends of Peter in the garden?" (fact/label question—classification) "Who were the enemies?" (fact/label question—classification) "When is a person a friend?" (convergent question—causality) "What would happen to Peter if Sparrow had not 'implored him'?" (divergent question—causality) "When you are in trouble,

without your parents, who can help you?" (divergent question—causality) "Was the mouse a friend or not?" (evaluative question—classification)

TEACHER BEHAVIOR CONTINUUM
Questioning (level 1—facts/labels) (Cognitive Content Area—classification)

EXPLANATION
The teacher uses the Cognitive Content Area of classification and level 1 (fact/label questions).

TEACHER BEHAVIOR
"What were the vegetables in the garden?" (fact/label question—classification) "What makes something a vegetable?" (convergent question—causality, classification) "What tools were in the garden?" (fact/label question—classification) "What makes things tools?" (convergent question—causality, classification)

How the Child's Mind Works

In order to understand just what is being taught through this questioning related to classification, you need some understanding of how the child's mind works—how concepts are learned.

Let's imagine testing young children, such as Piaget (Piaget & Inhelder, 1958) did in an attempt to understand how the mind works, by presenting to them a small box of wooden marbles, three blue ones and seven white. The teacher asks, "What if I move all of the blue marbles out of this box and put them in another box—what will be left?" Young children normally say "The white ones," and they would be correct. The teacher now states, "OK, pretend that I have put all of the blue ones back into the box. Now, if I take out all of the wooden marbles and move them over to this box, what will I have left?" Generally, children younger than age 7 reply, "The blue ones" or they simply do not know.

Unlike young children, adults have established in their minds an arrangement such as Figure 5.1 illustrates—a hierarchical classification system whereby higher categories (marbles), can be subdivided into sub-categories (wood, glass, plastic), and then these subcategories can be further subdivided (white and blue). To understand the preceding marble test, children must understand that marbles can be white and blue, the lowest subcategory, and are also members of a higher category, glass, wood, or plastic. A marble can have an identity of first-order, white, and of second-order, wooden, at the same time. Marbles can also be thought of as belonging to a still higher class of objects called toys.

Children under age 7 generally do not yet have this hierarchy of categories established in their minds; therefore, they cannot do a classification task correctly. We have heard of the young child who has a dog at home, and then rides out into the country for the first time and sees a cow, and shouts, "Look, Daddy,

FIGURE 5.1   Classification Ladder: Inductive vs. Deductive Thinking

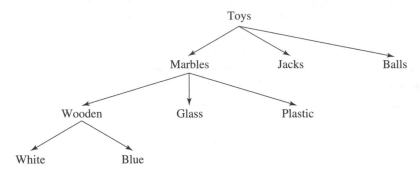

doggie!" or, the young child who opens the front door of his home to find an adult male and states, "Mommy, there is a daddy here." In both examples, the child does not have the mental ladder of relationships to classify animals or people. Thus, a hierarchical classification system must be developed before children can understand concepts such as dog, daddy, marble, and so on.

Inductive/Deductive Thinking

When a person senses an object (e.g., hears a motor start outside the window) and then applies an identity label (a word) to that sound, we say that the person is thinking *inductively*. From a real object to a label—inductive. But, if we say an object of less density than water will float while one with greater density will sink, and then demonstrate this with nails, rocks, corks, and wood, then we are hoping your mind will work *deductively*. Rules and labels followed by sensory experience—deductive.

Transductive Thinking

When your mind moves up a hierarchical classification system, you are thinking inductively; when it moves down a classification system, you are reasoning deductively. The young child who does not have this mental system jumps from one category to another arbitrarily: all men are daddies, all animals are doggies. We call this incorrect thinking *transductive thinking* (Phillips, 1969).

Let's take another example of transductive thinking by the young child. A 3- or 4-year-old picks up a piece of paper and waves it before his face like a fan, feeling the wind that is produced. The child reasons, "Moving paper causes wind." The child goes out into the playground, which contains tall, thin pine trees. A storm is approaching and the trees sway violently back and forth. The child feels the wind in his face, and transductively reasons, "Moving trees cause wind to blow" (Brearley, 1971).

Most early childhood programs aim to give children educational experiences that will enable them to move from transductive thinking to inductive and deductive thinking. Therefore, many early childhood education curricula require children to classify and seriate, and work with concepts of time, causality, and number. Of course, the methods for doing so vary according to the philosophies on which the programs are based. From the developmentally appropriate curriculum position, learning how to think more abstractly does not result from a simple input-output process of teaching, but would require children to be involved through play in direct and real experiences and activities.

Weikart Triangle

David Weikart (1971), drawing from the work of Piaget, used a triangle as a model to visually demonstrate the relationships between Piaget's representational stages of development and easily observable motoric to verbal levels of operation and corresponding classroom curriculum activities. Elements from each side of the triangle can be combined to create lessons at different levels of difficulty. *Cognitive content areas, levels of representation,* and *levels of operation* are terms that are heavily theoretical. In this chapter, these terms will be applied to the classroom situation in order to make them practical and meaningful. Other teaching techniques such as the questioning levels and the say, show, check instruction methods will be applied to classroom activities centered around the tale of Peter Rabbit, and related to the triangular constructs of Cognitive Content Areas, Levels of Representation, and Levels of Operation. The following discussion will be a practical application of what you can do with Piaget's theories in the real-world classroom.

Cognitive Content Areas

The Cognitive Content Areas (see Figure 5.2) contain the subcategories of classification, seriation/number, temporal, spatial, and causality, which denote processes through which people try to understand their world. It is through the development of the Cognitive Content Areas that the young child will later be able to move to higher levels of thinking.

In our introductory look at the reading of Peter Rabbit, we saw the teacher using questioning techniques, activities, and a three-step teaching procedure of

FIGURE 5.2   Weikart's Triangle of Cognitively Oriented Curriculum

Sign

Verbal

Symbol

Levels of Representation

Levels of Operations

Object

Motoric

Cognitive Content Areas

Classification   Seriation/Number   Temporal   Spatial   Causality

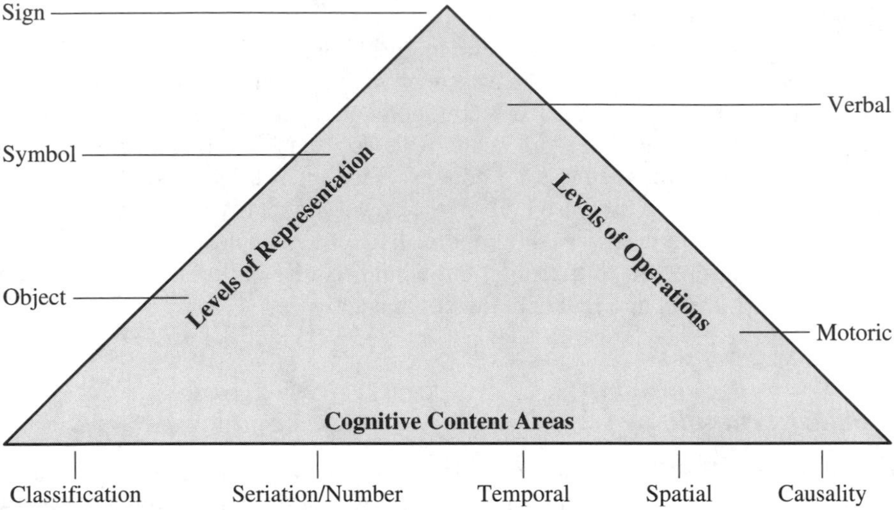

Source: The Cognitively Oriented Curriculum: A Framework for Preschool Teachers by David P. Weikart et al., 1971, Washington, DC: NAEYC. Reprinted with permission.

say, show, and check in order to help the children develop classification skills—using the concepts of tools, vegetables, and so on.

Here is an example of the use of the questions taxonomy as related to Cognitive Content Areas:

Temporal Relations

1. *Facts/labels:* What happened first in this story? What happened next? Then what?
2. *Convergent:* What happened after Peter's coat button got stuck in the gooseberry net?
3. *Divergent:* If Mr. McGregor had not found Peter in the watering pail, how long do you think he would have stayed in there?
4. *Evaluative:* When do you think would be a good time for Peter to return to get his jacket and shoes—next day, nighttime, or next winter?

Spatial Relations

1. *Facts/labels:* Where did Peter live? Where was the garden located? Where did Peter hide?
2. *Convergent:* Why didn't Mr. McGregor climb through the window after Peter? Why didn't Peter go under the gate like the old mouse?

3. *Divergent:* What would have happened if the window in the toolshed had been bigger?
4. *Evaluative:* If the watering pail had been empty of water would that have been a good place to hide?

Seriation/Number

1. *Facts/labels:* What happened first, second, next, last in the story?
2. *Convergent:* Who could place these pictures of the story in order? If Peter had time, how many carrots would he have taken home for his brothers and sisters?
3. *Divergent:* Who could name a smaller or larger animal, or enemy in the garden, that could have been about unseen and unheard?
4. *Evaluative:* If you were lost who do you think would be most helpful: a baby sister, your older brother, your teacher, or a police officer? Who would be least helpful?

Classification

1. *Facts/labels:* What were the vegetables in the garden? What tools were in the garden?
2. *Convergent:* Why are a jacket and shoes not tools?
3. *Divergent:* What other tools might be in Mr. McGregor's tool shed?
4. *Evaluative:* If you were to make a garden, what would be the most important tool?

Causality

1. *Facts/labels:* What did Mother say before leaving?
2. *Convergent:* Why did Mother tell her children not to go into Mr. McGregor's garden?
3. *Divergent:* What are other rules that Peter should follow to be safe?
4. *Evaluative:* Should Mother have punished Peter when he returned home, or given him tea?

Through increasingly abstract levels of questioning, the teacher tries to challenge the children to think at higher levels in the Cognitive Content Areas.

Let's return again to the Peter Rabbit lesson:

TEACHER BEHAVIOR CONTINUUM

EXPLANATION
The teacher uses symbols to work in the Cognitive Content Area of classification with low-level fact/label questions.

THEMATIC-PROJECT TEACHING
Step 1—Say; Step 2—Show

The teacher is prepared with flannelboard pictures of friends, enemies, vegetables, and tools. As the children call out the names in response to the teacher's classification questions (level of representation: symbols-pictures), the pictures are placed on the flannelboard.

"Who were the friends of Peter? Who were the enemies?"

EXPLANATION
The teacher begins another lesson that will follow the strategies of Say ("This word is *friend*"), Show (holds up card, modeling), and Check. In the Say step of instruction, the teacher introduces the highest level of representation as signs or written words, which also includes beginning letter recognition.

THEMATIC-PROJECT TEACHING
The teacher shows the children a 2-inch by 5-inch card with the word *friends* written on it (sign) in dark block letters. "Class, this word says, *friends.* Say this word, class." The children respond, "Friends," as teacher runs her hand under the word. "Yes, *friends.* Say it again, class." "Friends." (All of these are fact/label questions.)

EXPLANATION
The teacher Checks (modeling). The Cognitive Content Area of classification is being taught by combining the representation of symbols (pictures) with signs (written words), and this is carried out through fact/label questioning.

THEMATIC-PROJECT TEACHING
Step 3—Check

"What group of pictures (symbolic representation) on this board are friends?" (facts/label—classification) "Yes, I will put this word (sign representation) on top, here, and put all the friend pictures below it. Now, this word says *vegetable,* and I will put it up here. I will call on one of you to come up and move one vegetable picture underneath the word *vegetable.* Who can find the vegetable pictures?"

The teacher now repeats this sequence with *enemies* and *tools.*

EXPLANATION
This is a repeat of the third step, Check, in the three-step lesson of Say, Show, Check. It requires the children to classify (Cognitive Content Area), by applying symbols (pictures) to signs, with the teacher using directive statements ("Put your picture under *friend*").

THEMATIC-PROJECT TEACHING
The teacher takes away all pictures, leaving the labels *friends, enemies, vegetables,* and *tools* on the flannelboard. "Now, class, I'm going to give each of you a picture. Don't show it to anyone. When I call your name, I want you to come up and put your picture (symbol) under *friends* (sign), *vegetable, fruits,* or *tools.*" (directive statement) Each child does as directed, with the teacher reteaching it if a child has difficulty. This permits the teacher to check each child's understanding (classification).

Levels of Representation

After the child has heard the story, he has new information; the teacher then helps him process that information by using questions related to the Cognitive Content Areas. The next goal is to have the child learn to represent his ideas at increasingly abstract levels: first symbolically (pictures of friends, enemies, tools, and vegetables), then with signs (language—"friend," "enemies," etc.).

Symbols are representations, such as pictures, the objects a child makes in construction (such as painting Peter Rabbit), or pretend play (being Peter in dramatic play). Signs, which are also representations, are spoken or written words ("rabbit"). Developmentally, the child progresses through levels of representation as he matures and gains experience. These levels move from (1) real experiences such as feeding, petting, and caring for a real rabbit, or hearing a story, to (2) representations by the child of his ideas about the story through symbols, and finally to (3) signs used by the child in speaking and writing about his own stories (see Table 5.1).

TABLE 5.1   Levels of Representation

Level	Teaching Implications	Examples
3 Sign	Words: The word itself evokes vivid and meaningful mental images (verbal and written).	1. The spoken word *rabbit.* 2. The written word *rabbit.*

2 Symbol	3. Pictures (realistic to abstract)
	2. Clay models and drawings (child makes representation)
	1. Motor encoding
	  a) makes believe (uses objects) to represent other objects
	  b) imitation including onomatopoeia (child uses body to represent object or sound of object)
	  c) dramatic play (representation of familiar and/or common situations)
		3. a) Child recognizes picture of rabbit when only feet are visible.
		  b) Child recognizes picture of rabbit among other pictures.
		2. a) Clay model of rabbit.
		  b) Original drawing or tracing of rabbit; etc.
		1. a) Box stands for rabbit.
		  b) Child walks like rabbit.
		  c) Children play house.

1 Real objects/experiences	The child has an experience with the object (a rabbit) being studied in order to make mental images of it. The order of presentation should be (1) experience with real object, then (2) symbolize it, and (3) apply signs (Weikart, 1971, p. 5).	

Source: The Cognitively Oriented Curriculum: A Framework for Preschool Teachers by David P. Weikart et al., 1971, Washington, DC: NAEYC. Reprinted with permission.

In a thematic-project curriculum it is the teacher's role to encourage this representation, first in symbols and later in signs. Here is how this might be done with the rabbits theme:

	Rabbits	
Kinds of Direct Experience	Representation Symbolic Level	Sign
Child visits pet or rabbit farm; sees various kinds of rabbits	Paints rabbit, makes rabbits out of clay, sews rabbits from material	*Word Labels*: rabbit litter hutch
Habitat		
Care of rabbit (care for classroom rabbit)	Enacts rabbit in sociodramatic play	rodent hare family fur
Has read: *Habits of Rabbits* *Rabbits—A Complete Pet Owner's Manual*	Makes mural of rabbit information	long ears bobbed tail burrowing
	Makes diorama of habitats where different rabbits live	
Weighs rabbit weekly	Makes graph of number of pellets rabbit eats each day, and graphs weekly weight of rabbit	

TEACHER BEHAVIOR CONTINUUM
Acting (culminating experience)

EXPLANATION
Experience with a real rabbit is the culminating experience (modeling) for tying up the lesson. Teaching still continues.

THEMATIC-PROJECT TEACHING
The teacher quickly pulls a towel off a hidden box, opens a door, and takes out a young brown baby rabbit. "We have a new friend that has come to live with us in our classroom." The teacher has the children form a circle, allowing the rabbit to hop about, each child gently petting it.

TEACHER BEHAVIOR CONTINUUM
Naming (motoric to verbal level of operation)

EXPLANATION
The teacher is now working on the Levels of Operation from the triangle construct, by using *naming* or verbally encoding ("Fur is soft") as the child has a motoric experience (touching the rabbit's fur).

THEMATIC-PROJECT TEACHING
A rush of observations are made by the children as they first have a sensory experience with the rabbit (level 1—operational process: motoric) then encode this impression with words or language (level 2—operational process: verbal). For example, a child touches the rabbit and says, "He is soft; his nose is cold and wet; and he has sharp claws." He looks at the rabbit and says, "Big teeth, long ears, brown and white."

EXPLANATION
The teacher does not attempt to answer questions at this time, but keeps them in mind for later planning.

THEMATIC-PROJECT TEACHING
A flood of questions now come from the children: "What is his name?" "Where will he live?" "What will he eat?" "Is he a girl or boy?" "Does he have brothers and sisters?" "Where is his mother?"

Levels of Operation

The final side to the curriculum triangle is labeled Levels of Operation, the two levels being motoric and verbal (see Table 5.2). The operation can be thought of as a process experience—the child feeling the rabbit and seeing the rabbit. (Cooking, tasting, and smelling ingredients such as salt, pepper, and sugar would be another process experience.)

How do we know the physical world? The answer is by its motor meaning. The meaning of "cup" is the sensorimotor experience of one's outstretched hand clasping a cylindrical object, bringing it to one's mouth, and tilting one's head back. This sequence of behaviors (motoric operation) is mentally stored as the "meaning of cup."

When the child is told to "drink from a cup" (verbal level of operation), the child truly understands the verbal label "cup." The child climbs under the table

TABLE 5.2   Levels of Operation

Motoric	Verbal
Hear G bell then C bell	High vs. low
Feeling the rabbit's fur	Soft
Feeling the rabbit's claws (or polar concept with different senses)	Sharp
Touching sandpaper and silk cloth	Rough vs. smooth
Tasting a lemon and sugar	Bitter vs. sweet
Seeing two balls of differing sizes	Large vs. small

(motoric operation), and the teacher says, "You are going 'under.'" At times, as in the "going under," while the teacher encodes, the child is working at both levels of operation simultaneously (motoric and verbal), but generally the motoric experience must come first to give true meaning and understanding to the verbal.

To summarize, the Weikart triangle presents a construct for the teacher to use in carrying out lessons in the thematic-project curriculum. This triangle presents a model for the teacher to use in giving the children experiences of classifying, seriating, and so on, representing those experiences with symbols and later signs, and acting or operating on those experiences, motorically and then verbally.

Thematic-Project Teaching

We have just examined an introductory lesson on rabbits, with the central motivational vehicle and source of new information being the classic children's book *The Tale of Peter Rabbit*. In the thematic-project curriculum, the skilled teacher tries to stimulate learning around a theme, such as rabbits, in order to: (1) keep children highly motivated to learn; (2) encourage them to represent their ideas in symbols (drawings, clay, etc.) and signs (written words); (3) help them gain knowledge about their world and the ability to think about that knowledge with increasingly high levels of mental operations; (4) expand their vocabularies; and (5) help them acquire a true love of children's literature that will lead to developing a real readiness for reading. Children's literature is the hub around which the thematic-project curriculum is organized. The construct for organizing the curriculum is *webbing*.

Webbing

The teacher, with co-teachers or aides, plans the learning unit with the use of a system called webbing. The teacher begins by drawing a circle and writing in it the name of a motivational book, (e.g., *The Tale of Peter Rabbit*). The story is read and the children and teacher discuss it. Then the teacher draws a second, larger circle around the first one, and sections off the circular space like a spider's web (see Figure 5.3). In each section is listed a very general topic relating in some way to the story (e.g., rabbits, friendship, gardens, rules, and safety). These broad, general topics are called strands.

The teacher then searches the library for children's books, music recordings, or teacher resources on these broad topics (see Figure 5.4). After reading through the available children's books and again reflecting on the children's discussion of the first lesson, the teacher adds a third circle, filling it in with subtopics related to the second-strand broad topics.

FIGURE 5.3   Peter Rabbit Web

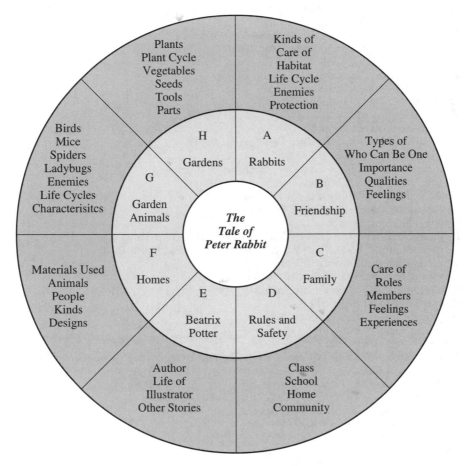

Note: A special thanks to Dr. Carolyn Schluck and her students, Doris Jean Whitten, Sue McDaniel, Krissy Gentry, and Tina L. Easterwood, for this web.

FIGURE 5.4   Books

Rabbits

Aesop—*The Hare and the Tortoise*
Anders, Rebecca—*Whiskers the Rabbit*
Anderson, Lonzo and Adrienne Adams—*Two Hundred Rabbits*
Bate, Lucy—*Little Rabbit's Loose Tooth*
Brown, Margaret Wise—*Brer Rabbit; Home for a Bunny Brown; The Golden Egg Book; The Runaway Bunny; The Sleepy Book*

(Continued)

FIGURE 5.4   *(Continued)*

Bruna, Dick—*Miffy at the Zoo*
Carroll, Lewis—*Alice in Wonderland*
Colby, Carroll—*Gabbit the Magic Rabbit*
Daniel, Kira—*Habits of Rabbits*
Delage, Ida—*Bunnyschool*
Dermine, Lucie—*The Rabbits Give a Party*
DeVault, Vere—*The Jack Rabbit*
Dunn, Judy—*The Little Rabbit*
Evers, Helen and Alf—*Fussbunny*
Fisher, Aileen—*Listen, Rabbit*
Friskey, Margaret—*Rackety That Very Special Rabbit*
Fritz, Jean—*How to Read a Rabbit*
Fritzch, Helga—*Rabbit-A Complete Pet Owner's Manual*
Gag, Wanda—*The ABC Bunny*
Galdone, Paul—*The Hare and the Tortoise*
Grimm Fairy Tales —*The Hare's Bride*
Henrie, Fiona—*Rabbits*
Heyward, DuBose—*The Country Bunny and the Little Gold Shoes*
Howard, Matthew V., and Earl W. Moline—*Blink the Patchwork Bunny*
Jackson, Kathryn—*Tawny the Scrawny Lion*
Kaufman, Elizabeth—*Bunnies and Rabbits*
Kohler, Julilly—*Collins and His Rabbits*
Lawson, Robert—*Rabbit Hill*
Memling, Carl—*Little Cottontail*
Moreman, Grace—*Walk Rabbit Walk*
Peters, Sharon—*Stop That Rabbit*
Potter, Beatrix—*The Tale of Peter Rabbit; The Tale of the Flopsy Bunnies; The Tale
    of Benjamin Bunny*
Sadler, Marilyn—*The Very Bad Bunny*
Scarry, Richard—*I am a Bunny; Nicky Goes to the Doctor*
Schlachter, Rita—*Good Luck Bad Luck*
Tufts, Georgia—*The Rabbit Garden*
Weil, Lise—*The Candy Egg Bunny*
Werner, Jane—*Walt Disney's Bunny Book*
Whithead, Pat—*What a Funny Bunny*
Williams, Margery—*The Velveteen Rabbit*
Wright, Betty Ren—*The Rabbit's Adventure*
Zolotow, Charlotte—*Mr. Rabbit and the Lovely Present*

Gardens

Baker, Sam Sinclair—*Gardening*
Beller, Joel—*Garden Experiments*
Chevalier, Christa—*Gardening Stories*
Creative Educational Society—*Vegetable Gardening*
Cutler, Katherine N.—*Gardening*
Gibbons, Gail—*Tool Book*
Hudlow, Jean—*Vegetable Gardening*

FIGURE 5.4   *(Continued)*

Jobb, Jamie—*Gardening*
Keller, Beverly—*The Beetle Bush*
Kramer, Jack—*Plant Hobbies*
Kratz, Marilyn—*The Garden Book*
Kraus, Ruth—*The Carrot Seed*
Lesson, Robert—*Tools*
Lavine, Sigmund A.—*Vegetable Gardening*
Manley, Deborah—*Gardening*
Parker, Bertha Morris—*Gardening; The Plant World*
Poling, James—*Tools*
Robbins, Ken—*Tools*
Smith, Ken—*Garden Construction Know How*
Swenson, Allan A.—*Vegetable Gardening*
Vallin, Jean—*The Plant World*
Vasiliu, Mircea—*One Day in the Garden*

Garden Animals

Berenstain, Stan—*Birds*
Blough, Glenn—*The Insect Parade*
Brandenbert, Aliki—*At Mary's Blooms*
Conklin, Gladys—*When Insects are Babies*
Cressey, James—*Max the Mouse*
Eastman, P. D.—*Are You My Mother?*
Gans, Rona—*Birds Eat and Eat and Eat*
Ipcan, Dahlov—*Big City*
Koening, Marian—*The Mouse*
Kraus, Robert—*The Good Mousekeeper; Whose Mouse Are You?*
Lobel, Arnold—*Mouse Soup and Other Stories*
Pole, Lavine—*Spiders Are Special*
Potter, Beatrix—*The Tailor of Gloucestor*
Raskin, Ellen—*Twenty-Two, Twenty-Three*
Wong, Herbert—*Where Can Red-Winged Blackbirds Live?*

Homes

Burton, Virginia Lee—*The Little House*
Cutts, David—*The House That Jack Built*
Green, Robyn, Yvonne Pollock, & Scarffe Bronuen—*When Goldilocks Went to the House of the Bears*
Heilbroner, Joan—*This is the House Where Jack Lives*
Hilbert, Margaret—*A House for Little Red*
Hutchins, Pat—*The House that Sailed Away*
Israel, Leo—*Our New Home in the City*
Palmer, Helen—*Why I Built the Boogle House*
Parkeks, Brenda & Smith, Judith—*The Three Little Pigs (retold by)*
Roffery, Maureen—*Door to Door*

(Continued)

FIGURE 5.4   *(Continued)*

Family

Berenstain, Stan and Jan—*The Berenstain Bears and the Weekend at Grandma's*
Berger, Terry—*Big Sister, Little Brother*
Blaine, Marge—*The Terrible Thing That Happened at Our House*
Borack, Barbara—*Grandpa*
Brindwell, Norman—*A Tiny Family; Clifford's Family*
Byars, Betsy—*Go and Hush the Baby*
Fehr, Howard F.—*This is My Family*
Flack, Marjorie—*Wait for Williams*
Galdon, Paul—*The Three Bears*
Hazel, Beth, & Dr. Jerome C. Harste—*My Icky Picky Sister*
Hoban, Russell—*The Little Brute Family*
Hogan, Paula Z.—*Will Dad Ever Move Back?*
Hutchins, Pat—*Don't Forget the Bacon*
Keats, Ezra Jack—*Pete's Chair*
Knoche, Norma R. & Mary Voell Jones—*What Do Mothers Do?*
Lindman, Maj—*Flicka, Ricka, Dicka Bake a Cake*
Low, Alice—*Grandmas and Grandpas*
Mayer, Mercer—*Just Grandma and Me; Just Grandpa and Me; Just Me and My Dad*
Melser, June & Joy Cowley—*Grandpa, Grandpa*
Myers, Bernice—*My Mother is Lost*
Reif, Patricia—*That New Baby*
Simon, Norma—*All Kinds of Families*
Stecher, Miriam B. & Alice S. Kandell—*Daddy and Ben Together*
Swetnam, Evelyn—*The Day You Were Born*
Wittram, H. R.—*My Little Brother*
Zolotow, Charlotte—*The Quarreling Book*

Friends

Aesop—*The Lion and the Mouse*
Aliki—*We Are Best Friends*
Anderson, Janet—*A Hug for a New Friend*
Anglund, John Walsh—*A Friend is Someone Who Likes You*
Arneson, D. J.—*A Friend Indeed*
Baker, Laura Nelson—*The Friendly Beasts*
Barkin, Carol—*Are We Still Best Friends?*
Battles, Edith—*One to Teeter-Totter*
Behrens, June—*Together*
Berenstain, Stan—*The Berenstain Bears and the Trouble with Friends*
Berger, Terry—*A Friend Can Help*
Bonsall, Crosby—*It's Mine . . . A Greedy Book; The Case of the Hungry Strangers*
Bornstern, Ruth—*Little Gorilla*
Bourque, Nina—*The Best Trade of All*
Carruth, Jane—*Making New Friends*
Cavanna, Betty—*Jean and Johnny*
Cohen, Miriam—*Best Friends; So What; Will I Have a Friend?*

FIGURE 5.4   *(Continued)*

Conta, Marcia Maher—*Feelings Between Friends*
Curry, Nancy—*My Friend is Mrs. Jones*
Deering, Janet—*Eddie's Moving Day*
Dalton, Judy—*Two Good Friends*
DeRegniers, Beatrice Schenk—*May I Bring a Friend?*
DeWitt, Jamie—*Jamie's Turn*
Fremlin, Robert—*Three Friends*
Gans, Margaret—*Pam and Pam*
Gehm, Katherine—*Happiness is Smiling*
Gould, Deborah—*Brenden's Best-Timed Friend*
Graham, John—*I Love You Mouse*
Harmey, Barbara—*I Used to Be Older*
Heide, Florence Parry, & Sylvia Van Clief—*That's What Friends Are For*
Hilbert, Margaret—*Not I, Not I*
Hott, Syd—*Danny and the Dinosaur; Who Will Be My Friends?*
Holland, Joyce—*Porter, the Pouting Pigeon*
Hughes, Shirley—*Alfie Gives a Hand*
Ichikawa, Satomi—*Friends*
Johnson, Gladys O.—*Jimmie, the Youngest Errand Boy*
Krasilovksy, Phyllis—*The Shy Little Girl*
Lavelle, Sheila—*My Best Friend*
Lobel, Arnold—*Frog and Toad All Year; Frog and Toad Together*
Masterson, Audry Nelson—*The Day the Gypsies Came to Town*
Mazer, Norma Fox —*B, My Name Is Bunny*
Minarik, Elsa—*Little Bear's Friend*
Moncure, Jane Belk—*Julie's New Home*
Oxenbury, Helen—*Friends*
Park, Barbara—*Buddies*
Peterson, Mike—*The Biggest Giraffe*
Rey, H.A.—*Cecily G. and the 9 Monkeys*
Robins, Joan—*Addie Meets Max*
Simon, Shirley—*Best Friend*
Slote, Alfred—*My Robot Buddy*
Steig, William—*Amos and Boris*
Tabot, Winifred—*Denny's Friend Rags*
Waber, Bernard—*Lovable Lyle*
White, E. B.—*Charlotte's Web*

Safety and Rules

Ady, Sharon—*We Didn't Mean To*
Alexander, Martha—*No Ducks in Our Bathtub*
Bendick, Jeanne—*Accident Prevention*
Berenstain, Stan—*The Bike Lesson*
Barry, Joy Wilt—*Accidents*
Grossman, Jill—*Bicycle Songs of Safety*
Hader, B. & Elmer Hader—*Stop, Look, and Listen*
Kessler, Leonard—*Last One in Is a Rotten Egg*

(Continued)

FIGURE 5.4 *(Continued)*

Leaf, Munro—*Safety Can Be Fun*
Marron, Carol A.—*Mother Told Me So*
Talanda, Susan—*Dad Told Me Not To*

Beatrix Potter

Crouch, Marcus—*Beatrix Potter*
Mayer, Ann Margaret—*The Two Worlds of Beatrix Potter*
Potter, Beatrix—*The Classic Tale of Peter Rabbit and Other Cherished Stories*

Teacher Resource Books

Carlson, Nancy—*Bunnies and Their Hobbies*
Hodgson, Harriet—*Toyworks Simple Toys to Make and Enjoy for Ages 3-7*
Lionni, Leo—*Let's Make Rabbits*
Warren, Jean—*1-2-3 Games No-Lose-Group Games for Young Children*
Wilmes, Liz, and Dick Wilmes—*Circle Time for Holidays and Seasons Book*

AV Materials

Records

Learning Basic Skills Through Music—Educational Activities, Inc.
Learning Basic Skills Through Music Vocabulary—Educational Activities, Inc.
The Tale of Peter Rabbit in Story and Song
Little Grey Rabbit Goes to Sea
Little Grey Rabbit's Christmas
The Rabbit and the Cat

Filmstrips

Bunnies' Easter Surprise
Dinosaurs Beware
I'm No Fool With Safety
Many Kinds of Pets
Rackety Rabbit and the Runaway Easter Egg
Watch Out—Learning Tree

Videos

Playground Safety: As Simple as A,B,C
Primary Safety: Bus Safety
Primary Safety: On the Way to School
Primary Safety: School and Playground
School Bus Safety and Courtesy

Note: A special thanks to Dr. Carolyn Schluck and her students, Doris Jean Whitten, Sue McDaniel, Krissy Gentry, and Tina L. Easterwood, for this list of rabbit books.

Strands

A	B	C	D
Rabbits	Friendship	Family	Rules and
kinds of	types of	care of	Safety
care of	who can be one	roles	class
habitat	importance	members	school
life cycle	qualities	feelings	home
enemies	feelings	experiences	community
protection			

E	F	G	H
Beatrix Potter	Homes	Garden Animals	Gardens
author	materials used	birds	plants
life of	animals	mice	plant cycle
illustrator	people	spiders	vegetables
other stories	kinds	ladybugs	seeds
	designs	enemies	tools
		life cycles	parts
		characteristics	

Under the heading of each strand, the subheadings indicate the interests of the children and the resource materials. The web, with its parallel list of books, is an outline of the course of study, backed by information sources. The web narrows down the content while at the same time graphing an interrelationship between the headings and strands.

The teacher may design many learning activities using the Cognitive Content Area constructs:

- Strand A—Rabbits: kinds of rabbits (classification), care of (seriating steps in caring for rabbit), habitat (causality—white rabbits in snowy places, brown ones in fields, etc.), life cycle (seriating stages of growth), enemies (classification—from the land, from air), protection (causality—camouflage, speed, quietness)
- Strand B—Friendship: types of friends for rabbits (classification—forest rangers, children), who can be one (causality), importance/qualities (seriate actions one might take to make friends), feelings (classification)

(Progressing in a similar manner with the remaining strands.)

Teacher Behavior Continuum: Thematic-Project Teaching

With an understanding of the web for organizing content knowledge, the taxonomy of questioning, and the triangle construct of Representational Level, Cognitive Content Areas, and Operational Level, you may now apply these concepts to the process of thematic-project teaching. You may visually represent the use of these constructs with the Teacher Behavior Continuum (TBC)—Thematic-Project Teaching (see Table 5.3).

TABLE 5.3   Teacher Behavior Continuum (TBC): Thematic-Project Teaching

Minimum Teacher Control (inductive)				Maximum Teacher Control (deductive)
Looking	Naming	Questioning	Commanding	Acting
	(1-b) Verbal encoding	(3-b) Levels of Questioning* 1. "What is this called?" (facts) 2. "Why does this happen?" (convergent) 3. "What would happen if we did this?" (divergent) 4. "What is the best for this?" (evaluative)	1. **Say** (1-a) "This is ____." 3. **Check** (3-a) "Pick out the ____."	(1-c) Read story books (motivational experience) 2. **Show** Levels of representation: Sign (written word) Symbol (picture) Object (real object: Rabbit)

*Questions would test the child's concepts of the Cognitive Content Areas related to classification, seriation, temporal, and so on.

Step 1—Say

Begin teaching new information with commanding statements, such as "This is a _____." Or begin by reading a book, which may also serve as a motivational experience. If the child is already motorically involved (petting the rabbit), you may verbally encode concepts for the child (levels of operation).

Step 2—Show

Next, show the child a model of the concept at any of the three levels of representation: a real object, a symbolic representation of the object (e.g., a picture), or a sign (spoken or written word, such as "rabbit").

Step 3—Check

Check to determine if the child understands the concept by asking questions, which progress up the taxonomy from facts/labels, to convergent, to divergent, and, finally, to evaluative. The questions relate to one of the Cognitive Content Areas (classification, seriation, temporal, spatial/number, causality). Checking can also be done by having the child motorically enact the concept (hop like a rabbit). The child might also be checked for learning by observing her level of representation as seen in her paintings, drawings, and so forth. Read again the introductory example of *The Tale of Peter Rabbit* to see where these teaching concepts would be applied.

A culminating experience, such as all the children having the opportunity to touch and observe a real rabbit, might occur after a daily lesson, or an art show or skit for parents might be presented at the end of the learning unit.

Let's take another example. The *garden* strand leads to the making of the children's own "Mr. McGregor's garden" in the corner of their playground (or on the windowsill). They have classified seeds, used spatial concepts in planting their seeds, and used temporal and number concepts in measuring and graphing the plants as they grew. They have also made a book related to gardens/vegetables using, of course, symbols and signs. The culminating experience might be making vegetable soup with the vegetables they have grown, and eating it for lunch.

Lesson Plans

A lesson plan (Figure 5.5) provides an outline to guide the teacher through content and method presentation and processes.

FIGURE 5.5   Lesson Plans

I. Theme Name _____

   Strand Name_____

   Lesson Number _____ (letter) _____ (no.)

   Teacher's Name _____

   Date Taught _____

   To Group: (circle) A B C D

II. Goals:

     1. _____

     2. _____

     3. _____

     4. _____

     5. _____

III. Key Vocabulary

     _____

IV. Materials Needed

     1. Teacher _____

     2. Child _____

V. Strategies

   A. Motivational Experience (adv. org.)

     _____

   B. Procedures (or steps)

     1. _____

     2. _____

     3. _____

     4. _____

     5. _____

     6. _____

   C. Follow-Up Lesson (or Culminating Activity)

     Go to: _____

VI. Methods of Evaluation

     1. _____

     2. _____

     3. _____

Lesson Plan (Introductory)

The top items—theme name, strand name, lesson number, teacher's name, date taught, and group—are self-explanatory. The lesson number keeps the lessons in sequence. Many plans will be made under the headings of each strand. Circling the group (A, B, C, D) provides a record of which students have been taught this lesson.

Goals

Goals are statements as to what the children should gain from their study of a particular strand. Implicit in these goals will be the Cognitive Content Areas, levels of representation, and levels of operation. Goals may also be related to level of thinking (facts/labels, convergent, divergent, and evaluative).

> *Example:* Children will gain the ability to classify (Cognitive Content Area) kinds of rabbits (Strand A) and their native habitat, and represent this through creating a diorama (symbolic representation) of snow, desert, and forest rabbits.

> *Example:* Children will be able to care for (Strand A) the rabbit (motoric operation) and graph the number (Cognitive Content Area: seriation/number) of pellets eaten and rabbit's weight. (Levels of representation—symbol and sign)

> *Example:* Children will be able to classify (Cognitive Content Area) vegetables (Strand H), a root (in soil), head (on soil), and veining (above soil) by making plant shapes (level of representation—symbolic) and placing them correctly in a garden picture.

Key Vocabulary

The key vocabulary contains the new words that the children will learn, and will come from the strands, Cognitive Content Areas, and levels of operation.

Materials Needed

As the teacher prepares to give the lesson, it is critical to have all needed materials at hand. A glance at the Materials Needed list can quickly reveal if anything is lacking. At times, the materials list is divided into teacher materials and child materials (to be used by the children).

Methods of Evaluation

Did the children understand the concepts taught? The evaluation methods listed here are general ones that might come at the end of the unit, but the evaluation should take place throughout the lesson. The Child-Play Behavioral Rating Scale (Figure 12.5) and Social Observation System (Figure 12.3) or written observations could be used to assess the children's knowledge or representational ability. See Chapter 12 on methods of assessment and evaluation.

Strategies

The subheadings under Strategies are Motivational Experience, Procedures (or Steps), Follow-Up Lesson, and Evaluation (or Culminating Activity).

Motivational Experience
The opening of a lesson should seize the children's attention. It also models what will be learned: "We will read Peter Rabbit and learn many new things about rabbits and their surroundings." The children now know where they will go in the journey (lesson) with the teacher. Although storybooks will often be used for motivational beginnings, other methods, such as audiovisual aids, could be used.

Procedures (or Steps)
An outline is written to help you follow the three-step lesson (say, show, check) and apply various aspects from the TBC (Figure 5.3), such as acting, commanding, questioning (facts/labels, convergent, divergent, and evaluative), naming, and looking.

Follow-Up Lesson (or Culminating Activity)
The culminating activity should require the child to use the new information gained, and should involve an element of fun. Another example for use with the Peter Rabbit unit would be having the children enact the story. A culminating experience for a cooking-science lesson could be to eat the bread (or other food) that the children made. Others might include making murals or books, and producing plays.

Evaluation
Evaluating the children's learning should be done throughout the lesson.

Symbols to Signs

In the thematic-project process, the child acquires new information and then represents his understanding first in play symbols (paintings, clay, sociodramatic play, etc.) and then with the use of written words. Symbolic development has been described in the play-activity curriculum. Painting and similar symbolic projects will move from random scribbling, to controlled scribbling, to the circle, and so on. You may use the Child-Play Behavioral Rating Scale (Figure 12.5) to assess where the child is in symbolic development. The projects that the teacher will set up and encourage the child to complete will involve all forms of expressive media (e.g., sociodramatic play; miniature life toys; murals; string painting; sewing; wire sculpturing; pasting, cutting, tearing; puppet making; collage, and carpentry).

The bridging to signs requires that you take the child's dictation after he has completed one of his theme-related symbolic projects. For example, the child has cut a rabbit shape from white corduroy materials and glued it onto a sheet of cardboard. He brings this to you and asks, "Could you write 'Peter Rabbit' on my picture?" The child is beginning to bridge from symbols (pictures he has drawn) to signs (words he wants written) in such paintings or drawings, which during the kindergarten year can be bound as "books."

Reading Readiness

It might be surprising to the beginning teacher to see that the child is actually writing before he can read. This is because we are following the Piagetian-Weikart construct for the developmental progression of representational ability. When is the child ready for formal reading instruction? Marie Clay has devised a Concepts about Print Test (1979) that is given in a one-teacher-to-one-child setting using a small child's book called *Sand.* With the use of the *Sand* book, the child is tested for his understanding of the print traditions that indicate readiness for formal reading instruction. The Concepts about Print Test asks whether the child knows:

> The front of the book
> The difference between illustrations (symbols) and print (signs)
> Print (not the picture) tells the story
> What a letter is
> What a word is
> The first letter of a word
> The function of the space
> Use of punctuation (periods, question marks, quotation or "talk" marks)

This individualized test is standardized and used by thematic-project teachers to determine when children are ready for more formal instruction.

Classroom Display Table and Murals

In most thematic-project classrooms, what is being studied is apparent as soon as you walk through the door! Displays of art or "construction" work are prominent, usually forming a classroom mural. This student-created mural would demonstrate what the children have learned. A mural on the Peter Rabbit unit, for example, might have on the left side a fir tree with a hole underneath Peter's home. This home "under the ground" would have a table with a fireplace in the background, and a bed for Peter when he is ill. There could be a road leading to Mr. McGregor's garden, with gates, tool shed, various vegetables grown, the gooseberry netting, the water can, the scarecrow with Peter's coat and shoes on it, and the various animals to be found in the garden (cat, mice, and sparrow). Of course, Mr. McGregor would be there, too.

Located near the front door of the thematic-project classroom one usually finds attractively covered tables and boxes that create a display area for those items the children bring in to share, such as books about rabbits, a "lucky" rabbit's foot, mounted pictures of various types of rabbits, and the like. These items are all shared at circle time and are on display for children and parents to inspect.

Traditional Subject Areas

Subject areas such as science, math, music, and reading are not taught separately in the thematic-project curriculum. Each of these subject areas is integrated into the webbing. The learning unit would contain music related to rabbits, science related to garden planting, and math as children seriate and use numbers to make graphs and charts.

Summary

A series of constructs has been provided for implementing the thematic-project curriculum. One of the primary teaching techniques is questioning, using the four-level taxonomy (facts/labels, convergent, divergent, and evaluative). With these types of questions, the students will develop knowledge that can be subcategorized as classification, seriation/number, temporal, spatial, and causality (Weikart's triangle). Once the children have acquired new information or knowledge, they will attempt to represent it, first through play (symbols) and finally through the written word (sign). The general content to be studied can be organized using the webbing process, with the central factor being children's literature and real-life experiences.

Activities

1. Read a high-quality children's book to a group of young children. When you have finished, question them using the question taxonomy, starting with lower-level questions and working your way up to greater abstraction. Repeat this with a new book, but this time select one of the Cognitive Content Areas from the Weikart curriculum

triangle, questioning the children with the taxonomy related to one of these content areas.

2. Locate yourself at an outdoor water table with a group of young children who are playing intently with the water. See if you can verbally encode their learning as they motorically interact with the water.
3. Make a webbing for these topics, selecting a book for the center of the web: bears, circus, musical instruments, dinosaurs, spaceships, the seashore, and the zoo.
4. Find the Concepts about Print Test by Marie Clay and give the *Sand* test to three children ages 4, 5, and 6.

References

Brearley, M., *The Teaching of Young Children.* New York: Schocken Books, 1971.

Briggs, C., and C. Elkind, "Characteristics of Early Readers," *Perceptual and Motor Skills,* 44 (1977).

Cazden, C. B., *Classroom Discourse: The Language of Teaching and Learning.* Portsmouth, N.H.: Heinemann, 1988.

Clay, M., *The Early Detection of Reading Difficulties: A Diagnostic Survey with Recovery Procedures.* Exeter, N.H.: Heinemann, 1979.

Cockran-Smith, M., *The Making of a Reader.* Norwood, N.J.: Ablex, 1984.

Cohen, D. H., "The Effect of Literature on Vocabulary and Reading Achievement," *Elementary English,* 45 (2) (1968).

Durkin, D., *Children Who Read Early: Two Longitudinal Studies.* New York: Teachers College Press, 1966.

Elley, W. B., "Vocabulary Acquisition from Listening to Stories," *Educational Leadership,* 36 (2) (1978).

Ferreiro, E., and A. Teberosky, *Literacy Before Schooling.* Exeter, N.H.: Heinemann, 1979.

Glazer, J. L., "Reading Aloud to Young Children," *Learning to Love Literature* (L. L. Larnme, ed.). Urbana, Ill.: National Council of Teachers of English, 1981.

Herrell, A., *A Child and an Adult Interact with a Book: The Effects on Language and Literacy in Kindergarten.* Tallahassee, Fla.: Florida State University, 1989.

Holdaway, D., *The Foundations of Literacy.* Sydney: Ashton Scholastic, 1979.

Martinez, M., and N. Roser, "Read It Again: The Value of Repeated Readings during Storytime," *Reading Teacher,* 38 (8) (1985).

Phillips, J. L., *The Origins of Intellect: Piaget's Theory.* San Francisco: W. H. Freeman, 1969.

Piaget, J., and B. Inhelder, *The Growth of Logical Thinking: From Childhood to Adolescence.* New York: Basic Books, 1958.

Smilansky, S., and L. Shefatya, *FacilitatingPlay: A Medium for Promoting Cognitive, Socio-Emotional and Academic Development in Young Children.* Gaithersburg, Md.: Psychosocial & Educational Publications, 1990.

Weikart, D., and others, *The Cognitively Oriented Curriculum: A Framework for Preschool Teachers.* Washington, D.C.: NAEYC Publication, 1971.

6

Understanding Direct Instruction and Instructional Design

VIVIAN FUEYO

As we enter the classroom, we see a small group of children seated in a half circle in front of the teacher. She is pointing to letters of the alphabet on a flannelboard. By each letter on the flannelboard she has placed a picture of a corresponding object. Next to the *A* is a red apple, next to the *B* is a blue ball, next to the *C* is a yellow cat. As we get closer, we can hear the teacher asking each child, in turn, to say the name and the sound of the letter to which she is pointing.

As the teacher points to the *A,* Frank says, "A, and it makes the /ah/ sound." She smiles at Frank, and then points to the *B* while looking at Marvin. He says, "B, and it makes the /buh/ sound." The teacher responds, "Nicely done," and looks at Lila. Lila answers, "C, and it makes the /cat/ sound."

"Lila," the teacher says as she points again to the letter *C,* "Tell me what *sound* the letter makes," and the teacher points to the flannelboard picture of the cat. Lila looks carefully at the letters and objects on the flannelboard and says, "Cat."

Why did Lila respond incorrectly to the teacher's request for a sound? Wasn't she paying attention? Isn't she developmentally ready for this? How can we understand the steps the teacher is using to teach this lesson? Next, we will analyze what happened in this small group lesson from the point of view of direct instruction.

Understanding Learning from a Direct Instruction Point of View

Direct instruction, based on the experimental analysis of behavior by B. F. Skinner, views student learning in terms of variables the teacher can control, including the level of student motivation, the difficulty of the response required of the student, and the sequencing of stimuli presented directly by the teacher. Before we go back to help Lila and her teacher, let's summarize the key concepts underlying the science of learning known as *behavior analysis.* According to Skinner, learning is the orderly, moment-to-moment change of behavior that is sensitive to change. The science of learning evaluates the probability of a response, or what is likely to happen next, and explores the conditions in which that will occur (Skinner, 1968). If Lila's teacher had understood the science of learning through direct instruction, she would have spent more time analyzing all the possible responses Lila could make to the letters and objects on the flannelboard. The teacher would ask herself whether Lila might respond to the color or the shape instead of the letter, or whether Lila would look at the letter on the flannelboard when the teacher instructed her to, or even whether the shape of the cat was the right object to use to teach the /cuh/ sound. Let's learn a little bit more about the science of learning before helping Lila's teacher.

The theoretical basis for direct instruction is Skinner's contribution to behavioral psychology of the concept of "operant." Unlike reflex-behavior, such as a knee-jerk reflex or Pavlov's salivating dog, operant behavior is just "emitted" by the child. *Emitted behavior* is the behavior teachers observe in students every day. For example, when children line up to go to the playground after the teacher's request, those who line up first get to go out first. If those children who lined up first had a good time on the playground, the next time the teacher makes the request, their "emitted" behavior would be to line up first again. If, on the other hand, one of the children fell on the playground and skinned a knee, this child might not hurry to line up the next time he heard the teacher's request.

Direct instruction is concerned with *S-R-S:* (1) the circumstances under which behavior occurs (the stimulus); (2) the behavior itself (the response); and (3) the consequences that the behavior produces (the stimulus). Because a stimulus can be any discernible event in the environment, what is important is when and how the stimulus is presented and the consequent response it produces. It is this S-R-S chain that forms the basis for direct instruction. In Table 6.1, we revisit our small group using an S-R-S analysis of the science of learning.

Table 6.1 gives us an idea of the myriad stimuli to which Lila could have been paying attention. Which one caught her attention? Was it the teacher saying, "Tell me the letter name and the sound?" Was Lila paying attention to what Frank and Marvin were saying when the teacher pointed to *A* and *B*? Or was Lila focusing on the teacher as she pointed to the shape of the cat? An educated guess would

TABLE 6.1   S-R-S

The Child	(S) Circumstances under Which the Behavior Occurs	(R) The Behavior Itself	(S) The Consequences the Behavior Produces
Frank	Sees the letter *A,* a red apple, the teacher pointing, all the other shapes and letters on the flannelboard	Says *A* and /ah/	The teacher smiles and goes on to Marvin.
Marvin	Sees the letter *B,* a blue ball, the teacher pointing and looking at him, all the other shapes and letters on the flannelboard; hears Frank say *A* and /ah/, and sees the teacher smile at Frank.	Marvin says *B* and /buh/	The teacher says, "Nicely done," and looks at Lila.
Lila	Sees the letter C, a yellow cat, the teacher pointing and looking at her, all the other shapes and letters on the flannelboard, hears Frank say *A* and /ah/, hears Marvin say *B* and /buh/; looks carefully at the letters and objects on the flannelboard	Says *C* and *Cat* Says, "Cat."	The teacher says, "Lila," and points again to the letter *C.* "Tell me the *sound* the letter makes," and points to the shape of the cat.

be that Lila was centering on the teacher pointing to the picture of the cat and not on what the teacher was asking or what Frank and Marvin had said.

Direct instruction does not require teachers to make educated guesses. Looking again at the information in Table 6.1, you can see that there is a long list of possible stimuli to which Lila might have given her attention. To ensure that Lila focuses on the precise stimulus that will result in her saying the letter sound correctly each time, the teacher needs to achieve stimulus control.

If a teacher understands the definition of stimulus control, then it will become clear that the process of teaching is about establishing a relationship between a certain stimulus and the child's responses. This understanding makes it all but impossible to maintain a one-sided view of teaching in which the only thing that is important is what a teacher says and does, and it is merely the child's job to respond. No teaching occurs where there is no learning. Teaching with stimulus control involves improving the teacher/student communication process so that the teacher is saying, "This is the important stimulus to pay attention to;

these other stimuli do not make much difference. This is the situation where you can apply and generalize these other stimuli; and these others are the situations where you cannot." The teacher's job is to determine whether communication has occurred. A message was sent, but was it received? The teacher knows if it was received by seeing if the child does, indeed, respond to the correct stimulus. If this happens, a relationship has formed between the stimulus and the child's response, and there exists stimulus control. If the child's response does not show stimulus control, as in Lila's case, then the teacher knows genuine communication did not happen, and the message must be adjusted accordingly. The teacher should use his or her knowledge of the science of learning to design instruction in order to achieve stimulus control.

A *stimulus,* then, is any discernible event occurring in the environment at a given point in time. The fact that a stimulus is a discernible event at a given point in time means that a child can perceive the event as an entity in time and space. A stimulus can be anything that occurs that prompts a child to say, "Yes, that's happening." For example, a teacher smiling at a child is a stimulus. In the classroom, a stimulus can be a phrase said by the teacher to give directions to pick up the blocks, a color cut-out on the flannelboard, an easel set up for painting, or a friend saying hello. What is important to remember is that a stimulus must be discernible. To check your understanding: When a teacher asks a child a question, what additional stimuli besides the content of the question could be prompting the child's response? Look at Table 6.1 to check your answers to this question.

Stimulus Control is when a given discernible event prompts a response or reaction by a child. In fact, most teaching is actually an attempt to achieve the best communication possible between a specific stimulus and the child's response. A teacher holds up a red object and asks, "What color is this?" If the child says, "Red," the teacher has achieved the desired communication between the stimulus and the child's response. This is stimulus control.

The Design of Instruction

Three factors provide the basis for the design of instruction: (1) a careful study of the individual learner, (2) the conditions under which learning takes place, and (3) the change in the learner that provides evidence of the learning. All teacher/ student communication in the well-known early childhood educational *direct instruction* and *behavior analysis* approaches is based on these instructional design principles.

You learned from the preceding example that Lila may have been paying attention to a wide variety of stimuli. Let's design instruction to teach Lila letter-sound recognition using the five-step process presented in Table 6.2.

Step 1: Identifying the Objectives for Learning.   The first step in designing instruction is to identify the learning objective. Objectives are important because

TABLE 6.2   Five Steps in Designing Instruction

Step	What the Teacher Is Doing	Why the Teacher Is Doing It
1	Identifying the objective for learning	To begin instruction at the level of the learner and to provide a clear picture of the learning the teacher wants the child to achieve
2	Identifying the critical element (concept development)	To analyze the essential aspect of the concept being taught in order to emphasize it in the teaching process
3	Conducting a task analysis	To break the learning down into all its steps
4	Sequencing the steps	To order the steps from simple to complex
5	Using instructional design strategies to teach the objective	To phrase instruction for optimal communication between the teacher and the learner

they (1) give the teacher an understanding of what the learner can do at the end of teaching; (2) give a basis for creating the teaching steps to reach the learning goal; (3) clear away unnecessary information and ensure clear communication between the teacher and the child about what is to be learned; and (4) provide enough specific information for the teacher to know when the teaching is completed (Nelson, 1990).

To ensure that all four goals are met when identifying an objective for student learning, each objective contain three parts: a performance, a condition, and a criterion for evaluation.

Performance

The *performance* describes what the child will be doing or saying in observable terms. When establishing the performance, the teacher uses verbs that paint observable pictures of the child in the learning situation—for example: *say, look, trace, point to, arrange in order, match, paint, draw, stand, circle, describe, tell, sing,* and so on.

Although verbs describing other goals for the children (e.g., *understand, appreciate, enjoy, develop,* and *respect*) belong in the curriculum, they do not belong in the objective because they fail to identify observable behaviors of the child in the learning situation. If the teacher has specified the final outcome of instruction, she knows when she has achieved her teaching aim. If the objectives are general and ambiguous (verbs such as *enjoy* or *appreciate*), then the teaching process is always in a state of uncertainty.

Table 6.3 provides a list of verbs that can be used for writing the *performance* portion of learning objectives to teach skills and concepts. The verbs are organized by the cognitive domain into which the learning objective falls.

In our example with Lila, we will separate teaching her the letter sounds (phonetic sound-symbol correspondence) from teaching her the letter names (alphabetical recognition). These are two different skills, and learning a letter name is not required for learning a letter sound. With some children, teaching the

TABLE 6.3   Bloom's Taxonomy and Performance Verbs

Areas of Bloom's Taxonomy	What the Teacher Does	What the Child Does	Verbs to Use in Writing the Performance
1. *Knowledge:* Recall or recognition of specific information	Directs, tells, shows, examines	Responds, absorbs, remembers, recognizes	define, repeat, list, name, label, recall, relate, record
2. *Comprehension:* Understanding of information given	Demonstrates, listens, questions, compares, contrasts, examines	Explains, interprets, demonstrates, translates	restate, discuss, relate, describe, recognize, tell, locate, relate, report, explain, express, identify
3. *Application:* Using methods, concepts, principals, and theories in new situations	Shows, observes, facilitates, criticizes	Solves problems, demonstrates use of knowledge, constructs	translate, interpret, apply, demonstrate, employ, use, practice, operate, illustrate, dramatize
4. *Analysis:* Breaking information down into its constituent elements	Probes, guides, observes, acts as a resource	Discusses, uncovers, lists, dissects	distinguish, differentiate, calculate, experiment, test, diagram, invent, criticize, debate, question
5. *Synthesis:* Putting together constituent elements or parts to form a whole requiring original, creative thinking	Reflects, extends, analyzes, evaluates	Discusses, generalizes, relates, compares, contrasts, abstracts	compose, plan, design, propose, formulate, arrange, assemble, collect, construct, manage, prepare, organize
6. *Evaluation:* Judging the values of ideas, materials, and methods by developing and applying standards and criteria	Clarifies, accepts, harmonizes, guides	Judges, disputes, develops criteria	judge, evaluate, appraise, rate, value, select, assess, measure, predict, estimate, choose, score compare

*The source for the levels of the taxonomy is Bloom (1956). The lists of suggested verbs in the other columns are original to the author.

two skills simultaneously may be very confusing. We can describe the *performance* for teaching Lila letter-sound correspondence as follows:

Performance: The child will *say* the letter sound.

Condition

The *condition* of the objective describes the circumstances under which the learning will take place. In our example with Lila, the condition describes the circumstances under which she will be expected to *say* the letter sound.

Condition: After being presented with a graphic representation of the letter, the child will *say* the letter sound.

Notice that the condition does not read, "After being presented with a *flannelboard* shape of the letter ..." In this learning objective, the flannelboard is only one way in which a letter shape can be presented, so it is not the flannelboard letter that is the important stimulus. It is the shape of the letter that is the important stimulus to include in the objective.

Criterion for Evaluation

The third part of every learning objective is the criterion for evaluation. The *criterion* describes the standard the teacher will use to evaluate the learning. For example, in the criterion, the teacher describes how frequently, how loudly, how accurately, or how completely the performance needs to occur to meet the standard for the objective.

Criterion for evaluation: After being presented with a graphic representation of the letter, the child will say the letter sound *each time the letter is presented.*

Let's put all three parts together and look again at our objective: **After being presented with a graphic representation of the letter** *(Condition),* **the child will say** *(Performance)* **the letter sound each time** *(Criterion)* **the letter is presented.**

To summarize, then, an *objective* is a clear statement of the learning to take place. To ensure that the teacher has a clear understanding, all objectives must have a performance, a condition, and a criterion for evaluation. To check your understanding, look again at the objective we just stated. Does it meet all the requirements? Now you know how to write a learning objective with all three components.

Step 2: Identifying the Critical Element.   After writing an objective, the next step in designing instruction is to identify the critical element. This process is also termed *concept development* (Nelson, 1990), or analyzing a concept to specify what to emphasize in the teaching process. The critical element is the stimulus that will prompt a correct response, or the discriminative stimulus. What is the most important feature of the learning on which a student should focus? Isolating the critical element of a learning task is a necessary first step in designing instruction. Let's look at some examples.

Stimulus	*Critical Element*
The sound of the letter *A*	The shape of the mouth (open, smiling)
When it is safe to cross the street	A green light, no traffic coming from either direction
Putting away blocks by correct size	The size of the block in the child's hand and the matching symbol of the block on the shelf

In some learning tasks, there may be a series of critical elements addressed sequentially to solve a task. For example, in the task of putting on a coat, the first critical element would be identifying such features as buttons or zippers that would indicate the front of the coat. The next critical element would be the collar to indicate the top rather than the bottom of the coat. The third critical element would be the location of the sleeves, and so on.

Because most teachers have already mastered the concepts and skills they are teaching (they already know how to put on their coats), in attempting to communicate to their students it is often difficult for them to think back to the first time they encountered this concept. Often, the discriminative stimulus aspect of the concept has been lost and the understanding of the concept has become automatic. It is essential that the teacher examine the critical element through the eyes of the child.

To determine the critical element, the most useful procedure is to examine the learning task from a logical standpoint and ask: What is the single most important element of this? The teacher could ask herself: When I respond, which aspect of the learning task would I pay the most attention to in order to respond correctly if I were the learner? The critical element is not the theme of a lesson. It is the specific aspect of presenting a question, object, or task that, when focused on by the child, will be the key to unlocking the solution or answer. In other words, it is the most important item that catches the learner's attention.

Let's go back to our objective for Lila and identify the critical element. The objective now reads: **After being presented with a graphic representation of the letter** *(Condition),* **the child will say** *(Performance)* **the letter sound each** time *(Criterion)* **the letter is presented.** What is the critical element of a flannel-board shape of a letter that will capture Lila's attention and prompt her to say the corresponding sound? Unfortunately, *the flannelboard shape alone is totally unrelated to the sound of the letter.* Knowing that, let's think again of the critical elements for the following letter sounds:

Stimulus	*Critical Element*
The sound of /ah/	Forming the mouth and lips to make the vocalization
The sound of /buh/	Forming the mouth and lips to make the vocalization
The sound of "c" at beginning of *cat*	Isolating the initial consonant sound of "c" from the word *cat,* and forming the mouth and lips to make the vocalization

Isolating a critical element helps a learner assimilate a concept or skill. Once the critical element has been identified, the teacher can emphasize this critical element in the teaching process. (Step 5, discussed later, addresses strategies for emphasizing the critical element.)

Step 3: Conducting a Task Analysis.   A task analysis is a description of the steps or subskills in the learning that are necessary for a student to accomplish a given objective. Teachers should conduct a task analysis of the learning objective to be certain that no important information necessary for student learning is omitted. The task analysis is produced by examining the behavior and thoughts of a student who competently performs the learning objective. A task analysis also isolates the skills a learner must possess or understand before he or she can begin learning a new concept.

A task analysis can be accomplished in several ways. Once way is to visualize the learner performing the objective perfectly. Once the image is in the teacher's mind, the teacher sequentially writes down the steps the child must progress through to perform the task. The teacher also logically thinks through the prerequisite skills before the child can start the first step.

When the learning objective involves a psychomotor skill or a manual task, such as climbing a playground structure or putting the blocks away in order by size, another task analysis method would be to actually perform the task yourself and record each step. You may also watch a child complete the task and record the steps.

In doing a task analysis, it is helpful to know that there is no single correct task analysis for any given learning objective. The number of steps is determined by the learners in your particular classroom.

According to Nelson (1990), a task analysis is conducted so that:

1. The teacher will not assume that students understand certain component skills or concepts that are essential to completing the task, but are automatic to the teacher.
2. Students will not be asked to complete tasks for which they do not have the prerequisite skills.
3. Teachers can design instruction that improves communication with the learner and ensures successful learning. Teachers use the information from a task analysis to plan instructional sequences, to diagnose initial learning and skill, and to diagnose ongoing student learning (Hunter, 1994).

Again, task analysis is listing the steps a learner would take (mentally or physically) to competently perform the objective. An example from the kindergarten curriculum shows how problems can arise when the teacher fails to conduct a task analysis. The learning objective is number-numeral correspondence. The task is for the children to look at a number of objects and then put a ring around a visual representation of the numeral that stands for the number of objects. In conducting a task analysis (through the eyes of the learner), the following steps emerge:

Sample Task Analysis: Counting Objects and Selecting the Corresponding Numeral

1. Look at the objects.
2. Count the objects starting at the left.
3. Say a number aloud or in the mind as each number is pointed to, starting with 1 and proceeding in sequence.
4. Remember the last number that was counted.
5. Examine the choices of numerals.
6. Remembering the number of objects counted, find the numeral that represents that number.
7. Put a ring around the number.

Does the teacher really need to take all this time to teach something as simple and straight forward as finding a numeral to match a given number of objects? For a moment, consider this task not through the eyes of a teacher but through the eyes of a 5-year-old. The first thing the young child must do is decide which aspect of the stimulus on the page or flannelboard should receive his or her attention. The young child discerns which parts of the stimulus go together to make up the task he or she is going to solve. Often, kindergarten teachers ask children to count objects and find the correct numeral, without knowing whether the children know the numeral's name or place in a sequence. The child may know how many objects there are, but he may not know the numeral *4* is the symbolic representation for the number of objects he just counted.

Some teachers experience frustration teaching such concepts, believing that the children cannot count. Instead, the problems is relatively simple—identifying the names of numerals. Now, let's put together what we've discussed and apply it to Lila's learning.

Sample Task Analysis for Letter-Sound Correspondence

Objective: After being presented with a graphic representation of the letter, the child will say the letter sound each time the letter is presented.

Critical Element(s):
The child recognizes that the shape of the letter corresponds to a phonetic sound.
The child is able to match the correct phonetic sound to the corresponding letter shape.
The child recognizes the phonetic sounds corresponding to the letter shapes are the same sounds used in speech.

Task Analysis:
1. Recognize that it is a letter-sound correspondence task.
2. Recognize the letter shape.
3. Say the phonetic sound that corresponds to the letter shape.
4. Recognize that the phonetic sound of the letter is the same as the phonetic sounds in speech.
5. Say the word that begins with the same phonetic sound.

Prerequisites:
1. The child can follow the teacher's verbal directions.
2. The child can recognize discrete shapes.
3. The child can recognize discrete sounds.
4. The child can say and repeat sounds.

The most common error in writing a task analysis is for a teacher to write down the steps that he or she will use in teaching a concept, *instead of the steps a child will take in learning the concept.* One technique to get yourself out of thinking this way is to speculate on what could be going on inside the child's head as he or she approaches a learning task. Using the information in Step 3, write a task analysis for the steps your students would need to go through to participate appropriately.

Step 4: Sequencing the Steps.   Creating a sequence is the basic art of designing instruction. The purpose of a sequence is to create an instructional progression to lead a learner to competence and accuracy in responding to a concept. The first step of a sequence is a skill or concept that the learner has already mastered. This ensures that the sequence progresses from what the learner knows to what is new. To lead the learner to the critical element, or discriminative stimulus, in a sequence, the teacher uses cues or strategies (In step 5, we will discuss the cues and strategies a teacher can use to focus the child's attention on the discriminative stimulus of the learning task.)

The cardinal rule in creating a sequence is: *Teach one thing at a time.* It is essential that each step in a sequence teach one skill or concept only. Otherwise, it is possible for students to become confused. Using our new vocabulary, the purpose of each step in the sequence must be to establish stimulus control of the discriminative stimulus and to help a student see the difference between the discriminative stimulus and the other irrelevant stimuli. In the science of stimulus control, irrelevant stimuli are referred to as *S-Deltas.* This term is used to identify the stimuli that, when responded to by a child, produces an undesired response. In this chapter, however, we will refer to these stimuli as irrelevant stimuli to distinguish them from the discriminative stimuli we want the children to deal with.

Sequencing, then, is creating a series of instructional steps that move from simple to complex to teach each concept or skill generated by a task analysis. To order the steps in a sequence from simple to complex, we use Bloom's taxonomy of educational objectives, as presented in Table 6.3 (Bloom, 1956). *Simple* and *complex* in instructional design refer to the level of cognitive simplicity or complexity of the learning involved. To progress from simple to complex as a learner, the student moves from the first level, *knowledge,* which involves recalling or recognizing information, to the most complex level, *evaluation,* in which the learner judges and evaluates information by developing and applying standards and criteria. The following sample sequence provides an example of teaching letter-sound correspondence to Lila:

Sequence to Teach Letter-Sound Correspondence

Step in the Sequence	*Cueing the Discriminative Stimulus*
1. Recognize the shape as a letter shape.	1. Point to a letter shape, trace the shape, and tell the child, "This is a letter."
2. Recognize that it is a letter-sound correspondence task.	2. Tell the child, "This letter makes the _____ sound."
3. Match the letter shape with its correct sound.	3. Show and tell the child, "Look at the shape of my mouth when I make the _____ sound."
4. Say the phonetic sound that corresponds to the letter shape.	4. Tell the child, "Say_____ (the letter sound)."

This sequence proceeded from simple to complex, from recognizing that shapes represent letters (recognition and recall) to the sound-symbol correspondence of a particular sound for a particular letter shape (analysis and synthesis). In each step of the sequence, the teacher cued the child or pointed out the relevant feature of the discriminative stimulus. It is equally important for the learner to recognize and ignore the irrelevant stimuli. Now let's move on to some sample strategies that serve two important functions: (1) alerting the learner to respond to the relevant stimuli and (2) alerting the learner not to focus on or respond to the irrelevant stimuli.

Step 5: Using Instructional Design Strategies to Teach the Objective. Instructional design strategies are rules that alert the learner to the critical element. Strategies give the child something to rely on when a teacher is not there to give assistance. Teaching a strategy also prompts a child to internalize a skill or concept instead of relying on the external prompting of a teacher or on rote memory. Strategies allow learners to be more self-directed in learning and also allow them to be independent of external instruction. Strategies also produce effective communication with students, because rules should be designed to emphasized the critical element. Let's look at some examples.

Teaching children to "look both ways before you cross the street" when teaching safety rules is teaching them a strategy. In this example, the critical element of crossing streets safely has two components: (1) recognizing that traffic goes in both directions and (2) recognizing that only when no vehicles are present in the street may the child cross safely. Once the children effectively learn the strategy as seen by the actions, the teacher does not need to repeat the rule constantly and the children become more independent.

Another example of the effectiveness of using strategies to assist learning comes from research comparing the sight and phonetic approaches to beginning reading. For example, a child must understand four prerequisite concepts before he or she can "read" a word and understand its meaning: (1) words can be "spoken" or "written," (2) written words in print correspond to words in speech, (3) words are made up of sounds, and (4) words are composed of letters that correspond to units of sound (Carnine, Silbert, & Kameenui, 1997). Each of these steps has a series of critical elements that, when learned, provides the child with strategies for reading and understanding new words encountered in print.

Two publications—*Learning to Read: The Great Debate* by Jean Chall (1967) and *Beginning to Read* by Marilyn J. Adams (1990)—reported that after one year of instruction, learners taught to memorize words by sight had a larger vocabulary than those taught by the phonetic approach. After three years of instruction, however, the children who had learned the phonetic method significantly outscored the sight method students in terms of being able to recognize words and comprehend what they read. The implication is that although it may take longer to teach students a strategy than to teach them to memorize information, once they learn the strategy, they can apply it independently to new information (Nelson, 1990).

Strategies for Designing Instruction

The following strategies are useful for cueing the critical element of the learning task and may be used alone or in combination when designing instruction.

Behavior Rehearsal

This strategy is practiced by the student learning the desired response. The practice is prompted by the teacher. Usually, behavior rehearsal is a routine, or a script, of teacher questions and student answers that result in the complete response. A behavior rehearsal can be designed to teach the rule of a strategy. Often, in behavior rehearsal, the teacher uses *modeling* (providing a demonstration) and *prompting* (providing a cue or asking a question to encourage the child to give the correct response); the teacher then gradually removes the prompting, or *fades* it out.

The following example uses behavior rehearsal with modeling and prompting to teach the following objective: *Given pictures of objects, the child will demonstrate one-to-one correspondence by counting the sets of objects as the teacher points.*

Behavior Rehearsal

Model	*Teacher Says and Does*
1. "One bike" (loud)	"This is a bike. Watch me point and listen to me count. One." (The teacher points to the bike.) "Now you count. One." (loudly with the child)
2. "One bike" (normal)	"Count again. One." (in a normal speaking voice with the child)
3. "One bike" (whisper)	"Count the bike. One." (The teacher says it in a whisper, while the child says it in a normal voice.)

This sequence continues as different objects are added to avoid having the child associate the picture of the bike with the number one. As each object is added, the teacher models by saying the number and prompts the response by pointing. As the child learns the concept of one-to-one correspondence, the teacher gradually fades the prompts.

4. "One bike"	"Count the bike." (prompt by the teacher)
5. "One boat" (loud)	(The teacher prompts the response by pointing and saying "Count the boat.")

When the teacher says the number while pointing to the picture of the object, she is modeling. When the teacher says "Count the bike" while pointing to the bike, she is prompting the child to say the number that corresponds to the number of objects.

6. "One boat" (normal)	(The teacher prompts the response by pointing and saying "Count the boat.")
7. "One boat" (whisper)	(prompt by the teacher)
8. "One boat"	(The teacher continues modeling and prompting until the child responds correctly on his or her own.)
9. "One tree" (loud)	
10. "One tree" (normal)	
11. "One tree" (whisper)	
12. "One tree"	The teacher points to one tree without saying anything.
13. **Model**	**(Teacher demonstrates)** "Two hammers." (loud)

As shown next, Steps 14 through 23 continue the same as in the preceding steps, with the teacher alternating between one and two objects, introducing different sets of objects such as two kites and two cats. Once the child can say the corresponding number when the teacher points to a set with one object or two objects, the teacher models sets of three objects using the procedures of modeling and prompting described earlier. The number in the behavior rehearsal is determined by the learner. Once the child responds correctly and consistently, the teacher may move on to the next step in the sequence or skip steps that the child already seems to have mastered.

14. **Model**   (**Teacher demonstrates**)
   "Two hammers" (loud)

15. "Two hammers" (normal)

16. "Two hammers" (whisper)

17. "Two hammers"   The teacher points to the two hammers without saying anything.

18. "Two kites" (loud)

19. "Two kites" (normal)

20. "Two kites" (whisper)

21. "Two kites"   The teacher points to the two kites without saying anything.

22. "Two cats" (normal)   The teacher is fading out the prompts and says "two cats" in a normal voice, instead of a loud voice.

23. "Two cats"   The teacher points to the two cats without saying anything, fading out the prompts by skipping the "whisper" step.

24. "One boat"   The teacher points to one boat without saying anything. By this step all of the prompts have been faded out, if the child is still responding correctly.

25. **Model**   (**Teacher demonstrates**)
   "Three snakes" (loud)   The teacher models this step because three items are being introduced.

26. "Three snakes" (normal)

27. "Three snakes" (whisper)

28. "Three snakes"   The teacher points to three snakes without saying anything. If the child is still responding correctly, the teacher adds the other stimuli to the flannelboard and begins pointing to sets of objects from one to three without modeling as the child says the number of objects.

Because behavior rehearsal takes time to develop, it is most beneficial for very difficult situations or for easily confused concepts (e.g., right and left) or for skills that are essential for later learning (such as number-numeral correspondence or sound-symbol associations). Use it to teach concepts or skills that are very difficult for a given learner. An adaptation of behavior rehearsal is using a rhyme or a song to emphasize the critical element of a learning task, as in the "Alphabet Song," which teaches the sounds of the letter names in alphabetical order. The song cues the learner to the critical element in alphabetical order and the name of any letter in the alphabet cues the name of the next letter in the alphabet, using melody, rhythm, and rhyme.

Scripts

Most commercial direct instruction programs, such as DISTAR, provide the teacher with scripts. Sometimes, teachers complain that using scripts is uncreative and restricts their professionalism. In fact, direct instruction developers feel quite the opposite is true. According to Doug Carnine, one of the most knowledgeable authorities in the design of instruction, the true mark of a professional is the ability to use scripts correctly. Some of the most creative professionals use scripts: playwrights, musicians, architects, dancers, and others. Carnine uses the following story to illustrate this point: Imagine you are running through an airport and collapse suddenly because of a heart attack. You are rushed to the nearest hospital and find yourself on the operating table. The cardiac surgeon says to you, "I am a creative surgeon, and I never use a script!!" Ask yourself, would you want such a surgeon to treat you? Clearly, then, there is nothing inherently wrong with scripts, as long as they are used appropriately.

Cueing

Cueing is a technique for adding information to a stimulus or emphasizing a particular feature of a stimulus, either through the teacher's words or through visual presentation of the stimulus. This is done to alert the learner to the critical element of the task. It helps the learner to remember information, decrease errors, and focus on the most critical aspect of the learning, the discriminative stimulus. In our examples of teaching Lila letter-sound correspondence, using as cues a picture of an apple or a real apple, or a picture of a cat or a cat-shaped stuffed animal, the teacher would focus Lila's attention on the shape of her mouth when making the sounds /ah/ and /cuh/. In contrast, using an unrelated cue such as color to cue the different letter sounds would not focus Lila's attention on the critical elements of /ah/ and /cuh/, and are not useful as cues. There are several forms of cueing, including model-prompt and superimposition.

Model-Prompt

When a teacher demonstrates the response that is expected, it is called a *model*. When the teacher tells a student the response, or some portion of the response, right before or during a learner's response, it is called a *prompt*. In the earlier behavior rehearsal, the teacher used a model-prompt strategy to cue the correct response.

Superimposition

The teacher adds, or superimposes, a visual or verbal prompt to the stimulus to aid in learning. This strategy is best used to help children learn sounds, words, names, and numbers. To make superimposition most efficient in prompting a response, choose a discriminative stimulus that prompts a response similar to the one desired in the teaching situation. In our example with Lila, if we placed the letters *a* and *c* on the shapes of an apple and a cat to teach Lila to say /ah/ and /cuh/ correctly, we would be using superimposition. When using superimposition, it is important to choose a cue that emphasizes the critical element and is related to the desired student response. In our example with Lila, we used pictures whose names began with the same sounds as the letter sounds we were teaching. Using a color, for example, would have been unrelated to the letter sounds and would not help Lila focus on the critical element. In superimposition, as in the model-prompt strategy, the cues are removed gradually, or faded out, until all that remains is the original stimulus, or, in Lila's case, the letter shape for *a* and *c*. Table 6.4 provides a summary of verbal, visual, and physical prompts and examples of how to gradually fade them.

Here, we have put all the steps together to design instruction to teach Lila letter-sound correspondence.

Designing Instruction to Teach Letter-Sound Correspondence

Objective: After being presented with a graphic representation of the letter, the child will say the letter sound each time the letter is presented.

Prerequisites:
1. The child can follow the teacher's verbal directions.
2. The child can recognize discrete shapes.
3. The child can recognize discrete sounds.
4. The child can say and repeat sounds.

Critical Element(s):
Each unique letter shape corresponds to a letter sound.
Each letter sound requires that the mouth and lips be placed in a certain position.
Phonetic sounds are the building blocks of words.

TABLE 6.4   Prompting and Fading Strategies

Types	Definition		Fading Prompts and Examples
Verbal Prompting	Signals what to do or how to do something. Keep prompts short, use simple words, and be consistent in your use of words.	full prompt	1. "Point to the letter c!" (said loudly) 2. "Point to the letter!" (said loudly) 3. "Point to the letter." (said normally) 4. "Point to …!" (said normally) 5. "Point! (in a whisper)
		no prompt	6. (make no action)
Visual Prompting	Adds a visual dimension to a stimulus in order to make it easier to discriminate from other stimuli, changing color, texture, location, size, etc.	full prompt	1. Superimposing the letter A on a red apple shape 2. Slightly cutting away the shape of the apple on which the letter A is superimposed 3. Cutting away more of the apple shape behind the letter A 4. Cutting away more than half the apple shape behind the letter A 5. Cutting away more than two-thirds of the apple shape behind the letter A
		no prompt	6. Presenting the letter A without the apple shape behind it
Physical Prompting	Physically helping or "leading the child" through the behavior	full prompt	1. Taking the child's hand and moving it as he or she traces over a line 2. Taking the child's hand and guiding it as he or she traces over a line 3. Touching the child's hand as he or she traces over a line 4. Lightly touching the child's hand as he or she traces over a line. 5. Barely touching the child's hand as he or she traces over a line
		no prompt	6. Not touching the child's hand at all as he or she traces over a line

Step in the Sequence	Critical Element	Strategy to Cue the Critical Element
1. Recognize the shape as a letter shape.	1. Each letter has a unique shape.	1. Point to a letter shape, trace the shape, and tell the child, "This is a letter!" (model-prompt).
2. Recognize that it is a letter-sound correspondence task.	2. Each unique letter makes a different sound.	2. Tell the child, "This letter makes the ____ sound, just like the ____ (picture of a) ____ " (model). The letter shape is superimposed on a picture that begins with the same sound as the letter sound (superimposition).
3. Match the letter shape with its correct sound.	3. Each unique letter shape makes a different sound that sounds just like the sounds in familiar words.	3. Show and tell the child, "Look at the shape of my mouth when I make the ____ sound."
4. Say the phonetic sound that corresponds to the letter shape.	4. Associate the correct sound with the letter shape.	4. Tell the child, "Say ____ (the letter sound) and in ____" (the object) (model prompt and superimposition).
5. Say the word that begins with the same sound as the letter.	5. Associate the sound with a familiar word.	5. "Say ____ " (the name of the object) (model-prompt).

The teacher continues to present letter shapes superimposed on familiar objects, beginning with the same phonetic sound as the letter. The teacher prompts and models, fading out the prompts and models as the child responds correctly on his or her own. Opportunities for practice ensure mastery. Let's say you have studied French for two years. What would you say if you were asked if you are fluent in French? If your answer is "no," you probably haven't had enough opportunity to practice. Knowing vocabulary in a foreign language does not lead to fluency; properly using vocabulary in appropriate situations defines fluency. The only difference between the two is practice. The same applies to young children's learning: Practice ensures mastery.

The instruction we designed to teach letter-sound correspondence will ensure that Lila pays attention to the correct feature of the stimulus every time. When the teacher says to her, "Lila, what sound is this?" as she points to the letter *C,* Lila will answer "/cuh/" if she has learned the concept. Because the teacher also has provided opportunities for Lila to practice this new learning, Lila has effortlessly and errorlessly mastered an essential concept in prereading—phonetic awareness.

Assessing Student Learning in Instructional Design

With Lila's success at her new learning task, we have seen instructional design provide a step-by-step approach to meeting the needs of an individual learner. Because each step in the learning sequence has been identified, it is easy to keep track of what materials the child has and has not learned. A criterion checklist to indicate the prerequisites for the learning task and the steps in the sequence (as in Figure 6.1) can be used to monitor children's learning. For each step in the sequence, the teacher indicates whether the child performed the step with prompting by the teacher (P) or independently (I). Initially, all of the steps may be followed by a *P*. After practice, the child will be able to perform the steps independently, and the teacher will mark an *I*.

Other Applications of Instructional Design

Designing instruction has many applications in a school for young children. Have you ever had to spend time reminding children to come to circle time? Have you ever had to wait more than five minutes for a child to join fellow preschoolers on the rug? In the following example, we have designed instruction to teach children to come quickly to circle time.

FIGURE 6.1   Assessing Learning of Letter-Sound Correspondence

Objective: After being presented with a graphic representation of the letter, the child will say the letter sound each time the letter is presented

Child's Name	Prerequisite Skills	With Prompting (P) or Independently (I)	Steps in the Sequence	P I
Lila	1. Following verbal directions		1. Recognizing the shape as a letter shape	
	2. Recognizing discrete shapes		2. Recognizing that it is a letter-sound	
	3. Recognizing discrete sounds		3. Matching the letter shape with correct sound	
	4. Saying and repeating sounds		4. Saying the phonetic sound that corresponds to the letter shape.	
			5. Saying the word that begins with the same sound as the letter	

Designing Instruction to Teach Children to Come to Circle Time
(see also pages 142 and 143)

- *Step 1: Write an objective.*
  Objective: When the teacher signals circle time, each student will find his or her seat on the rug within 30 seconds.
  Prerequisites: Following directions, recognizing verbal commands

- *Step 2: Identify the critical element(s).*
  Critical Element(s): The teacher's signal indicates that (1) something different is going to happen and (2) the child will be expected to act differently than before.

- *Step 3: Conduct a task analysis.*
  Task analysis:
  The signal is given for circle time.
  The child hears the signal for circle time.
  The child stops what he or she is doing.
  The child puts away what he or she is doing or leaves the activity area (like the sand table).
  The child comes to the rug area.
  The child sits on the rug in the appropriate place.
  The child pays attention to the teacher in front of him or her.

- *Step 4: Create a sequence that moves from simple to complex.* (See the following list.)

- *Step 5: In each step in this sequence, use strategies to cue the critical element.*

Step in the Sequence	Critical Element	Strategy to Cue the Critical Element
1. The signal for circle time is given.	1. The signal indicates circle time and nothing else.	1 and 2. The teacher says, "Circle time means stop, put everything away, and come to the rug." As the teacher says this, she motions in cadence to the three steps in the instruction: (1) stop, (2) put away, and (3) come to the rug (model).
2. The child hears the signal.	2. The signal is loud, different from any other signal, and means circle time and nothing else.	

3. The child stops what he or she is doing and follows the teacher's model.	3. Stop what you are doing when you hear the signal.	3. With elbows at her sides, the teacher pulls up both hands with palms in front of her chest facing out in a stopping gesture, and says, "Stop, and do what I do!" (model-prompt).
4. The child puts away what he or she is doing or leaves the activity area (like the sand table).	4. Put away toys or other materials that are out of place.	4. The teacher gestures as if she were stuffing imaginary items into a box as she says, "Put away. Put everything away!" (model-prompt).
5. The child comes to the rug area.	5. Come to the designated place on the rug for circle time.	5. The teacher gestures as in an invitation and says, "Come to the circle!" (model-prompt).
6. The child sits on the rug in the appropriate place.	6. Sit in the appropriate place on the rug.	6. The teacher puts tape on the rug, indicating where children should sit for circle time (cue).
7. The child pays attention to the teacher in front of him or her.	7. Follow directions in circle time.	7. The teacher tells and shows the children what they're doing in circle time (model-prompt).

In addition to the model-prompt strategy and the cues, the teacher could also use behavior rehearsal to teach the children the three-step strategy for circle time: (1) stop, (2) put away, and (3) come to the rug. Table 6.5 provides an example of using a behavior rehearsal script to teach the prompt-model strategy and to help ensure that the children had paid attention to each of the critical features. The script is written in a question-answer format.

The behavior rehearsal is an effective way to teach the three-step strategy. As the teacher models for and prompts the child, the child performs each step. The teacher gradually fades out her modeling, as the child does the motions and says, "Stop, put away, and come to the rug." Each of the steps in the three-step strategy emphasizes what the child should focus on in order to arrive quickly and ready to participate in circle time: The child should stop and listen the minute she hears the signal; she should pick up whatever she is working with and put it away at that time; and she should come to the rug and find her place there. By analyzing this important classroom procedure using instructional design, we identified the critical elements of this task and designed meaningful instructions to teach it.

TABLE 6.5 Behavior Rehearsal Script

What the Teacher Does and Says	What the Child Does and Says
1. *The teacher says,* "Circle time means stop, put away, and come to the rug." As the teacher says this, *she does* the motions in cadence.	1. The child looks at the teacher and listens to the three steps in the strategy.
2. "Now, it's your turn. Say it with me. What do we say?"	2. *The child says,* "Stop, put away, and come to the rug."
3. "Now, it's your turn. Do the motions as we do and say it together. What do we say? Stop, put away, and come to the rug."	3. *The child does* the motions *and says,* "Stop, put away, and come to the rug," along with the teacher.
4. *The teacher does* the motions *as she says,* "Again, let's say and do it together. What do we do and say? Stop, put away, and come to the rug."	4. *The child does* the motions *and says,* "Stop, put away, and come to the rug," along with the teacher.
5. The teacher *says,* "Your turn. What do you do and say? Show me." (The teacher does the motions without saying the instructions.)	5. *The child does* the motions *and says,* "Stop, put away, and come to the rug."

Effective instructional design is not enough however, to ensure that the child continues to follow these directions every time. Once the child gets to the circle, the teacher needs to be ready to involve him or her in an activity or dialogue to increase the likelihood that the child will arrive quickly the next time.

Remember our discussion of S-R-S psychology? It is concerned with (1) the circumstances under which behavior occurs (the first *S*, in this case the model-prompts for the three-step strategy for circle time); (2) the behavior itself (the *R*, in this case the child doing what was modeled and prompted in each step); and (3) the consequences, or consequent response, that the behavior produces (the second *S*, in this case the child's behavior the next time the teacher uses the three-step strategy).

A Word about Consequences and Reinforcement

As we discussed earlier, to sustain a child's successful performance, it is not enough to have effective instructional procedures. We have learned that the consequences that follow a child's actions or learning affect the likelihood that the child will continue to perform that action successfully or will perform it the next time under the same circumstances. In S-R-S psychology, there is no such thing as a reinforcer. What makes a reinforcer out of an action or concrete object—a teacher's smile, the chance to go outside first, a toy, a cookie—is the effect it achieves. Only if a particular action or object, when presented following the child's behavior, increases the likelihood of the child performing that activity again will we know that it was reinforcing.

Let's consider an example. Say you love Key Lime pie. If you have just had a big meal, however, nothing could make you eat a piece of Key Lime pie because you would not have the room. Therefore, you could not say that Key Lime pie is a reinforcer after a big meal. In fact, if the only opportunity you ever had to eat Key Lime pie was at the conclusion of a big meal, you would soon stop liking Key Lime pie. No given action, object, or activity is always a reinforcer; the potential reinforcing value depends on its effect.

Table 6.6 shows categories of potential reinforcers to consider in designing instruction. Do not assume that any or all of these will be reinforcers for every child, or on all occasions. You need to observe the effect each one has on a given child in order to determine if it serves as a reinforcer. An easy way to do this is to make anecdotal notes about the effect a potential reinforcer has on a child's behavior. For example, you could make notes of the games, toys, or centers a child goes to for free-play time. You may love the science table, but very few children go to it during free play; in fact, when you call them to come over to the science table, it takes some children a little longer to get there each day. You could conclude that the opportunity to observe at the science table is not reinforcing for some children. Your anecdotal notes would have given you that information, so you'd know which of the areas the children prefer. As you observe, you can identify the activities, materials, objects, and opportunities that children seem to enjoy. When provided as a consequence, these will increase the likelihood of the children performing the desired behavior the next time.

Use instructional design when you want to be certain that the child has successfully learned a task, especially one that is a building block for subsequent learning. Table 6.7 provides examples of instructional design to support learning, and suggests when you do not need to use it. You will see that instructional design is not a curriculum, so it does not have a scope and sequence. It is a set of tools for you to use in planning effective communication between you and the children in the school for young children. Instructional design and direct instruction give you, as a teacher of young children, the tools you need to individualize instruction for every learner.

Activities

---

1. Observe feeding and bathroom routines in the classroom. Do they seem cumbersome and take too long? Do they flow smoothly and effortlessly? If the answer to the first question is "yes" and the answer to the second question is "no," design an instructional sequence to teach feeding routines and another one for bathroom routines.
2. Observe children's transitions in and out of the classroom, such as going out to the playground, leaving the school to take walks, or coming into the classroom in the

TABLE 6.6   Possible Consequences and Potential Reinforcers

Type	Definition	Examples
Food		Whole-wheat pretzels, small pieces of fruit, or similar food items fortified with ingredients such as a whole-grain flour, oatmeal, wheat germ, or bran
Tangible items to be used alone or as part of a token system	Children receive tangible items throughout an activity or at the end of the activity	1. Parts to form a teddy bear (body, head, two ears, two arms and two legs, two eyes, nose, and mouth) 2. Other pictorial forms with parts: jack-o-lanterns, flowers with petals, artist's palette with colors, soup bowl with vegetable shapes 3. Earn actual tokens to be traded for opportunities to play in a preferred activity
Preferred activity or opportunity	After certain "learning" or directed activities are completed, the child is permitted to participate in certain "free" choice activities around play	Water-play, sand-play, cooking, using adult objects, taking turns at being the "teacher" in charge, and the like
Social consequences		1. Pats, squeezes, hugs, winks 2. Getting called on to "show and tell" or help 3. Statement of approval 4. Having work displayed 5. Notes sent home
Task-imbedded consequences	The task is designed to have a novel or attractive item in the activity	1. In motor activity, a target for throwing balls in a lion's "mouth" 2. Putting away snack items 3. Doing adult tasks, (i.e., running the vacuum cleaner, etc.)

morning or afternoon. For several days, take anecdotal notes, writing down how long each transition takes. Note the shortest transition time and the longest. Can you identify the critical elements for each of the transitions? How could you cue the critical elements for each transition to decrease transition time?

3. Interview an experienced teacher about potential reinforcers and consequences. Ask him or her about activities, events, and objects that children find reinforcing. How many new ideas can you collect in each of the five categories presented in Table 6.6? Try out some of these potential reinforcers and observe their effect on the children's behavior. Keep a list of each child and review it periodically.

TABLE 6.7   Guidelines for Using Instructional Design

Use It to Help You Teach This	You Won't Need It to Teach This
Climbing a particular piece of equipment, using fine motor skills to operate a microscope, safety rules	Developing large and small muscle skills
Holding a brush, behaving in the art and music areas, listening and observing	Aesthetic development; music and art appreciation
Sequencing events in a story, number-numeral correspondence, teaching concepts like *before* and *after*	Cognitive development
Following directions, classroom routines for going outside, putting away blocks, taking turns, going on a field trip	Social skills development
Listening skills, taking care of books, letter-sound correspondence, letter formation	Language development and literacy
Teaching acceptable and unacceptable behavior, rules for helping	Social-emotional development
Bathroom behavior, feeding and eating routines, napping routines, hygiene tasks	Health, safety, and nutrition
Routines for parent volunteers and paraprofessionals to support the implementations of the curriculum	Curriculum development and long-term planning

4. As an extension to activity 3, ask that same experienced teacher how he or she keeps track of the potential reinforcers that seem to be reinforcing for most children most often? Can you think of another way to keep track of them?
5. Spend an afternoon in a classroom with 3-, 4-, and 5-year-old children. Using the guidelines in Table 6.7, identify at least five learning objectives for which you would like to design an instructional sequence to improve the teacher/student communication process. Does each of the five objectives contain a performance, a condition, and a criteria for evaluation? Compare your performance verbs to those listed in Table 6.3.

References

Adams, M. J., *Beginning to Read: Thinking and Learning About Print.* Cambridge, Mass.: The MIT Press, 1990.

Bloom, B., *Taxonomy of Educational Objectives.* New York: Longman, 1956.

Bredekamp, S. (Ed.). *Developmentally Appropriate Practice in Early Childhood Programs Serving Children from Birth through Age 8.* Washington, D.C.: The National Association for the Education of Young Children, 1977.

Carnine, D., Silbert, J., and Kameenui, E. *Direct Instruction Reading* (3rd ed.). Upper Saddle River, N.J.: Prentice-Hall, 1997.

Chall, J. *Learning to Read: The Great Debate.* New York: McGraw-Hill 1967.

Cummings, C. *Teaching Makes a Difference.* Edmonds, Wash.: Teaching.

Englemann, S., and Carnine, D. *Theory of Instruction: Principles and Applications.* New York: Irvington Publishers, 1982.

Epstein, R., (Ed.). *Skinner for the Classroom: Selected Papers.* Champaign, Ill.: Research Press, 1982.

Hunter, M. *Enhancing Teaching.* New York: Macmillan, 1994.

Kameenui, E., and Carnine, D. *Effective Teaching Strategies That Accommodate Diverse Learners.* Columbus, Ohio: Merrill, 1997.

Nelson, A. *Curriculum Design Techniques.* Dubuque, Iowa: Wm. C. Brown Publishers, 1990.

Skinner, B. F. *The Technology of Teaching.* New York: Appleton-Century-Crofts, 1968.

Checklist for Designing Instruction

_____ 1. *Write an objective.*
- A clear understanding of student's learning.
- Describe your long-term expectation for a student's learning.
- Identify when students have learned what you are teaching.
- A performance, condition, and criterion for evaluation are included.

_____ 2. *Identify the critical element.*
- What is the essential feature of the learning?
- If the learning involves a series of steps, can you identify the critical element for each step?
- Can you cue the critical element(s)?
- How do you make the critical elements concrete?

_____ 3. *Conduct a task analysis.*
- Visualize a child performing the objective.
- List the steps the child goes through in performing the objective.
- List the prerequisite skills the child needs before instruction can begin.

_____ 4. *Create a sequence that moves from simple to complex.* (Make sure that recognition always precedes recall.)

_____ 5. *In each step of your sequence, use strategies to cue the critical element.* The following questions are designed as prompts to assist you in designing your instructional sequence. As you read each question, ask yourself if the answer applies to your instructional design sequence. Choose those that apply:
- How can you *cue* the *critical element?*
- Can a *strategy* be taught? If so, which strategy?
- Does it make sense to use *behavioral rehearsal?* If so, write a script with questions and answers.
- Will you *model and prompt* the correct response? Can you use superimposition?
- How will you fade out the cues?

_____ 6. *Review the final design of your sequence to make sure it contains all the necessary features.* After you have arranged your sequence of steps from simple to complex, make sure you have given attention to the following important features of your instructional sequence. These will be included in every instructional sequence.
- How will you provide *opportunities for practice?*
- What are the irrelevant stimuli? What are the examples you can present to the learner to make sure the learner can discriminate between the discriminative stimuli and the irrelevant stimuli?

_____ 7. *Revise your sequence (if necessary).*

- After you have taught your objective using your instructional design sequence, do you need to make any adjustments for future learners?
- Did you cue the critical element correctly?
- Did the learner focus on the discriminative stimulus and not the irrelevant stimuli?

7

Playground and
Outdoor Space

The father of early education, Fredrich Froebel, called his early school for young children the kindergarten, or children's garden, because in fact it was located during large amounts of the day in a garden. Our "garden" or playground, as we now call it, is a space that historically has been given little to no thought. Critics have called them asphalt deserts! Some adults consider that playgrounds are places where children are taken out for a 15-minute period to "run off steam" before getting back to the important learning inside.

We must be careful that such attitudes and traditions do not guide the design and use of outdoor space for young children. It is our position that the outdoor space is just as important as indoor space, and in some aspects we can achieve many things outdoors that could never be accomplished indoors. Primarily, the outdoor space will be organized around the play-activity curriculum constructs, but with the addition of much more equipment and materials to support fundamental movement patterns in sensorimotor play.

The arrangement of outdoor space is based on the classification of play as symbolic, fluid-construction, structured-construction, and restructuring construction, with greater space and equipment for sensorimotor play, and applying the unit-play potential measure of simple, complex, and super-complex units (Krichevsky, 1969). Outdoor equipment, once built, is difficult to rearrange because many pieces of equipment (climbing towers, decks, and poles, for instance) are permanently cemented down; thus, it is critical to plan carefully. Grid paper, as used for our indoor diagram, can also be used for the outdoor plan, with one square equal to one square foot.

Laws in some states stipulate a minimum amount of square footage of usable, safe, and sanitary outdoor play area per child in any group using the play area at one time.

A number of variables must be considered when arranging your equipment to support play:

Slope and water runoff
Sun and shade
Ground surfaces (concrete, P-gravel, sand, grass, etc.)
Visual supervision
Storage of props

Before beginning your plans, consider the use of drainage pipes to permit water to drain quickly, and retaining walls, which will stop erosion. Children love to climb banks and slopes, but their feet soon kill the grass and erosion occurs. These slopes can add to the variety of surfaces in a playground, and if they can be terraced properly, this can be considered a climbing or running area. If you are inexperienced in such matters, check with a landscape expert or a construction specialist; one of your student's parents might have this expertise and a parent-teacher playground planning committee could be formed.

Sample Playground

To explain the dos and don'ts of playground building we will use the sample playground (see Figure 7.1), which is 40 by 60 feet and has been divided into six zones (A1, A2, B1, B2, C1, and C2). Every school's outdoor space will present unique problems—harsh sun in Phoenix, fire ants and insects in Orlando, and so on—so the teacher or playground committee may want to read in depth such excellent books as *Children's Play and Playgrounds* (Frost & Klein, 1979).

Zone A1: Upper Body Exercise

The northeastern zone (A1) of our playground map contains a large maple tree, an adult park bench, a three-tire pyramid, an L-shaped frame made out of treated 6 inch × 8 inch × 8 foot wood beams held up by three uprights at each corner, 6 feet off the ground surface for hanging ropes, ladders, and rings. The surface can be sand, but P-gravel is best because it never hardens up, and it moves when children fall on it. The drawback to P-gravel is that since it does move, it needs to be 14 to 18 inches deep and well-framed in by wood beams (dotted lines on the map). We do not recommend the new chip rubber surfaces for young children

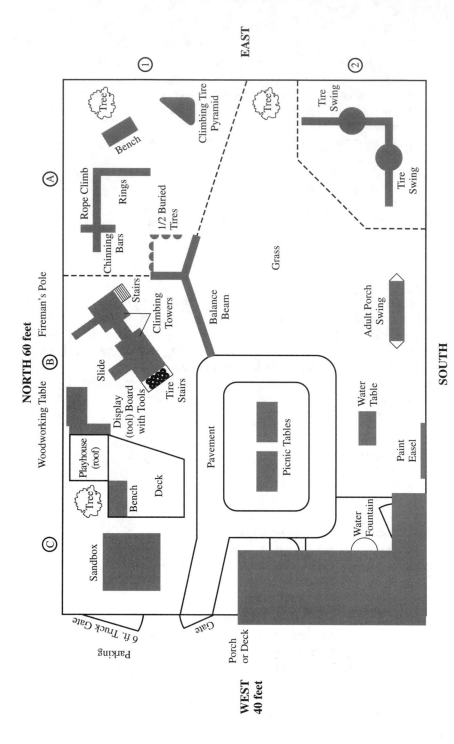

FIGURE 7.1 Sample Playground

because they put chips in their mouths to chew, which, like foam balls, may get stuck in their throats.

The adult bench is located well under the tree in order to take advantage of its shade (remember that we will have the sun in the east in the morning and setting in the west in late evening). The first step on the TBC is visual *looking,* and the two benches, the adult swing, and the picnic table will be located with this in mind. When children challenge themselves on this equipment, they will quickly check these teacher observation points, make eye contact with the teacher, and "know that a teacher is watching" to keep them safe. This shaded bench is also a good place to snuggle with children and read stories with them.

Hanging from the east side of the L-shaped frame are two chinning rings on chains. The rings are mounted at the height that the tallest child can reach. One or two wide but small tires (drilled with holes to permit water to escape) can lie about in the area to be used as step-stools for the smaller children to reach the rings.

From the north side of the L-frame hang three 1-inch cotton ropes and a rope ladder with wooden steps. In order to create different physical motor problems, one rope has knots tied every 6 inches and the second every 12 inches apart, with the ends touching the ground left untied and free. The third rope's knots are also 12 inches apart, but the bottom end is buried in the ground, creating a fixed rope. The rope ladder is made up of two similar ropes hanging free at the bottom, and running through 1½-inch thick wooden dowels, creating steps. The steps are at graduated distances, one 6 inches apart, the next 8 inches, the next 12 inches, the next 18 inches, and the last 24 inches. On the crossbeam above each ladder is mounted a small "dinner bell" with a thick string hanging from the clapper. This is a reinforcer: The children climb to the bell, grab the clapper rope, and pull to ring the bell. For young 3-year-olds, the clapper string can be lengthened.

On the west support beam are mounted three galvanized bars 1 inch thick, in a cross-arrangement, for chinning. The lowest bar of the three should be at the height of the full reach of your smallest child, and the highest at the full reach of the tallest child. The third bar should be placed equidistant from the two. This climbing apparatus should be 5 to 6 feet from the fence or bench.

The last item in this zone is a tire pyramid three tires high. The inside space of the pyramid provides a "secret" place for the young child to be alone at times. All tires need to be drilled with holes to permit drainage. Although some people feel that tires are unattractive, they make excellent climbing surfaces for children. We discourage the use of metal climbing frames or any metal outdoor equipment. In hot climates, the metal surfaces burn children, and in freezing climates, the children unfortunately put their tongues on them. A climbing frame should permit a child to fall freely, not hitting any bar. An upright or a half-globe shape will permit unobstructed falling. (Holes should be 1½ times the size of the child's body.) A square multibar honeycombed apparatus strikes the child in the face and neck as he falls through it; it is the most frightening piece of equipment seen on the playground for children of any age.

The play potentials can be counted as:

3 ropes/1 ladder	4 simple units	4
1 bench	2 simple units	2
3 chinning bars	3 simple units	2
1 tire pyramid	1 complex unit	4
		total 12

Zone A2: Swinging

In Zone A2 is located an L-shaped support beam for two swivel tire swings (purchase good quality swivels with greased fittings). We discourage back and forth swings, which often strike and injure children. Also, from a programmatic point of view, young children historically had their parents or other adult to push them, and we would not want to use teacher time this way.

The tire swings, on the other hand, require cooperation of two or more children, and create a natural need for cooperation if everyone is to ride. Much is learned on a tire swing by very active, assertive children. P-gravel or sand is a good surface, boxed in by beams on all sides. The beams should be at least 12 inches above ground level, which will section this zone off. If a child is running, he will need to stop or slow down to step over the beam, and will thus be less likely to run through the swing area. The upright support beams need to be 10 feet apart with the crossbeam located 6 to 8 feet above the ground, depending on the age of the children. The fence and terracing beam should be well back from the swing so that a child would not fall on them, if he should fall off the swing at its highest point.

The play potential is:

2 tire swings	2 complex units	8
		total 8

Zone B1: Climbing Towers, Balance Beams, Carpentry Table

Located in Zone B1 are, first, two climbing towers (platforms) standing no more than 3 feet above ground level. Each tower should have two entrances/exits with an upright board ladder at the southeast end of the small tower. If ladders are not upright, and placed at an angle, falling children will hit each rung of the ladder with their chins; upright ladders permit them to fall free.

The other exit, on the north side of the small tower, is a fireman's pole. Also, at the step-off point a predrilled tire should be mounted on the outside in such a manner that if the child does fall backwards, his head would hit the rubber tire, not the wood platform. The pole should be positioned 18 inches away from the tire, requiring the child to reach out and providing much clearance.

On the large tower is a two-tier upright ladder for entering or exiting, and the second exit is a 3-foot-wide slide providing a steep slope into a sand pit. Notice that this slide, which has a great deal of surface area, is facing northwest, away from the sun, and is also shaded by the tower. When children commit themselves to going down the slide, you want them to slide quickly, not to stop halfway with other children behind them. We warn against narrow, freestanding metal slide-ladder combinations. These slides are among the top three most dangerous pieces of play equipment (Frost & Klein, 1979). The children become "drunk" and competitive, like rats in a maze—sliding, running quickly to get back in line, climbing quickly, and pushing those in front of them off at the top, where there is no platform. Wide slides combined with platforms create greater choice and complexity.

We suggest that this area be framed in by groundbeams 6 to 8 inches high. (*Note:* Be careful where you purchase sand, because in some areas of the country the sand might contain industrial toxic waste. If practical, get the seller to provide in writing that the sand has been tested and is free of harmful materials.) The towers may be walled in on one or two sides (north side will section it off from the sliding areas) making clubhouses under each tower. If a floor is not put in children will play with sand under these towers. Ask experts in your area about the best wood to use in the platforms where children will be seated. Some treated wood gives off a chemical that can be absorbed by children's bodies, and some soft wood, when weathered, dries out, producing lots of splinters.

The landscaping beams that section this zone off on the southeast corner can be used for balance beams by also including upright half-buried tires as "stepping stones." You may want to raise one end of the beam to create a balance uphill problem, but keep all beams close to the ground.

At the northwest corner of this zone is a carpentry table with a tool display board against the fence on a small deck. The display board should have locks and silhouettes of the tools so control of error with these potentially dangerous tools can be maintained. Ideally, if the display board has doors that can be locked, these tools will not need to be taken in each evening.

The play potential is:

2 towers	2 complex units	8
slide	1 simple unit	1
fireman's pole	1 simple unit	1
carpentry table	1 complex unit	4
balance beams	3 simple units	3
2 clubhouses	2 complex units	8
		total 25

Zone B2: Open Grass, Porch Swing

Nearly 80 percent of Zone B2 is made up of a tricycle sidewalk-oval and an open space with grass. This can be considered "potential" space, and boards, wooden barrels, and boxes can be placed here, permitting the children to build their own structures. (See Gerhardt, 1973, for a thorough understanding of such materials.) The wooden adult porch swing supported by two uprights and one cross beam is another seated area for teachers to observe and have children join them. Leave plenty of space between the swing and the fence.

The play potential is:

open grassy area with props	2 complex units	8
2 swings	2 complex units	8
		total 16

Zone C1: Sandbox, Deck, Playhouse, Large Blocks

Zone C1 contains the entrance gate with a sidewalk that takes visitors from the parking area to the front of the school, and the tricycle sidewalk-oval. We would suggest a 6-foot fence with a 6-foot gate, the latch mounted as high as possible to permit easy access by adults and prevent children from opening the gate and slipping out of the playground unnoticed. The 6-foot fence with a lockable gate gives the playground greater security from vandals at night and on weekends. We like the primary entrance and exit to the classroom for school parents to be inside the playground fenced-in area, giving us double protection if the child should go out the school door unnoticed. If there are back doors that do not open onto the fenced-in area, teachers should discourage its use by parents and children.

There is a second gate on the west side, a 5-foot locked gate, which can be opened to permit a truck to back in and deliver sand. We would strongly suggest the outdoor sandbox be located in the shade in hot climates, in the sun in cold climates, where a sand truck can back up to it, and never under the edges of roofs from which water drips. Many sandboxes in playgrounds are sandless from a lack of time or strength or money to get 6 tons of prewashed sand wheelbarrowed in; sand is inexpensive, but labor for wheelbarrowing is not. And one can always depend on sand to disappear every fourth month, stolen by sand fairies to be found on the floor of the parents' cars or on the bed where the child takes off his jeans.

The sandbox should be covered by a strong canvas tarp or retractable wooden top to prevent animals from fouling it at night. Prop storage should be nearby. In our example, props are kept in a large wooden box with wheels, stored in the shed in Zone C2, which can be brought out by pulling an attached rope or pushing by the children across the tricycle sidewalk. The tree in this zone provides all-day shade to the sandbox, the adult park bench (A), the deck, and the playhouse, which are all areas where children tend to be seated or engage in less active play.

The deck is raised 1 foot above the level of the tricycle sidewalk, thus preventing the tricycles from being ridden on the deck. Three sides of the deck are further sectioned off by a low rope fence. On the south end of the deck are large wooden blocks with an auto steering wheel mounted nearby. Also included are baskets of cars and trucks and miniature life toys and furniture. Children may use the blocks for structured-construction or dramatic play, or props can be brought over from the playhouse for sociodramatic play with the large blocks.

A playhouse is found on the north side of the deck, walled off with lattice on three sides and covered with a roof. Mounted inside are shelves, an old porcelain sink, and a host of domestic props that are of limited value and are permanently stored under the shelving.

The play potential is:

sandbox	super-complex	8
large blocks	complex	4
props	complex	4
playhouse	super-complex	8
bench	2 simple units	2
		total 26

Zone C2: Storage Shed, Water Table, Paint Easel

In the final zone, C2, is a water fountain with a faucet for attaching a hose. Concrete leads to the tricycle sidewalk, and, without any step, into the storage shed. When the door to the storage shed is open, the tricycles, wagons, and balls can be brought out by the children. Once the equipment is out, the door is hooked open, so children can drive the tricycles into the shed and make it a playhouse. Teachers planning to use this storage shed must organize it together, deciding where to paint marks on the floor where tricycles will be parked, labeling storage boxes, and painting silhouettes where equipment will hang. If this is not done, children will not know where to return the equipment, and things will just be thrown inside by the children and tired teachers at the end of the day. This will destroy equipment, cause conflicts with other staff who must use the equipment, and limit play because the props just won't get out of the shed.

On the south side of the zone is a double painting easel mounted on the fence. Under the easel is a wood-framed trench containing P-gravel (2 feet deep), so that the easel can be hosed down and colored water contained in the trench. Nearby is a water table, the ground surface covered with grass. A circular sidewalk, wide enough for two tricycles, channels the wheeled toys around the painting space. In the center of the tricycle oval are two picnic tables, one containing structured construction materials and the second used for pasting, cutting, and other restructuring-construction. These tables can also be used for snacktime.

The play potential is:

double paint easel	2 simple units	2
water table	1 complex unit	4
storage shed as playhouse	1 complex unit	4
3 tricycles	3 simple units	3
1 wheelbarrow	1 simple unit	1
1 wagon	1 simple unit	1
1 picnic table (st-con)	1 complex unit or 4 simple units	4
1 picnic table (re-con)	4 simple units	4
		total 23

Adding the play potentials, we get 110 units on the playground; add 15 more units for other simple unit props from the storage shed (e.g., hoppity-hops) and we have 125 units. Dividing by the 2½ play units required for each child, we have now designed a playground to hold 50 children at one time. Notice, also, that we have sociodramatic play, structured-construction, restructuring-construction, fluids, and many sensorimotor play items for a balanced play-activity environment.

It is also important to point out that we have four observation points from which the teachers will be able to keep watch over and facilitate the play activity of the children. First is the bench (A) under the tree in zone C1, which would also be an excellent spot for the teacher to be located first thing in the morning and at the end of day to greet parents arriving and departing, as well as to supervise the sand, deck, and play areas. The teacher on bench (B) in zone Al would monitor that zone plus the towers and large structures. The teacher on the porch swing (C) would monitor the swings, the large grassy areas, and part of the tricycle oval. Finally, the teacher standing or seated at the picnic table (D) would monitor the water table, paint easels, storage shed and water fountain, and also would greet parents.

Porches and Enclosures

In climates with extreme heat or cold, or heavy precipitation, a roofed porch is an important addition to the school space. When children are confined indoors for many days, the movement to a protective nearly-outdoor space with fresh air, where they can use "outdoor" voices and larger motor behavior, seems to help children to relax. If this space is limited in size, the teachers may rotate the daily play between various play classifications.

The storage shed and large structures have been located in corners so they do not create "dead" areas in which children cannot be observed. Locations of teacher observation points must be clear to staff and children, thus facilitating visual supervision.

Finally, storage is an important consideration. Outdoor playgrounds should not consist only of statically arranged permanent equipment, but must also have props so that children can play imaginatively.

Summary

With a well-organized outdoor space, the teacher can now use the observation system or do a play-behavior rating to see how children are performing outside, and then set goals for play facilitation, using the Teacher Behavior Continuum.

The sample playground is one way of organizing space and equipment, and has permitted us to demonstrate ways in which variables (shade, surfaces, etc.) may be used. Every outdoor space will be unique with its own problems and strengths. For more reading in this area, consult the references that follow. With these constructs, the teacher is well on the way to organizing a playground, but more reading might be needed to handle unique situations.

Activities

1. Locate and visit a playground designed for children younger than age 6. Score the play potentials using the Kritchevsky system. Select the playground facilities that scored highest and lowest in this system, return to each for ½ hour, and keep a running tally of the aggressive or conflict incidents for each playground, and compare them. What differences did you find? Why? Now, using Parten's stages, observe each child and place a tally mark under the social stage in which each child is performing. Does this playground support higher-level social play? What would you recommend?

2. Visit three preschool playgrounds where children are active and teachers are supervising. Draw a map of the space, and then, with a marker, for a 15-minute period, draw a line on your map to record the moving events of the teacher. What space in the playground is being monitored and facilitated? What equipment or materials are in this space? What space is not visited by the teacher? What equipment is in this space?

3. Visit a preschool playground. List all the equipment and materials under the play classifications (symbolic, construction, etc.) and determine what is underrepresented. How would you change it? How does the sun help or hinder the activities in the playground? How would you change it? What are the surfaces under each type of climbing equipment? Would each surface create any danger to children if they should fall on it?

4. Interview an experienced teacher of young children, and ask him or her what children are expected to get from a playground experience. Ask what his or her role is, and why the school has the equipment it does.
5. Find an inadequate playground used by young children and, using grid paper and symbols, organize this space as if you had limited funds, using the constructs introduced above.
6. Select five catalogues selling playground equipment for young children. Pick out from each catalogue one piece of equipment you like that is not on the sample playground and one that you feel is definitely inappropriate, and show these to two experienced teachers of young children. Ask them to evaluate the 10 items.

References

Florida Administrative Code, Chapter 1OM-12, *Child Day Care Standards*. State of Florida, Tallahassee, Fla.: Department of Health and Rehabilitative Services, 1986.

Frost, Joe L., and Barry L. Klein, *Children's Play and Playgrounds*. Boston: Allyn and Bacon, 1979.

Gerhardt, Lydia A., *Moving and Knowing: The Young Child Orients Himself in Space*. Englewood Cliffs, NJ.: Prentice-Hall, 1973.

Kritchevsky, Sybil, and others, *Planning Environments for Young Children: Physical Space*. Washington, D.C.: NAEYC, 1969.

8

Discipline and
Child Guidance

For all the happy, well-adjusted children we see at a school for young children, there will be some who pose a far greater challenge. Let's contemplate just a few. Preschooler Linda sucks her first two fingers constantly; eats crayons, producing a "rainbow" of colored teeth; masturbates repeatedly; spends most of her time daydreaming; rarely bathes at home; and demands lap-time cuddling late on a hot Monday morning. Oliver's vicious bites produce bluish sets of teeth marks on the arm of a hapless passerby. And, after we make a minor request for Kathy to come inside out of the rain, she shouts, "I hate you.—I hate you, Ms. Anderson. You're the meanest teacher in this whole school. No one likes you!"

These three children are typical of some of the challenging children teachers face as early as preschool/kindergarten. How shall we view these types of behavior, and what actions should be taken? In discussing methods and techniques of discipline and child guidance, we take the position that all children, especially at the preschool age, need to feel loved and accepted by adults and by the other children in their classroom. All children need to be able to use language to be understood and to get the wider world to respond to their needs—simple needs, such as to use a toy or materials, to keep a toy once they have it, to get their fair share of snack, to receive help in toileting, to get a "hug" from the teacher, to be a coplayer with other children in the classroom, and so on.

If children feel unloved, unaccepted, and helpless in the classroom, possibly these feelings developed before they started school because of poor early care or unfortunate life experiences. These children act out in negative ways: excessive daydreaming, physical aggression such as biting, or verbal aggression such as swearing or "I hate you, Ms. Anderson!"

Rudolf Dreikurs, the psychiatrist who developed a practical program for dealing with misbehaving children, would say that they are motivated by one of four forces: attention getting, power, revenge, or helplessness. He might propose that introverted Linda feels helpless and unworthy in her world, and simply wants to be left alone. Oliver, with his biting and physical aggression, might be considered a child who feels so hurt by the world that he simply wants to get even. Kathy, on the other hand, might be motivated by power: She wants to do what she wants to do, when she wants to do it! A simple request to leave the sandbox to come in out of the rain threatens her overwhelming need for power and she strikes out by physically refusing to come in, and by being verbally aggressive when the teacher carries her in.

Acting out may also take the form of a constant quest for attention and approval ("Look at this, Ms. Anderson," "Do this for me, Ms. Anderson"). Other attention-getters perform a host of naughty actions like spitting out food at snacktime, making bizarre noises at rest time, or disrupting story times. Basic to all these children may be feelings of inadequacy in their world. They may, perhaps unconsciously, decide that if they cannot be accepted as the best "good" student or friend, they will become the "best" bad child in our classroom.

Why Do Children Misbehave?

A simple, but accurate, answer to Why do children misbehave? is that children misbehave because of past experiences and negative learning. Erik Erikson's theory proposes that what people are like today as adults or as young children is the result of early socioemotional stages. These stages, theoretically, have two pushing and pulling forces that later affect people's personalities. Young preschoolers, ages 3, 4, and 5, have passed through the stages of trust versus mistrust (birth to age 1) and autonomy versus shame and doubt (ages 1 to 3), and would currently be struggling with feelings related to initiative versus guilt.

Initiative versus Guilt

We may speculate that misbehaving young children are those who have an overdeveloped sense of mistrust; that is, they are not sure that their needs will be met or that those who care for them are dependable. The same children possibly could have a strong residue of shame and doubt about their own actions and lack the independence or belief that they can master the world. The acting-out behaviors or misbehaviors are an attempt to get individual attention, or power, and to make up for early inadequacy. Some children will have been so hurt by their world that they may be vengeful, or may have retreated helplessly from the world about them.

Our goal in attempting to help misbehaving children is to reestablish their basic trust in their caregivers or teachers, and to create many opportunities for them to have power over their world. We would resist actions and statements that would heighten a child's sense of guilt.

Setting Limits

When students act out in a manner that requires us as teachers to set limits for them, there is a high degree of risk that we might damage our relationships with those children. We can hear an angry parent or teacher shouting, "Get your feet off that table immediately—I mean now!" Such harsh commands, possibly even justified, breed hostility and anger in children. The problem for the teacher of young children is how to set limits or "get those feet off the table" in a manner that not only shows respect for the child, but also enables the teacher to take care of the "table" or classroom.

Actions taken by a teacher toward a student who is misbehaving are based on *degrees of power*. Minimum-power actions alert the child to the teacher's desire for a change in behavior with the hope that time and the suggestion of a wide range of acceptable alternative behaviors will bring the desired change. Maximum teacher power is exerted when a teacher demands a specific action within an immediate time period, specifying a punishment that will swiftly follow noncompliance. The problems with using power behaviors toward students stem from the danger of "overshooting" the amount of power used—or from using too little power in a serious misbehavior situation.

Personally, we wish to grant the student the initial autonomy to self-correct his or her actions, using as little coercive power as necessary. But if the student fails to take advantage of the opportunity to self-correct, we gradually, in a purposeful way, increase our power actions in order to get the behavior necessary to maintain good classroom discipline. The general method we use involves escalation and de-escalation of power, as illustrated (at a teen-age level) here:

The teen has just turned 16 and is going out with the car on his first date.

Teenager: "What time should I be home?"

Mother: "You are old enough now to drive and be responsible. You know what is reasonable." (minimum power)

(Teenager returns home at 3 A.M.)

Mother: "What are you doing? This is unacceptable and this needs to change. What is a reasonable hour that we can both agree upon? Let's make a contract!" (escalating power)

(Teenager returns at 3 A.M., again.)

Mother: "I need you to be home with the car by 12 midnight. If not, this _____ will occur." (Escalation of power; if need be, the car is taken from the teen.)

If we continued to follow the plight of this teenager, we might see the mother begin to give back (de-escalate) some power in the form of freedom to make decisions, once the teen had begun to show responsible behavior by obeying the rules.

In the case of the mother setting limits, we saw three positions taken toward her child's misbehavior. The first was a trusting Relationship-Listening (R-L) position. The mother started out with the belief that the child could be trusted and was rational about evaluating his own actions (how late to stay out); thus, she gave him nearly total decision-making power. The second position, although simplistic in our example, was one of Confronting-Contracting (C-C). The mother insisted that the son agree to a contract with her to specify his curfew. Finally, because of continued misbehavior, she took a third stance, moving to a Rules and Consequences (R-C) position.

The R-C position recognizes that the child has demonstrated a lack of ability to rationally reflect on his own actions and to correct himself in a reasonable manner. Note that the *locus of control* shifts in each of the three positions. The child holds the locus of control in the Relationship-Listening position; there is a shared locus of control in the Confronting-Contracting position; and an external locus of control by the adult exists in the Rules and Consequences stance, where external rewards and sanctions are used to get a desired behavior from the child. If the teen begins to show responsible behavior, the mother can de-escalate her power, moving from an R-C stance to C-C. Still later, with continued success, she could move to an R-L position of interacting with her son.

In the classroom application of limit setting, we propose a "gear shifting" process of escalation (or de-escalation) of power as used in the preceding example. The use of power by the teacher can be thought of as moving along a Teacher Behavior Continuum from minimum to maximum power (see Table 8.1). The power interactions on the continuum would move from Relationship-Listening techniques of (1) Looking and (2) Naming, to the Confronting-Contracting techniques of (3) Questioning, and finally to the Rules and Consequences techniques of (4) Commanding and (5) Acting or physical intervention.

Relationship-Listening

Looking

Obeying rules requires students to listen to inner-messages of *no* and to make quick decisions to control their actions or seek what they want in an acceptable way. The younger the child, the less permanent this memory of *no* seems to be. The

**TABLE 8.1   Teacher Behavior Continuum (TBC):
Child Guidance**

Minimum Teacher Control				Maximum Teacher Control
Relationship-Listening		Confronting-Contracting	Rules and Consequences	
Looking	Naming	Questioning	Commanding	Acting
• Visual cueing • Tactile cueing	• "I-messages" • Active listening • Door openers	• Three levels of Questions 1. Facts: "What did you do?" 2. Convergent: "What was the rule?" 3. Divergent: "How will you change?"	• Tell what to do, not what *not* to do! • Preparatory to a logical consequence	• Time-out (relax) chair/space • Mirroring • Lap-time • Body to toy, play, work

young child tends to become carried away with enthusiasm when working or playing with peers and can easily miss those inner-messages. When we make our presence known to the child, this memory often quickly returns and behavior changes.

The teacher's "looking" is a minimum-power technique through which the teacher simply moves toward the student and emphatically, but in a nonaggressive manner, makes her presence known. This is the first step in setting limits for an individual child. The teacher's presence radiates a zone of safety and control for children. The students feel that within this adult observation zone their rights will be protected.

The effectiveness of "looking" can be seen when teachers and students are traveling on the bus during field trips, when they are sitting in the auditorium during school assemblies, when they are on the playground, and so on. There are some children whose sense modality is not visual, and the teacher may need to touch these children's shoulders or tactilely cue them in a nonpunitive way to get their attention.

Spheres of Communication

It is helpful to think of the attention of the teacher, when looking or verbally cueing, as creating a "sphere of communication" or "bubble" in which the teacher and children will feel varying degrees of warmth and acceptance. The first sphere is created when we deal directly with one child who gets our total attention as we listen to and communicate with her. In this sphere, one teacher and one child appear to be in a relationship "bubble," cut off from other actions going on around them. Communication flows from child to teacher and back again, with encouragement for the child to express his or her thoughts, ideas, and feelings. This is much like the infant/mother relationship.

The second sphere is a small-group relationship where we have one teacher and three to six children communicating. The child feels less intimacy and communication with the teacher than in the one-to-one sphere, but still feels included. The communication flows between the children and the teacher and usually they must keep to a shared topic. This is much like the family relationship with mother, father, child, and siblings.

The third sphere of communication involves the teacher with the entire classroom of children. All children must stop their actions and focus on the teacher as she or he speaks or lectures to them. The teacher's attention is diffused to all, and thus minimal intimacy is felt by the child. The communication goes in one direction, teacher to child, as in formal classroom relationships.

Studies have demonstrated that large numbers of school-age children receive communication only in the third sphere for days and weeks at a time. For weeks, then, some of these children are never spoken to by any child, teacher, or school staff member in an intimate way. We have to be especially careful when dealing with children in schools for young children and even more so in day-care centers, so they do not become cut off from intimate communication with adults and peers. We need to balance the daily schedule so that the children can have large blocks of time in the first and second spheres, where they can express their ideas and feelings and can experience close relationships with others.

"Bringing Them Back Alive"
On a bus trip, a teacher with a group of young children should sit on the last seat of the bus, while a "room parent" or aide sits in the middle of the bus on an aisle seat. If the teacher is seated in the first seat of the bus, trouble is on its way! The children can see her but she can't see them. "Trouble" is generally not the result of calculated rebellion, but of the restlessness of young children who are flooded with enthusiasm but unable to move around. The same is true in the cafeteria or auditorium, or on the bleachers at sporting events—where teachers should distribute themselves throughout the body of students.

"Showing the Flag"
Where teachers should be placed to supervise playgrounds or similar situations depends on where the students and other teachers are: positions of supervisors shift to maintain a fairly even distribution of teachers among students. Teachers gradually circulate, making their presence known—"showing the flag."

"Dining at the Ritz"

Group snack or other meal periods should be valued times for first- and second-sphere communication. Rather than teachers disappearing on coffee breaks, they need to be seated at tables with children, conversing. Sharing food and conversation, or "dining at the Ritz," is a common adult behavior and can be very beneficial to young children.

Naming

We often assume that the student is old enough and has been taught the rules often enough that he *should* know the rules and be following them. However, human behavior, especially for younger children, is regressive: Developmentally, children seem to take three steps forward and two back. There will be times when the child is emotionally "flooded" (possibly by events at home, by being angry with others, or from gnawing feelings of inadequacy) so that this emotional flooding washes away the memory of *no* or the "rule." Before escalating use of teacher power, we need to give the student time to self-correct. Naming statements are a minimum intrusion to "awaken" the memory of the prohibition without the child's feeling guilty or fearful of punishment.

The two techniques under Naming statements are *I-messages* and *active listening* (Gordon, 1974). These techniques are used by the teacher to help "flooded" children reflect on their actions. When students do not respond to the first steps of cueing (looking), we advance to the Naming statement, or the I-message. First, we ask ourselves as teachers, "What is the misbehavior?" Second, "What direct and concrete effect is the misbehavior having on us as teachers? Is it stopping us from teaching? Is it damaging property for which we are responsible?" Finally, "How do we feel about it? Are we upset, frustrated, fearful, ... or what?"

Let's take an example. A young child is standing at an easel and begins to flip paint with his brush, first at the paper and then at other children passing by. The teacher moves toward the child, cues visually, and touches his shoulder. He doesn't stop. She says: "When paint is thrown, it makes our floor and clothing messy, and I have to clean it up—and that makes me angry!"

Notice that this I-message does not contain a "you" accusation for the student ("You are throwing paints ...!"). What the teacher is doing is bringing to the child's awareness the problem *she* is facing as a result of the student's actions. Since the problem is hers, she uses *I* rather than *you*. You-messages should be avoided because they suggest guilt on the student's part and can only be destructive, worsening the child's feelings about himself—making him feel less capable of being a worthy student.

Let's look at this from another perspective. When a teacher communicates or transacts with students, that teacher unknowingly uses one of her own ego states of *parent, adult,* or *child.* For example, when a student has spilled a pot of paint, the teacher, pointing to the large, red pool on the floor, may say:

"How disgusting! What a mess you have made again."   (Parent)

or

"What is needed to clean this up?"   (Adult)

or

"Oh, what am I going to do, another mess for me!"   (Child)

The parent-like communication from the teacher implies guilt and failure. The child-like statement from the teacher shows that he or she feels helpless, vulnerable, and inadequate to deal with the student's actions. The adult-like statement keeps to an assessment of the facts and a statement of a problem to be solved. The I-message is the most refined of the adult statements teachers can use toward students who are misbehaving. It raises students' consciousness about the effect of their actions and permits time for them to act positively.

When we transact with an I-message, we dramatically increase the likelihood of getting a self-correcting behavior, but this does not always happen. Sometimes, students are emotionally flooded with anger or resentment and they respond to us or transact back from one of their ego states. For example, if the teacher uses an I-message as follows:

Teacher: "When paints are thrown, I am afraid. . . . "

Student: "I don't care!"   (Parent)

or

"Oh, I didn't know that."   (Adult)

or

"Let me wipe this up."   (Adult)

or

"Tommy did it, not me!"   (Child)

The student's use of the adult-like statement shows rational thinking and understanding, while the student's parent-like statement ("I don't care!") is definite and hostile, and the child-like statement ("Tommy did it . . . !") is "whining" and makes excuses. When we hear parent and child statements coming from students, we know that they still do not have their adult ego state or rational thinking in gear. Such responses may even include hostile language such as swearing as the initial attempt of the child to communicate. We respond with active listening.

Active listening is a process of summarizing what we think the child is saying to us by "saying it back to him" in nondirective naming terms:

Student: "I don't care!" (shouting)

Teacher: "You're angry when you're asked to stop."

Student: "It is my turn to paint. I didn't get my turn!"

Teacher: "You are worried that someone will take your turn away from you."

Active listening is a helpful technique whenever children are emotionally flooded and cannot rationally discuss or reflect on their own actions. It is a non-punitive way of responding to verbal aggression, hostility, and even swearing. It simply helps to elicit and clarify communication from the child, and to demonstrate that the teacher is listening and is offering a caring, one-to-one relationship to that child.

A third set of techniques called *door openers* can be placed under the relationship-listening stance. Door openers are simply questions asked of children to get them to talk about what might be upsetting them: "Carol, I can tell by your face that you are very unhappy this morning. Would you like to talk about it?" Once the child begins to talk, teachers suppress the tendency to lecture them, give suggestions, and so forth.

Confronting-Contracting

Questioning

Our goal is to use the minimum amount of power toward a misbehaving child to get the child to self-correct. If need be, we escalate our power. After we have used naming statements with no results for a reasonable period of time, we then increase power through questions. The questioning of the misbehavior is to have the child think out what he is doing and consider ways of changing behavior.

The questions strategy involves three levels of questions that require an increasing degree of abstract thinking by the child. First, "fact" questions are asked; then "convergent" questions; and finally "divergent" questions.

Fact Questions
Simply ask for the facts. We ask a misbehaving child, "What are you doing?" This forces the child to consciously reflect on and acknowledge her actions. Young children, when flooded with emotion, do not necessarily reflect on their behavior. When they say, "I don't know!" they really may not know consciously what they did. Our questioning is used to guide them to think about their previous actions. Many children will respond to us with "fogging" to divert us to a side issue:

"Tommy did it first!" or "I didn't get my turn!" We simply ignore these "fogging" statements and continue (like a broken record) with, "What did you do?"

After a reasonable period of time, if the child cannot or will not state what he did, we simply tell him, "Jim, this is what you did. You kicked down the block arrangement." This is not said in a hostile way by the teacher but in a controlled, purposeful manner so that the behaviors that are unwanted can be identified.

Convergent Questions

Next, we ask the *what-rule* convergent question: "Jim, what is the rule about blocks?" If we receive no reply, the question is repeated; we ignore any "fogging" statements made by the child. We want the child to consciously bring to memory and state the rule that has been previously taught to him or her. If this does not come from the child, we would clearly state the rule. "Jim, our rule here is that we do not knock others' blocks down."

The process of questioning requires us to suppress any wish we might have to moralize, lecture, or preach to the child, since such statements might heighten the child's feelings of naughtiness or guilt—which, according to Erikson's theory, are part of the pulling-pushing force (initiative vs. guilt) for the child ages 3 to 7.

Divergent Questions

After a verbal summary of the child's actions and a statement—by either the misbehaving child or the teacher—of a pertinent rule, we now "push" for a contract: "How will you change?" or "If this happens again, what will you do?" The fact questions had the child reflect on the past event; now, the divergent questions require the child to think about how he or she will behave in the future, and this will become the basis for a contract. Teachers working with school-age children would be able to have the students actually write out an agreement, which would then be signed by both parties. For the young child, however, a verbal agreement with a handshake would be more appropriate.

To summarize, questioning is used to get the children to consciously reflect on and to verbally summarize errant behavior, and then to state applicable rules they have learned. The teacher suppresses any desire to preach, moralize, or express opinions about the child's actions, simply using questions—in a repeated, "broken record" manner, if necessary. Finally, the teacher pushes for a contract.

Rules and Consequences

Commanding

The next step on the Teacher Behavior Continuum is the use of directive statements as commands. At this point, we have accepted the position that the child cannot or will not verbally summarize his actions, and it has become imperative to bring about a behavioral change. We therefore tell the child what we want him to do in specific terms: "Keep the paint on the paper!" In making such a statement, we need to have the child in the first sphere of communication, look him directly in the eye, say his name, gesture, touch him in a nonhostile manner, and state what change is necessary.

We always attempt to tell the child what *to* do, not what *not* to do. "Keep the paint on the paper!" will more likely get results than will "Don't throw paint!" The latter is highly likely to encourage the child to react to the verb *throw* by doing so! Again, if the child does not comply, we may have to sound like "broken records" and keep repeating the directive statement.

After a number of repetitions of the commands have proved fruitless, we may escalate to a more powerful position and state a "logical consequence": "If I see you throw the paints again, it will tell me that you do not know the painting rules and I will have to ask you to play in another area." This is not a threat of punishment, but an expression of "logical consequence." Let's look at the difference.

Both *punishments* and *logical consequences* are actions taken in response to the breaking of a rule. They differ in these ways (Dreikurs & Cassell, 1972):

Logical Consequences	*Punishment*
A learning process	A judicial proceeding
Teacher plays the role of an educator	Teacher plays the role of police, judge, and jailer
Distinguishes between the deed and the doer	Denotes sin
Expresses the reality of the social order	Expresses the power of authority
Is intrinsically related to misbehavior	Has an arbitrary connection to misbehavior
Is appropriate in a democratic setting	Belongs only in an autocratic setting

If a child is put in time-out for throwing paint, this is punishment, because the sanction has little relationship to the misbehavior. On the other hand, we are using logical consequences when we state, "Throwing paint wastes it and there will not be enough for others. If that occurs again, you will have used up your share and will have to leave the paint area until you learn the rules."

As adults, when we are driving a car and come to a stoplight, we usually stop. Why? Is it because we are afraid of getting a ticket and fine? If so, we are operating from a lower moral position—from fear of punishment. On the other hand, if we obey the stoplight because we wish to promote a safe system of traffic regulation, we are operating from a higher moral position: Groups of people need certain rules in order to function effectively and safely. We obey rules not from fear, but from a desire to promote the general welfare. We do not want children to obey rules out of fear—but because they have been made aware of how their actions affect others. It is in school that children have the time and opportunity to grow morally.

If the child acts positively as a result of our command statements, we may use encouragement, which is not to be confused with praise.

Encouragement versus Praise

"Jim, look what you have done! You have worked all morning with your group of Bob, Carol, and Alice, and you have built a castle with the blocks. You must feel proud that you're now able to work with friends." This is an encouragement statement, and is quite different from praise, such as, "What a beautiful castle. I am so proud of you!" *Praise statements* take a moral position, make value judgments on those less powerful, and focus on actions and end products; *encouragement statements* are made to help the child become aware of how he or she is growing and becoming more effective, so that these strides in themselves are reinforcing. The idea is that the "process is more important than the product." Here are other examples of encouragement versus praise:

Encouragement	*Praise*
How nice that you could figure that out for yourself!	Aren't you wonderful to be . . .
	I'm so proud of you for . . .
Your skills are growing.	You're my favorite student.
You're working hard on that painting.	What a beautiful painting.

As positive changes in the child's behavior become apparent, we may use encouragement statements to help her become aware of her own progress, valuing her efforts rather than a product.

If the misbehavior continues after using the preceding escalation of power techniques, the situation would seem to call for an additional escalation to physical intervention as acting behavior. But before this action, we always give a preparatory command as the last step under command statements. The preparatory command is usually stated as a contingency, followed by a logical consequence. "Tommy, if the blocks are knocked down again, it's telling me that you still have not learned the rule on using blocks, and I will need to take you from the block area to play somewhere else." If the child again knocks down the blocks, we will tell him to move to another area and, if he refuses, we will follow through with the logical consequences before escalating to physical intervention or requiring us to *act*.

Acting or Physical Intervention

Acting as physical intervention—that is, picking up or bringing a child by the arm or hand to a new area—is seen as a strong use of power on the TBC continuum. This should not be done with anger or in any hostile manner, but simply as a routine. If the child complies and moves off as requested, the intervention is completed; but many children may respond with physical defiance, such as screaming or kicking. We, as teachers, should not be surprised by such aggression. But how do we understand and deal with it?

After a misbehavior, many children expect that their bodies will be hit or dealt with in a rough physical manner. They expect to be hurt! They feel mistrust and possibly shame or guilt for their actions. We, as teachers, must recognize that children's actions toward us are not necessarily directed at us personally. The child has learned responses long before she arrived in our classroom. Our goal in working with a violent or hostile child is to *refuse to return* this hostility and to reestablish feelings of trust and safety in the child. We state clearly as we physically intervene, "I'm not going to let you hurt others (or destroy others' work), I'm not going to let you hurt me, and I'm not going to let others hurt you! And I am not going to hurt you." We repeat these safety statements several times. If the child can accept this verbal assurance and complies with our request, the intervention is over. But if he continues to defy us we have two choices: Move the child to a chair or personal space, or use mirroring techniques.

Relax-Chair or Personal Space
When a child has a temper tantrum or loses emotional control, we say he is flooding. *Flooding* means that the child is overwhelmed with guilt and fear, and cannot rationally think or process information or stimuli. Using a relax-chair, not to be confused with a time-out chair, or personal space (a corner of the room or floor space) is a way of excluding stimuli and giving the child some personal time to "defuse" and get himself under control. We simply give the child space to relax. When the "emotional storm" has subsided, we may approach the child to have him begin to rethink the actions he has taken. In doing this, we work our way through the TBC using naming and questioning.

The child is seated quietly on a chair.

Teacher: "I can see that you have had an angry morning. (active listening) When blocks are kicked over and thrown, I am afraid that children will get hurt, and that frightens me as the teacher."

If the child begins to talk, the teacher could for a period of time continue with active listening, permitting him to "talk it out." If no discussion comes from the child, the teacher may escalate to questions.

Teacher: "Tommy, I want to talk to you about what happened this morning. What did you do? (fact question) What was the rule? (convergent question) What will you do next time?" (divergent question) (pushes for a contract).

As the example shows, the use of the relax-chair or personal space is not for punishment, but to permit the child to gain self-control and to be reapproached for rational discussion. Once the contract is made, the child is free to move back into the full space of the classroom. If the child will not talk or respond to these techniques shown here, it means that he is still full of anger and needs more time in a personal space—perhaps as much as an entire morning. We simply say, "We must talk about the things that happened this morning. You can tell me when you're ready, or I will check back with you later."

Mirroring

A second technique to be used with the flooded young child is called *mirroring*. Bring the child before a large upright mirror so she can see herself, her own actions, and you. Again, we would want to repeat the safety statements, "I'm not going to let you hurt others (or destroy others' work). I'm not going to let you hurt me, I'm not going to let others hurt you, and I will not hurt you." We would also, through directive statements, say to the child, "Look at your face. It tells me that you're really angry. Look at my hand. I am holding you so that you can be safe, but my hands are not hurting you. You are safe!"

The image in the mirror helps us not only to limit the amount of stimuli the flooded child is receiving, but also helps the child see herself and her actions. The mirror gives another perspective. We may need to do many mirror interactions with a mistrusting child until she begins to believe that she can even be "naughty" and we will not hurt her. In this way, the world of the young child can become a safe place where this child can become attached to and trust in us as teachers.

Lap-Time

A young child awakens early in the morning, dresses quickly, eats quickly, is driven by a rushed parent through heavy traffic, and comes through the school door at 7:45 in the morning. The child enters the classroom like a bowling ball, bounding from one play area to another, knocking over equipment and clashing with other children. This child needs *lap-time*.

Children live, hypothetically, in three worlds: one, an inner-world full of thought and feeling; a body world where they can physically feel power in running and climbing, or enjoy the warmth of a bathtub; and an outer world where they produce, create, and work with others. We, as adults, freely move back and forth among these three worlds. When we are tired, we pull up our favorite chair and magazine, kick off our shoes, and retreat to an inner world; at other times, we enjoy playing and using our bodies vigorously; and at still other times, we go into the outer world and work with others. The young child, however, can get "stuck" in one of these worlds, unable to retreat "inside" to relax.

The "bowling ball" child entering our classroom in the morning may be stuck in the body world. Therefore, we may say, "James, I see that you need some lap-time this morning! Come sit with me for a few minutes as I show you this book." In our laps, we can feel James relaxing into the inner-world. Once relaxed, he can go out into the classroom and become productive. For the child who lacks trust in his world and repeatedly floods, large amounts of lap-time may help to reestablish trust in others and in himself. Physical intervention is not only physically removing children as a logical consequence, but also requiring them to come to our laps to cuddle and relax before they flood or emotionally explode.

Diversion
The third way of handling a misbehaving child is the widely used method of diversion. We divert the child from the potential problem area or activity to a different activity that he might work on successfully. Our prescription for diversion is "from the body to the toy; from the toy to play; and from play to work," following the normal development of play observed in young children (A. Freud, 1968). How does this work? We see the child buzzing aimlessly about the room. He is into everything but doing nothing productively. The teacher moves to the child using directive commands and physical intervention: "I see you going around and around the room. Come with me and I will show you where you can go around and around."

Taking the child to an area or corner that can be sectioned off, the teacher gives him some small miniature cars and encourages him to sit on the floor and "make the cars go 'round and 'round." The teacher has moved the child who might be stuck in the "body world" to the toy. The child's first use of the wheeled toys might be aggressive, but the vigorous activity in defined space permits the child some release of possibly pent-up tension or emotions. Later, the teacher might say, "Oh, now your cars need a road and a garage; see if you can use these blocks to make them!" The child has now been moved from the toy to play. In the play level, other children can join him in his activity and, if this works out, we have helped the child through play to be a cooperative "worker" with others.

Aggression

Aggression can be simply defined as energy misdirected. Our way of handling that aggression is diversion (from body to toy, etc.) Other examples of channeling aggression are working with clay, vigorous play with make-believe animals, and hammers on the carpentry table (see Figure 8.1).

Biting

Encourage the biting child to transfer his "bite" to microsymbolic toys such as alligator puppets or miniature animals (tigers/lions) with teeth (body to toy). At first, the themes of this miniature toy play will be violent and aggressive: The tiger or alligator puppet eats up "the world." We then intervene with the techniques on the TBC to attempt to have the child move out of violent themes to more positive themes. We may ask such questions as: "Could your alligator puppet keep the people safe today? Does your tiger have any baby tigers that she could keep safe today?" (toy to play). Once the child is using positive themes, we may encourage other children to join him to produce true sociodramatic play (play to being a cooperative worker with others).

Spitting

Spitting is aggression with the mouth; therefore, we may follow the suggestion made for biting. Also, we find many "spitters" who are afraid of fluid play materials, so we might gradually and deliberately introduce the aggressive child to fingerpaints, easel paints, clay or water, and the like (body to toy). The painting may at first be actually an aggressive use of the material, such as rubbing right through the paper in finger painting; but after a while, the child should become comfortable with these materials, and when that happens, we intervene, attempting to

FIGURE 8.1   Channeling Aggression

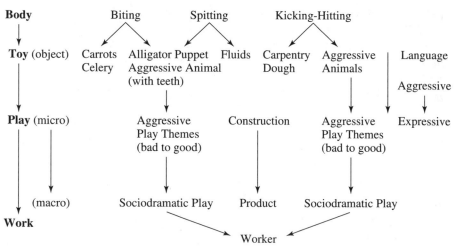

have the child make symbolic products with these materials (toy to play). Borrowing from Anna Freud, we believe that the child can move from play to work through the ability

> *(a) to control, inhibit, or modify the impulses to use given materials aggressively and destructively (not to throw, to take apart, to mess, to hoard), and to use them positively and constructively instead (to build, to play, to learn, and—in communal life—to share);*
>
> *(b) to carry out preconceived plans with a minimum regard for the lack of immediate pleasure yield, intervening frustrations, etc., and the maximum regard for the pleasure in the ultimate outcome (A. Freud, 1965, p. 82)*

Kicking or Hitting

The same pathway would be followed for dealing with children who are kicking or hitting. Figure 8.1 suggests that we would introduce carpentry and/or clay to facilitate construction play, or aggressive animals (body to toy) for symbolic play. The materials would be used aggressively (ripping the clay apart), and then the child would gradually move to construction or dramatic play themes (toy to play), and finally to products or sociodramatic play with other peers (play to work).

Some teachers use punching bags, toy guns, inflatable dolls, and similar hitting or aggressive items to give children opportunities to vent aggression. However, the trouble with punching bags and similar play items is that they are a "dead end," limited to aggressive use. In other words, we may move the child from the body to the punching bag, but we cannot move the child's hitting of the bag into more positive forms of play, in which others may join.

Social Engineering

Case History

During the first year of school, Carol and Janey were the closest of friends; in fact, their relationship was so exclusive that they rarely permitted other children to play with them. Then, during summer vacation, the friendship broke off. In the new prekindergarten class, Janey kept attempting to renew the friendship—but Carol had joined with a small group of other children, a clique, and would not permit Janey into the "special" group. Janey soon became a classroom discipline problem.

One morning, the clique, led by Carol, was being especially mean to Janey, taunting her and calling her names. The teacher witnessed this and decided to use some social engineering. "Janey, today we are going to make Thanksgiving cookies and I am going to give you the job of being the boss of cookie making. Pick three friends and come to the mixing table and we will go to work." The teacher refrained from directly instructing the girls, but positioned herself behind "the leader," Janey, coaching her periodically and dividing jobs among other cooperating students.

Now, Carol and her little clique no longer found what they were doing as interesting as what the girls making cookies were doing, so they wandered over and said to the teacher, "Ms. Anderson, can we make cookies, too?" Ms. Anderson responded, "I am not the boss of the cookie making, Janey is. You will need to ask her." They did, and after three or four long seconds of thought, Janey said yes.

The teacher continued to coach from the sidelines, making sure that Janey maintained her power in the cookie-making process, and the result was that the clique and Janey had a great time working together and later passing out the cookies to the other members of the class. The teacher, through social engineering, had endowed the powerless student with power—made her special. This experience, along with a few other similar incidents, helped Janey find new friends and become a cooperative worker with peers rather than going down the "black hole" of being labeled a discipline problem.

Social engineering occurs when we, as teachers, set up fun tasks to be completed, deliberately putting together certain students with a misbehaving student who lacks power and social skills, coaching him from the sidelines to help him gain social skills. This could involve such activities as painting a mural, making Christmas decorations, being a member of a class play, and so on. The teacher's role in dealing with young children who seem to have special problems is to help them find positive solutions.

Another form of social engineering is modeling reality solutions for children who have social conflicts or emotional concerns. Since the child has limited language capacities, the teacher must turn to symbolic expression such as modeling with puppet play, flannelboards, or children's literature. The teacher can enact scenes of mother/child separation, arguments between children over possessions, and other daily incidents that cause children difficulty.

In using puppets to enact, for example, a mother/child separation, the teacher dubs one of the puppets "mother" and the other ones "child" and "teacher." The teacher makes the puppets play out an incident in which the "child" cries, "No, no, Mommy, don't go! I want you to stay!" The "mother" responds that she will stay for a few minutes, but then must leave. "Mother" also gives the child her "handkerchief" to keep, and assures him that she will return.

After the "mother" leaves, the "teacher" states, "You look very unhappy. You're sad because your mother had to leave, but she will come back. I'm here to help you." The puppet drama continues until "mother" returns and they are reunited.

Such dynamic enactment (or, more likely, reenactment of actual incidents) allows the child to participate vicariously and perhaps discover a solution to a dilemma. Reenactment through the use of puppets or flannelboard characters allows the teacher to dramatize immediate classroom situations. Children's literature dealing with death, divorce, fear of the dark, nightmares, making friends, and other topics that children may have difficulty with presents some solutions and may encourage children to verbalize solutions of their own.

The key to modeling reality solutions is to enable the child, without reaching a too-high level of anxiety, to verbalize his concerns and to see certain ideas for resolving problems. While there are many incidents such as death and divorce that are not easily resolved, such symbolization can help the child gain a greater emotional and cognitive understanding of these happenings.

The Most-Wanted List

The child who is our Johnny (or Janey) No-Good is the child who has acquired a reputation that keeps him or her buried in a hole of isolation. When this happens, the student heightens his or her level of misbehavior, thinking, "If I can't be the best good star, I will be the best bad star!"

Although we may not admit it, such a child can actually frighten us as teachers. We are afraid that we are failing him, and we can lie awake at night worrying. One way to help this child would be to change the attitudes of the teachers and all other adults in the school who, have contact with Johnny so they will stop "shunning" him or ignoring him, and will begin actively, verbally accepting him. Not just an in-classroom process can accomplish this—a schoolwide campaign is needed. How to proceed?

The classroom teacher, director or principal, counselor, or any other adult takes a photo of Johnny and pastes it onto cardboard. Underneath is written all the factual information that can be obtained on Johnny: pets, brothers or sisters, parents' names, hobbies or talents, out-of-school activities, and so on. The card is then passed around at a faculty meeting of all the working adults, including the janitor, cafeteria workers, playground supervisors, and teachers.

With this information, every adult is to pretend that Johnny is a "new boy" in school; thus, he is given a clean slate. Each time the adults pass him in the hall or have any minor contact with him, they meet him eye to eye, say hello, use his name, touch him in a friendly manner, if possible, and, if there is time, inquire about his interests. Thus, we "give him the time of day." Imagine what effect this can have on Johnny, who, day in and day out, has felt disliked by all teachers and adults in his school. At first, this may seem unnatural to some teachers, but if all adults in the school can maintain this friendliness for two or more weeks, we will begin to find that Johnny No-Good is not really a little devil, and that real friendships can and do follow. In turn, it throws Johnny completely out of kilter. People are actually acting *nice* to him! How could this be? A change of behavior on his part will be almost inevitable as he begins to feel worthy and accepted and gains a sense of belonging.

The "Most-Wanted List" refers to those one or two children who are the greatest discipline problems for the entire school. Our position is that they do not feel wanted by the school and that is why they misbehave; so, we focus on them as individuals in need of our affection and acceptance. The adults in the school must change their attitudes toward these children if they want them to change.

Conflict over Possessions

The class has just gone out to the playground. Kate has found a shovel in the sandbox and is just about to fill a bucket. Mark, seated nearby, has a bucket but no shovel. His solution: reach out and take Kate's shovel. How should we handle such incidents, which are seen again and again in the early childhood classroom? Though many teachers may not be aware of it, incidents such as this present some of the most important "teachable moments" in daily classroom life!

Our goal is to have Kate use language to retrieve the shovel, and for Mark to realize that others have rights and that he needs to respond to language. Here, the TBC can be used to gain a perspective on the use of power in mediating conflicts.

Looking

We begin by bringing the children together either at a private corner of the sand-box, or by simply holding one of each child's hands and bringing them face to face. Now we "look," allowing some time for the children to settle their argument without any more teacher intervention. Our target is Kate, because she has the immediate problem—she lost her shovel! Kate can respond in a number of non-productive ways: by being passive (leaving or surrendering the toy), or by being physically aggressive (striking out at Mark), or by being verbally aggressive (calling Mark names, swearing, etc.). However, we want social conflict to be resolved through impulse control and expressive language (see Figure 8.2); so if Kate does not assert herself, we move up the TBC to naming statements: "Kate, I can see by your face that you are unhappy, you have lost your shovel." We have verbally encoded both Kate's feelings (much like active listening) and the problem needing to be solved, without being directive.

If there is no reaction from Kate, we escalate to the question strategy: "Kate, what could you say to Mark?" We then retreat to looking, to give Kate some time to think and respond. Then, if she still doesn't react, we move to directive commands: "Tell Mark what you want." After a period of "wait-time" we move to modeling: "Tell Mark, 'No, that is my shovel. I was using it, I want it back!'"

FIGURE 8.2   Impulse Control as a Developmental Process

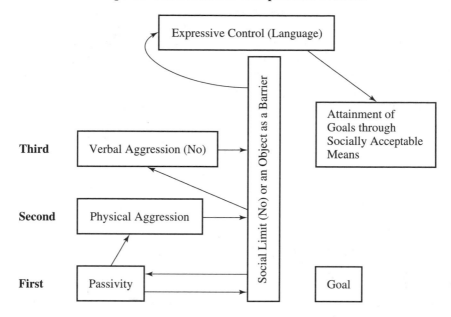

At this point, if Kate does not respond, we might say: "You are having a difficult time using words with Mark. Would you like me to tell him for you this time?" If she indicates yes, we repeat the language model directly to Mark: "Mark, Kate wants me to tell you that she was using the shovel and wants you to give it back to her." We do this for the child only once. From that time on, we will continue using the TBC techniques, but after verbal modeling, we will simply leave, telling the child that she must use language to get what she needs.

Some teachers feel that this is unfair and that Mark is getting away with something; but there will be many other occasions to deal with Mark, and right now Kate needs a lesson in asserting herself. If we relieve Kate of all the stress in the situation, getting what she needs *for* her, she will have no need to learn to act for herself. If our overdeveloped sense of "fairness" pushes us to play judge and jury, to return all objects to the rightful owners, we will be continuously exhausted because all the children in the class will be pulling at our skirt or pants to have us settle a thousand and one conflicts daily! Rather, when clashes over possessions occur, we will continue to intervene using the TBC techniques, until one day "Kate" will assert herself and gain the power to use language in the context of conflict. There can be no more valuable lesson, and, developmentally, 3-year-olds should be ready to begin learning this skill.

Backtracking a bit, if Kate *does* respond or simply says, "No, stop. That is mine!" the target child becomes Mark. Mark must learn to respond to the language of peers, and we help teach him this by using the TBC. First, we simply look as the children stand face to face, giving Mark time to think and act.

If a sufficient period of time brings no action on Mark's part, we move to naming statements, such as, "Mark, it is hard to give up toys that you want so much to keep." After thus encoding his probable feelings, if there are no results from Mark, we move to questions: "Mark, do you need my help to return the shovel?" If he says yes, we take the shovel from his hand and return it to Kate. If he says nothing we give him "wait-time," and then move to directive command and modeling: "Mark, Kate said give it back, she was using the shovel." Finally, after some "wait-time," we move to physical intervention, taking the shovel and returning it to Kate. If Mark then has a temper tantrum or attempts to strike us, we would use mirroring and diversion (body to the toy, etc.), as previously explained. Notice that in this resolution there is no attempt to discuss guilt or improper behavior. Our ultimate goal is to teach the children to use expressive language to resolve social conflicts.

Swearing, Bathroom Talk, and Verbal Aggression

It is Thanksgiving dinner and Grandma and friends are at the table. William states, "Mommy, I want my dessert." "No, not now, dear, you may have it after dinner." "Now, Mommy, now!" William screams. Mother ignores and William resorts to name calling and swearing. Hearing this unacceptable language coming from a 3-, 4-, or 5-year-old sends our pulses rushing! At first we feel helpless and then angry at the child.

If our middle-class values cause us as teachers to "flood" when such language is used by a child, we have unknowingly played into the child's power trap. The developmental stages of impulse control (see Figure 8.2) move from an attempt to use expressive language ("I want dessert now") to verbal aggression, to possibly physical aggression or passivity.

We will look at the problem of children's swearing from two aspects: (1) making a moral judgment and (2) preventing disruption of the social situation.

Moral Judgment

If the child should pick up some rocks, or perhaps some peas from his dinner plate, and throw them at another person (physical aggression), the emotional response he would get from adults would be dramatic. If he were verbally aggressive (using, for example, the "F" word), he would get the same dramatic effect. So, for the young child, still a transductive thinker, swearing has the same concrete meaning as direct physical aggression. When one child screams at another,

"I'm going to cut off your head," the other may scream and run, truly afraid that the words might make this happen.

When children are verbally aggressive with other children, we believe they talk this way because they cannot call up, under the emotional pressure of the moment, the correct language to get their needs met. We, as teachers, then, do not make a moral judgment, but simply provide them with the correct language model to express what they want to say. For example, if Kate screams at Mark after he takes her shovel, "You butt face!" the teacher responds, "Kate, Mark can't understand what you want with those words. Tell him to give it back—you were using it." Thus, when one child is aggressive to another, we simply provide the child with the socially acceptable language model. We are teaching her to move from aggressive language to expressive language.

When aggressive language is directed to us, we do not fall into the power trap set by the child. Consider the case of Kathy, who was asked to leave the sand play and come inside immediately because of the threat of rain and dangerous lightning. When she refused, her teacher picked her up and carried her into the classroom.

Kathy: "I hate you, Ms. Anderson. You're a @#*%@#!"

Teacher: "Kathy, I need to bring you in quickly to keep you safe from the lightning. It is OK to be angry with me. Maybe you will want to be friends tomorrow."

The teacher makes no moral judgment on the child's behavior, giving her permission to have the strong feelings that she does have and promising that the adult friendship will still be there.

Disruption of the Social Situation

The second aspect of the swearing, or verbal aggression, is the disruption of the social situation. Repeated verbal attacks coming from a child may make it difficult for a class to carry on with an activity. When this happens, give a preparatory command (from directive statements on the TBC) and then follow through with a logical consequence if the misbehavior occurs again: "Bill, if you disrupt our lunch with those words once more, I will have to move you to the kitchen to eat so we don't have to be interrupted." Again, no moral judgment is made, and we are attempting to teach the child the logical consequences of his actions.

At a later time, in a knee-to-knee discussion with the swearing child, we would go back through the TBC, much as we have described in the previous use of the relax-chair. "You have had a difficult time at lunch. (nondirective statements) What is the rule at the table? (questions) The rule is . . . " (directive statement).

Summary

Many of the ideas in this chapter dealing with discipline and child guidance will be new to beginning teachers; most of us are much more familiar with the methods applied to us by our own parents and teachers. Thus, when we are in conflict situations with young children, those familiar, even ingrained, methods will come to us as knee-jerk responses. But what we tend to want to do immediately is usually just what we should *not* do, because it would lead us into power traps.

We view children as gradually developing impulse control and the ability to handle frustrations. With the preceding ideas and techniques, we have the perspective to look at the actions of children and then to intervene in a nonjudgmental and nonhostile manner to help them. To set appropriate goals for each child, we use the Adjustment Behavioral Profile found in Chapter 12.

Activities

1. Spend a morning in a classroom with 3-, 4-, and 5-year-old children, observing one child who in the first half-hour has looked like a possible difficult child. Do the Adjustment Behavioral Profile (found in Chapter 12) by closely observing the child's departure and reuniting with parents, snack, rest time, circle time, and general play activities.
2. Select one discipline incident that you have recently observed, and with the TBC, design a strategy for setting appropriate limits with this child if this incident would occur again.
3. Visit a young children's classroom. First, interview the teacher to identify the five best-behaved children and the five most difficult children in the room. What are the methods by which the well-behaving children get attention and power? What are the methods that the difficult children use to get attention and power? Try to determine the motivations of the difficult children: attention, power, revenge, or helplessness (Dreikurs & Cassel, 1972).
4. Observe an experienced teacher working with young children, and watch for a discipline incident. Try to record the teacher's language responses with children. Number them in the sequence in which they occurred. Classify them with the use of the TBC as looking, naming, questioning, commanding, and acting. What percentage was in each category of behaviors? Is this a Relationship-Listening, Confronting-Contracting, or Rules and Consequences teacher?

References

Alberti, R. E., *Your Perfect Right: A Guide to Assertive Living.* San Luis Obispo, Calif.: Impact Publishers, 1982.
Canter, Lee, and Marlene Canter, *Assertive Discipline: A Take-Charge Approach for Today's Educator.* Seal Beach, Calif.: Canter and Associates, 1976.

Dreikurs, Rudolf, and Pearl Cassel, *Discipline without Tears.* New York: Hawthorn Books, 1972.

Erikson, Erik, *Childhood and Society.* New York: Norton, 1950.

Freud, Anna, *Normality and Pathology in Childhood: Assessment of Development.* New York: International University Press, 1968.

Glasser, William, *Schools Without Failure.* New York: Peter H. Wyden Publishing, 1969.

Gordon, Thomas, *T.E.T.: Teacher Effectiveness Training.* New York: Peter H. Wyden, 1974.

Harris, Thomas A., *I'm OK, You're OK: A Practical Guide to Transactional Analysis.* New York: Harper and Row, 1969.

Piaget, Jean, *The Moral Judgment of the Child* (trans. Marjorie Gabain). New York: Free Press, 1965.

Wolfgang, Charles, *Helping Aggressive and Passive Preschoolers through Play.* Columbus, Ohio: Charles E. Merrill, 1977.

Wolfgang, Charles, *Solving Discipline Problems: Strategies for Classroom Teachers.* Boston: Allyn and Bacon, 1986.

9

Daily Schedule

In other chapters we discuss methods for organizing space, objects, and materials for successful teaching through play. Another essential element in planning the daily activities for classrooms is time. The following is a look at how some of the events of the school day can be scheduled and managed to avoid placing unnecessary stress on children, parents, and teachers.

Arrivals

To adults, the movement from home to school or from parent to teacher and classroom seems a simple matter. For young children, however, especially for 3-year-olds (A. Freud, 1968, 1971; Mahler, 1970, 1975), these changes may be considered "culture shock" (Speers, 1970). If you, as an adult, were transported suddenly to a foreign country with a different language, different foods and rules about eating it, different clothing, and the like, you would be under great stress—or culture shock (Toffler, 1971). The school, a new place to live and work with others, places similar stress on the young child, who must be asking himself: Where do I go to the potty if I need to? Who will keep me safe here when my mother is gone? Will others take my toys from me? Where do I sleep and eat?

This fear of the school as an unknown will produce a variety of behaviors on the child's part, and may reappear periodically even after the child has become a regular member of the school "community." Here is an example of a successful preschool adaptation, with the child progressing through various stages of adjustment (Speers, 1970).

Lap Period

Three-year-old Kate enters the classroom door, tightly holding her mother's hand. After she and her mother are warmly greeted by the teacher and silently observed by the other children, the full meaning of "going to school" and "mother leaving" begins to dawn on Kate, and she climbs on her mother's lap and buries her face in her mother's chest. For a few minutes she refuses to look at this new world. This is called the *lap period* of adjustment. The teacher encourages the mother to take the rocking chair to a large upright mirror mounted on the wall, and suggests that when Kate feels more relaxed, her mother might demonstrate some of the toys to her. Then the teacher leaves, stating that she will be back shortly to help.

Customs Inspection Period

Kate soon begins peeking over her mother's shoulder to watch the classroom activities through the mirror. She begins to point things out to her mother, and the two chat about what is occurring. This is called the *customs inspection period* (Mahler, 1970, 1975).

Practicing Period

After looking about the room for a while, Kate suddenly slips from her mother's lap, runs out into the classroom to grab a toy, and brings it quickly back to her mother. Then, standing at her mother's knee, she watches to see if anyone will intervene—making eye contact with the teacher. The teacher smiles an OK at her.

"Oh, this is a toy dog," Mother says, "It goes 'ruff-ruff' and walks like this." Three or four times Kate runs out, grabs an object, darts back, and puts it in her mother's hands; her mother responds by telling her the name of the object and demonstrating its uses. This is called the *practicing period*—practicing being separated from mother for short periods (Speers, 1970; Mahler, 1975).

Teacher-Approach Period

Notice that the teacher did not "throw" herself at the child, but permitted the child and parent time to relax and gradually separate physically. During the gradual separation, the teacher was observing the parent/child interaction, noting the sense modalities employed by the mother (see Mahler, 1970, 1975):

Hearing: Is the mother trying to reassure the child by using language to explain, "This is what we are doing," "This is what will happen next," and so on? (If so, this may be a verbal mother.)

Touch: Is the mother cuddling and caressing the child, as well as exploring objects with her own hands and encouraging the child to do likewise? (This may be a tactile mother.)

Visual: Is the mother signaling the child with her eyes, telling her to "go ahead and pick up the object," just by using her eyes and facial expressions? (She may be a visual mother.)

The teacher has just learned something about the sense modality or combination of modalities that she may now use to make this child begin to feel comfortable in her new preschool world. For example:

Hearing-Verbal Child: The teacher tells what is happening or going to happen ("We are going to read a book about...," "You will sit near me so that you may hear the story," etc.).

Tactile-Physical Child: The teacher brings a furry puppet to the child, or takes the child to the classroom rabbit, encouraging her to touch.

Visual Child: The teacher signals with her eyes that there is a free chair, toy, or materials available, and encourages the child to use them.

If the child and mother communicate well verbally, but there is little or no touching, an attempt on the teacher's part to cuddle with or physically cue that child may be seen by the child as frightening or intrusive.

Why is it that when there are two or three teachers in a classroom, each child seems to gain a solid emotional relationship with one or two teachers and will shy away from or reject a relationship with another teacher? It may sometimes be that a certain child and teacher share a form of sensory communication, whereas the rejected teacher may unknowingly be attempting to communicate in the child's weak or underdeveloped modality. We, as teachers, might attempt to decide which are our own strong modalities, and begin to practice ways of "shifting gears" deliberately, moving into different modalities, in order to try to communicate with different children. Later in the child's school years, his favored modality may become his best learning style.

Parent Departure

Once communication is established between child and teacher, the parent may depart with minimal stress for the child. The preceding example demonstrated initial fearfulness and a demand for mother to remain. These stress indicators are viewed as positive, because they show that there is a healthy attachment between child and parent. The crying and demanding are simply an indication of love (Speers, 1970). If the child is given time to regress to more infantile behaviors, such as becoming a lap baby, she should gradually emerge from the arms of mother and be able to join the other children.

Surprisingly, the children who act like "little men" or "little women" and show no emotional stress when mother departs often have greater difficulty in making good long-term adjustments in the classroom. These "I don't need mother" children often refuse later to be cuddled or comforted by the teacher, need excessive teacher attention, behave in "run-and-chase" fashion, put themselves in dangerous situations, and engage in stereotypic play—failing to progress developmentally (Speers, 1970).

The point is that signs of stress, such as crying and demanding, are normal. Your role is to find ways of bridging the child gradually from home to school. One way this can be done is by giving the parent time to stay with the child in the first hours or days of school. Another way is to pin Mother's handkerchief with her perfume on it to the front of the child's clothing, so the child may finger it and smell "Mother" all day long. You might even permit the child to call Mommy by telephone during the day, hearing in her mother's voice reassurance that she will return. Another possibility is to ask the parent to bring a family photo for the child to keep and to show around. You also could let the child bring a "transition object"—a blanket à la the "Peanuts" character Linus or a cuddle toy—to carry around for the first few days. These "transition objects" give sensory reminders of home, permanence, and Mother, helping the child make the adjustment from home to school (A. Freud, 1971).

Another help in this transition is having the teacher and child play "Mommy and Child" with the use of a toy telephone. The teacher carries on a conversation with the new child, reassuring him that his mother is thinking about him and will not forget to pick him up at the end of day (Peller, 1959).

Similar dramas may be played out with puppets, making one puppet the child and the other the parent. In the puppet modeling by the teacher, the child puppet pleads, "Please don't go, Mommy." The mother puppet explains that she must leave in order to do such and such, and that Ms. Anderson will keep him safe until she returns. A teacher puppet now appears and helps the child puppet "go potty," eat, sleep, and play. Finally, a knock is heard at the door and the mother puppet has returned to reunite warmly with the child puppet.

Here are some further suggestions for helping children make initial adjustments to school:

1. Have the teacher visit the child's home, watch for parent/child cueing modalities, and learn to communicate with the child on familiar ground.
2. Have parent and child make a visit to the classroom when no other children are there, possibly after school or on weekends. Have mother encourage the child to use the small toilets, to sit with teacher and mother for a quick snack, and to take toys from the shelf and play with them. Have the child take some object home with him that he will bring back the first day, such as an inex-

pensive toy, piece of play-dough, or crayon with paper. Label the child's storage cubby or cot with his name and, if possible, a photo. (*Note:* Some children, when visiting a store where things are on display shelves, have been told not to touch and have even been disciplined harshly. The classroom, with things stored on shelves, will appear similar to children, and some will be fearful of touching or taking things from shelves. Parents and teachers must communicate that it is safe to take and use the classroom objects.)

3. With a small group of already adjusted children, play a series of imitative games, such as Thumbkin or Simon Says. The object of the play activity is for the new child to be directly introduced to a group of children, so they will at least know each other's names.

4. Cut a large silhouette of the new child, paste a photograph of him on it and display it in a prominent place so all can see it, including parents arriving in the classroom.

5. Prepare the parents on what routine they should follow when they bring in the child for the first time. Explain to them that the school views the early signs of stress as positive, and that they should expect the periods of separation, lap, customs inspection, and practicing before the teacher-approach period. Remind the parent, though, that some children might not go through these separation processes the first day of school, but may wait until later in the school year, after a long weekend or holiday period.

Some parents say, "He did so well the first two weeks, but now he doesn't want to come to school and makes a fuss!" The child is just now beginning truly to separate; if the parents are aware of this beforehand, they will not be disturbed by these new behaviors. Parents may consider removing the child from the school, if they have not been previously warned to expect some stress.

The Message Book

A very good communication aid is a message book (Phelps, 1984) placed on a stand inside the arrival door, high enough so that an adult may stand and write. The parent writes a message in this book each morning, as well as tells it to the morning teacher or head teacher. All staff members arriving to work throughout the day are required to read the message book as they come in. Also on the stand should be an enrollment roster with spaces after each child's name for initialing the child in and out, so that there will be a written record of the child's departure. Children may slip away to another classroom, to the bathroom, or to the playground; the initialed record indicates if they are actually in school. Also, if one parent arrives at the end of the day wishing to pick up the child, not knowing that the other parent picked her up just before lunch, and now demands, "Where is my child?" the sign-in/sign-out sheet is a lifesaver—literally.

A parent message bulletin board near or above the message stand is another must. Besides messages to parents, all requests to give children medication can be posted (on a standardized form). The forms should be filled out each morning by the parent, and the medicines stored in only one location familiar to all staff and parents. Since it is impossible to give medication to two or more children at staggered times throughout the day, the school should make known to all parents the established times when medications are given. Parents can then inform physicians or pharmacists, and dosages can be adjusted based on these time periods. It is recommended that only one staff member be in charge of giving medication (with a back-up person), and that this staff member initial the parent medication request, creating a record of the transaction.

Snacks and Eating

Mid-morning and mid-afternoon snacks not only provide bodily nourishment for highly active young children but they also bring children together to further a sense of group belonging. It is critical that snacktime be a pleasant experience for children because, if not, the situation may give rise to competition and aggression. Eating periods are not times for teachers to have breaks, leaving behind the less-trained and less-experienced teachers or aides to carry on. If negative instances occur at home between parent and child, they will most likely occur at the dinner table or when going to bed at night. Therefore, snacktime and lunchtime (and, in preschool, naptime) are prime periods for the child to become "difficult," expecting to carry out power struggles with teachers, just as with parents at home.

Group Snack

In organizing for snacktime, the concepts of control of error and degrees of freedom are used. You do not want the children to play with food, but you do want them to become accustomed to a routine that is nonrepressive and easy to follow.

What Not to Do at Snacktime

- In classroom X, the teacher instructs a mature child to set out the napkins and cups before each chair at the table. The children come to their seats, which have their names taped on. The teacher, seated at the end of the table, makes an announcement or, where permitted, says grace. Then, extending a wicker basket of a food such as celery or cookies, and not permitting the children to pass the basket, the teacher instructs each child to take one. (If any food remains, the basket is removed from the table so the children will not fight over it.)

- The children are instructed to set the snack on their napkins and wait until all are ready to eat. Next, the teacher appears with a pitcher of milk or juice and, moving behind the children, fills their 7-oz. paper cups. After the teacher is again seated, the children are told that they may begin.
- The children are required to eat and drink everything they have been given, and to wait at the table until everyone else is finished. Then one child travels around the table gathering the used cups and napkins. Such is the classroom "kingdom" where the teacher rules in a regal manner.

Such a rigid snacking procedure indicates that the teacher does not believe that children can learn responsibility, and has an overriding fear that an accident will occur. The teacher shows a limited understanding of control of error as she plays food server to passive children.

Snack materials should be engineered to allow children to eat with minimal pressures from adults. First, two plastic cups with pouring lids, holding approximately three cups of juice or milk each, are placed on a cafeteria tray, along with two snack-filled wicker baskets lined with napkins and a stack of 3-oz. drinking cups. The lidded pouring glasses will keep spills to a minimum. Also on the tray are napkins in a weighted holder, which keeps the napkins from being blown about. Approximately 30 percent more snacks than there are children should be provided. These items are previously prepared by the teacher (or cook, if the school is lucky enough to have one).

The responsibility for bringing the filled cafeteria tray to the table belongs to the children who have finished clean-up from previous activities and have washed their hands. They bring the tray carefully from the kitchen to the center of the snack table.

Round tables, each seating eight children, are ideal, allowing each child to see the faces of all the others and have equal access to the cafeteria tray. Rectangular tables always seem to leave the end child out of conversations and access.

After washing up, the children seat themselves as desired, select napkins and cups from the center of the table, pour their own juice or milk, and pass the container to a neighbor. Snack items are then taken from the basket with plastic prongs (for health reasons) and passed from one child to another.

Children are permitted to take more than one food item, and the small, 3-oz. cups make it necessary that they refill their cups repeatedly. The teacher is seated at the table or at a nearby table and models behavior by carrying on light conversations and eating and drinking the snack as she or he wishes the children to do. Coffee cups and soda cans used by the teacher at the snack table would be inappropriate modeling.

When children have had enough food and conversation, they may get up at will, drop their napkins and cups in one of several plastic-lined waste cans nearby, and move to some quiet activity, such as reading or looking at picture books. This procedure gives the children freedom and control. The teacher is not a food server or "boss," but an equal member of the group.

Open Snack

At some child-centered programs, the children are all "herded together" for snack, regardless of whether they are ready to eat. Why not give the children total autonomy over eating by using an open-snack arrangement? For example, from 9:00 A.M. until 10:30 A.M., a child-sized table with two chairs are placed in the corner of the classroom, arranged with snack materials, as previously described, with 3-oz. cups, lidded pouring cups, and snacks in baskets—but this time covered with a see-through plastic lid with a handle. During this open-snack period, a child is free to find a friend, wash hands (a container with soapy water and paper towels is nearby), and eat a snack when desired. The only rule is that the child must bring a friend. If she cannot find a companion that morning, the teacher may eat with the child—and then help that child make a friend in the next few weeks.

On the wall near the open-snack table is a class roster, where the teacher keeps a record of the time each child eats a snack and with whom. Open snack is especially useful during the beginning of a school year, when many children are making an initial adjustment; it may be alternated with group snack for variety, so that the children may benefit from the advantages of both methods.

Eating Difficulties

Some children become "Mr. Hyde" when they come to a group setting to eat. These carryover behaviors from home (Dreikurs, 1964) are rooted in power struggles, and generally are seen in the form of the child who will not eat or who becomes aggressive—both verbally (calling others names) and physically (jabbing others with his or her finger)—harasses others, and hoards snacks.

The attitude toward such children should be to consider this "misbehavior" as a sign of basic insecurity and fear of the eating and group situation. The children should not be viewed as simply bullies or as "just being mean." Your goal is to have all children become comfortable and to eat and socialize with others.

Start by permitting the difficult, passive, or aggressive child to eat in a one-to-one relationship with a friend or adult at a small table. This should not be done in such a manner that the child views it as isolation or punishment, but as a special time with a friend or teacher. Later, a second child can be invited to the small table, with others gradually joining over a period of days or weeks until the child finally is eating with a group. Even after the child has adjusted to the large group setting, there may be "bad days" when she might be permitted to revert to a smaller group for eating.

While the child is making these initial adjustments, few eating demands should be made of her; the other children will serve as good models of behavior for her. If she refuses to eat, make no demands. Simply clean up when snack is over and move on to other activities. Some teachers worry that if a child has not eaten she will become malnourished; however, the failure to eat at school will only occur over a two- to three-week period, and with a well-balanced day of active play, the child will develop a healthy appetite. When the child knows that the pressure is off, she will eat. As a teacher, you must have faith that this will occur (Dreikurs, 1964).

It is not surprising to discover that it is the "non-eating" child's parents who, at the end of the day, will often demand a full report of the child's eating performance ("Did Jon eat all of his lunch today?"). This is symptomatic of a power struggle between parent and child at the eating table. The parents' emotional intensity may be strong and possibly intimidating to the teacher, attempting to bring the teacher into the power struggle. You must resist. Your response to the parent should be an encouragement statement ("He did better today!" or "He is becoming more comfortable at snack and gradually eating more; we are confident that in a few days he will be eating a full serving"). Then move on to other positive topics with the parent, telling her or him of the other activities in which the child is doing well. Modeling positive expectations for the child is the best support you can give to parents who appear to be overconcerned.

Always attempt to be truthful with parents; however, some incidents may require otherwise. We were told about an incident in which a parent inspected his child's lunchbox at the end of the day and, finding items not eaten, verbally exploded, reprimanding the child for not eating. As a result, the child's teacher, for a period of two weeks during initial adjustment, deliberately removed uneaten items from the lunchbox. The parental reprimands stopped and, without this parental pressure, the child began eating his lunch and asking for more—much to his parent's delight. Deciding whether the teacher was "right" or "wrong" in this case presents a moral dilemma exemplary of those that must sometimes be faced by teachers of young children.

For the hoarding child who takes far too much from the shared snack basket, during the initial period provide items that are very small (e.g., nuts, dry cereals, or trail mix) rather than one large blueberry muffin. Announce to all children, "Take all that you can eat and leave in the basket all that you cannot eat. You may take seconds, and I will always make sure that everyone gets enough to eat." Remember, tell the child what to *do,* not what *not* to do." Resist the natural tendency to say, "Don't take so much, Tommy. You are not going to eat all of that." Permit the child, for a period of days or even two or three weeks, to continue to hoard without any comment. For the hoarder, there is a basic "not OK" view of the world, and his outlook is that the world is denying him and he must fight to get his needs met (Harris, 1969).

At the end of snack, during clean-up procedures, go to the hoarding child (who will have a large pile of trail mix in front of him, uneaten), make eye contact, touch the remaining food with your hand to focus his attention on what you are talking about, and then reassuringly state, "Take all that you can eat and leave in the basket all that you cannot eat. You may take seconds, and I will always make sure that everyone gets enough to eat."

Over the next weeks, begin to "back down" the TBC with the child:

- *Modeling:* Have the child eat with others who exhibit good eating behaviors.
- *Commanding:* Before the child takes from the basket of food, state directly, "Take all that you can eat and leave in the basket all that you cannot eat. You may take seconds, and I will always make sure that everyone gets enough to eat."
- *Questioning:* Again, just before the child takes from the shared basket, ask, "Tommy, what is our rule about snacks from baskets?"
- *Naming:* As the basket is passed, say to the entire group, "We have a rule for taking snacks." Such nondirective reminders simply bring to the child's awareness the desired rule before he acts.
- *Looking On:* Such difficult children need the teacher nearby during snack, radiating a zone of safety and control. If a teacher must supervise a number of tables, he or she may choose to eat at the table where the target child is seated for a number of weeks. This "looking on" is not done with an attitude of "I have to keep an eye on him every moment or he will get out of hand," but rather "I want to establish a supportive, helpful relationship with this child."

Acting Out While Eating

Once the child has become relaxed and adjusted to eating with others, there will be times when she, or other members of the class, might begin to disrupt the eating situation in a manner that necessitates direct action by the teacher. This will be done, again, by escalating up the TBC.

Carol has been "silly" all morning, giggling, challenging the teacher's limits, and generally refusing to fit into routines. At snack time, she is excessively loud, prevents the child next to her from eating by calling her "bathroom" names, and makes the entire eating atmosphere unpleasant.

- *Looking On:* The teacher changes her seating, moving into the direct view of Carol. If need be, she touches Carol or uses any other nonverbal actions to make Carol aware that she is present. Just looking might get Carol back on track; if not, the teacher escalates up the TBC.

- *Naming:* The teacher announces in a nondirective statement, "At snack time, we need to remember to use our 'inside' voices."
- *Questioning:* Increase the intervention by moving up the TBC to questioning: "Do you need my help to remember rules at snack?" or "Do you need to move to a smaller, quieter table to be able to eat your snack this morning, Carol?"
- *Commanding:* The teacher tells the child exactly what he wants her to do, not what not to do. If the child continues to be defiant, the teacher follows with a preparatory command or promise to take action in the form of a consequence: "Carol (uses name, touches her on shoulder, and makes direct eye contact), I want you to turn around, sit up in your chair, put your food in your mouth, and use an 'inside' voice that does not hurt ears" (Canter, 1976). She remains defiant. "If I see that done again, it is telling me that you do not know the rules for eating snack with others and I will ask you to move to another table, or leave snack time this morning" (logical consequence) (Dreikurs, 1964).
- *Acting/Physical Intervention:* If the child continues to refuse, the teacher now intervenes physically, if need be, to move the child away from the situation in a nonpunitive manner. (See Chapter 8 on discipline and child guidance for techniques in handling temper tantrums, which are likely to occur when the teacher uses very strong intervention.)

Recommended Meal Patterns

In planning meals for 3-, 4-, and 5-year-old children, the total daily food needs of children must be considered. What to serve and how much depend on the ages of the children and their length of stay at school. Children in school for four to eight hours will require one nutritious, well-balanced meal with one snack for mornings and one in the afternoon. This provides one-third to one-half of the recommended dietary allowances. Children spending more than eight hours, such as those in day care, would be provided additional food in the form of two meals and two snacks, providing two-thirds to three-quarters of their daily dietary requirement. Table 9.1 may be used in planning nutritious, well-balanced menus.

Rest/Sleeping Time

It is recommended that for all-day programs, 3- and 4-year-old children might require at least two hours or more of afternoon rest or sleep, while 5-year-olds might need a minimum of 45 minutes of quiet, lie-down-on-a-mat rest. Resting is another area where power struggles are fought between parents or other adults and the child, and these patterns will often be brought into the school during sleeping and resting periods (Dreikurs, 1964).

TABLE 9.1   Recommended Meal Patterns

Food Components	Children 3 to 6 Years
Breakfast	
Milk, fluid	¾ cup
Juice or fruit or vegetable	½ cup
Bread (enriched or whole grain)	½ slice
or cereal	
cold dry	⅓ cup
hot cooked	¼ cup
Mid-Morning or Mid-Afternoon	
(Snack supplement)	
(select two of these four components)	
milk, fluid	½ cup
meat or meat alternative	½ ounce
Juice (full strength) or fruit(s)	½ cup
or vegetable(s)	
Bread or cereal	½ slice
cold dry	⅓ cup
hot cooked	¼ cup
Lunch or Supper	
Milk, fluid	¾ cup
Meat or meat alternative (lean meat, poultry, or fish, cooked)	1½ ounces
or cheese	1½ ounces
or egg	1
or cooked dry beans or peas	⅜ cup
or peanut butter*	3 tablespoons
Vegetable(s) and/or fruit(s)	½ cup (total)
Bread	½ slice

Source: From the guidelines of Dept. of Health and Rehabilitative Services, 1317 Winewood Blvd., Tallahassee, Fla. 32309-0700

**Caution:* Peanut butter on dry bread and popcorn are items that have caused many choking incidents in centers for young children.

Again, children (as well as adults) live in three worlds: an inside world of thought and feelings, where the focus of attention is internal; a body world, where activities such as swimming, running, or simply relaxing in a bathtub are enjoyed; and an external world, in which the focus is on play, work, and the world around us. A healthy form of regression (A. Freud, 1971) for the adult at the end of a very busy day is to crawl into a large comfortable chair, kick off tight shoes, and feel one's tired body relax (the body world), then perhaps to daydream or think over the day (the inside world). Adults and children move in and out of these three worlds throughout the day.

In order to sleep, young children must give up being attuned to the external world of others and objects, move through the body world to feel themselves physically relax, and then move into an inner world of thoughts that finally lead to unconscious sleep. Overactive children, children who are frightened by the new school situation, or children who have patterns of engaging in power conflicts centered on napping will not be able to move normally through these three worlds. Thus, rest period is not a time to be left to inexperienced staff; teachers need to be present—to rub backs, to talk to children, and to reassure them that they are safe and secure.

The difficult child, when asked to lie on a cot, cannot give up an external awareness because his perceptions are outward and defensive. To help counter this, each child should have a cot labeled with his or her name, located at the same spot each day (for health reasons children should not sleep on each other's cots). This is truly a private space, and other children should not be permitted to invade it by putting their hands or feet on the cots. The teachers should scatter themselves over the sleep area, kneeling near the children who are having difficulty relaxing, helping them with appropriate sensory measures. Soft music without words can be played to mask inside and outside noise. Perhaps even some children will need headphones to listen to soft music to screen out external sounds. The teacher should remove them once the child is asleep.

The child who is visually stimulated may be placed near a wall, shelving, or small movable screen, so that distractions will be kept from view. For some tactile children, gentle back rubbing will help bring on relaxation. Once the children are relaxed and quieted, teachers may depart the sleeping room, leaving behind one adult, who will always be seated in the same location during rest. This is important, because children will awaken, look to the "adult chair," see the teacher, be reassured, and return to sleep. If that chair is deserted, the child who sits up to look for the teacher will have a very difficult time getting to sleep again.

There are rare children at this age who seem not to need sleep. Their behaviors and personalities are productive throughout the school day, and being on a cot is, for them, like being in jail. Such children should be required to attempt to rest and sleep, but if they cannot after 15 to 20 minutes and your best attempts to help them relax have not worked, then give them picture books or miniature toys to use quietly on their cots. Then, if the children still act as if they are in jail, allow them to leave the sleeping room quietly and do some tabletop activities (clay modeling or drawing, for example) in another room. Do not harshly reprimand, causing the children greater tension and making it even more difficult for them to relax. This would be a real contradiction of your action and goals.

Circle/Story Time

Bringing together a group of 5-, 4-, or 3-year-old-children and getting them to focus their full attention on one adult takes great care and technical understanding. It might be helpful to reread Spheres of Communication described in Chapter 8.

One to All

Group time provides third-sphere communication (one to all), whereby the teacher requires all attention to focus on him while his emotions and responses are diffused to all members of a group—generally not to one child. Thus, each child is required to inhibit his or her own egocentric desires and become a part of the collective activity. This is socially very demanding for the young child, who is still quite self-centered. You must carefully regulate the amount of time children will be required to maintain themselves in nonpersonal, directly controlled situations. Circle/story time is one such situation. If well-managed, this activity can lead the child toward a greater ability to handle direct instruction.

The transition into and out of group time is critical. If all 15 or 20 young children run into the rug room and try to grab a favorite spot, pushing and shoving will occur, with some danger of minor injury.

Let's look at a better way of making a transition from, for example, snack time to circle time (see Figure 9.1): The teacher in charge of circle time collects three to six children who have finished with their previous activity and have cleaned up. She directs them to follow her to the rug. Once at the rug, the teacher must take a power position, much like a judge in a courtroom, placing herself higher than the children, on a piano stool, rocking chair, or the like.

Circle time must be engineered with an understanding of "control of error." Each child should know the rules about what he or she should and should not do, and there must be some definition of individual seating space. Two large half-circles, taped or painted on the floor, or a circle design in the rug can indicate where each child is to be seated with legs tucked under. The first children will take the

FIGURE 9.1 Good Transitions

1. Generally, young children should not wait or stand in line.
2. Move children in groups of three to six, with the first group accompanied by the "point" teacher, who has these children get the new area ready for those who follow.
3. The last teacher to leave the space, such as the rug room where story time occurs, uses the remaining three to six children to clean up, before moving them to a new location.
4. When children are making transitions to a new space, before they leave their present space they should know where they are going and what they will do when they get there.

inner circle, closest to the teacher, while the later children will take the back circle, refraining from trampling over children already seated. The motor rules and circle on the floor are structured to control error; if there is no structure, the children will be randomly scattered over the rug, rolling over, lying down, and getting up and down.

The teacher should not wait until everyone is present and ready (this would cause the waiting children to find negative ways of amusing themselves), but should simply jump into a finger game, songs with physical actions, or something similar. Once everyone has joined the circle, reading from a storybook can begin.

While circle time is in progress, other teachers or aides need to be present at the back of the circle. If certain children cannot relax, and begin to disrupt the story, the helping teachers would move closer to them, touching them on their backs or drawing them into their own laps, generally helping them to relax. Or these teachers may move very physically active children to child-sized chairs at the end of the circle. These children literally hold themselves onto the chairs until they gain control of their bodies.

If repetitive disruptions by one or more children do occur, the in-charge teacher who is reading or conducting the activity must take some action, and that action will be based on the TBC.

- *Looking:* The teacher may simply signal with her eyes to the off-task child that she wants his or her attention. This is also a signal to the helping teacher on the sidelines to move in and help with this child.
- *Naming:* At this point, it is important for the teacher to understand the concept of high-profile and low-profile correction in a direct teaching situation. If the teacher stops the activity and reprimands one child directly, she is disrupting the shared fantasy of the story for all others, as well as possibly making the other children feel empathetically tense and uncomfortable. "Johnny, you are not listening and you are disrupting the story for everyone." The eyes of all other children now turn to Johnny. This is a guilt-inducing statement. The reprimand has probably disrupted the story more than Johnny's original actions.

  In using low-profile correction, the teacher simply looks at Johnny, says his name, and points out some aspect of the book or object she is sharing: "Johnny, you will notice (pointing to the picture) that the troll is hiding under the bridge. . . . " By using low-profile corrections, the teacher can utilize the child's name, touch, and visual focus, and continue with the rhythms of the story.
- *Questioning/Commanding:* If disruption by the "difficult" child continues, the teacher moves up the TBC to questions and to even more directive action, which will require a high profile. But keep in mind that when two or more adults are teaching in the classroom, the in-charge teacher can depend on the sideline teacher to help with children who need "looking." The teacher then

questions all children, "What are our rules of behavior at circle time?" Then she commands, "Show me that you know the rules!" Finally, a preparatory command to the off-task child: "Johnny, you are showing me this morning that you have not learned the rules for story-time, and if _____ occurs again, I will ask you to go to the next room and choose something else to do."

- *Acting/Physical Intervention:* If the misbehavior continues, the in-charge teacher will have the sideline teacher remove Johnny from circle time. Since a high-profile correction is needed, the teacher may choose to stop the story and play or sing a finger or hand game, and then reintroduce the story.

Later, in a nonpunitive manner, the in-charge teacher will approach Johnny, moving through the TBC again, with child and teacher seated in chairs facing each other, knee to knee. "You had a really difficult time in circle time this morning. (naming statement) What are the rules for circle time? (questions) In circle time, I want you to sit on your spot on the line, look at me, and listen to the story." If the teacher feels that the child truly does not understand the rules, the two of them could go to the rug room and the teacher could reteach the rules (modeling). This knee-to-knee follow-through lets the child know, in a nonpunitive manner, exactly what is wanted.

Departing from circle time can be done quickly and in an orderly manner. Generally, it is best to dismiss children in groups of six to eight. The in-charge teacher may continue with a simple hand game, while the sideline teacher signals a small group of children and leads them to a definite location. The in-charge teacher dismisses another group of six to eight who will "go to Ms. Anderson" at snack or her location. Finally, the in-charge teacher has the remaining children clean up the room and then follow her to the new location. Notice that no one has had to stand in line. Waiting in lines should never occur in early childhood practice. Children at this age do not move well in herds!

Departure

There are some children who do well all day long, until the first parent appears at the end of the day to pick the child up. Then the Dr. Jekyll and Mr. Hyde syndrome appears, with crying, temper tantrums, and defiance toward the teachers. Why is this so? We speculate that after the first parent of the day comes for his or her child, the "Mr. Hyde" child worries about whether he will be picked up by his own parents. For him, the question is: Will my mom forget me? This is not an extraordinary worry, but will be a concern for all children at this age.

Your goal is to occupy the children's minds (perhaps with a story) and possibly hands (using structured-construction materials such as puzzles) in some activity that keeps their minds off their worry and separation fears. This can be done by having a small, intimate circle time with the six to eight children who are picked up late. Find a comfortable corner on a rug where children can be on your lap or physically close to you. Read stories, play hand games, and carry on lively conversation, permitting individual children to depart from the circle at natural break points when you are aware that the parent has arrived. This should be done whenever the parent is truly late. If you simply leave the last child to be picked up on her own while you go about cleaning up, she will have a real feeling of loss. Engage her, if possible, in helping you clean up, or take time for some one-to-one communication with her until the parent arrives.

Suggested Schedules

The rule of thumb for arranging the daily schedule of activities is to balance physical-activity time with quiet time (see Figure 9.2). This section discusses some additional guidelines.

Active/Passive Times

Consider the amount of physical activity of a child and try to balance this with a passive activity. Children tend to get "stuck" in outside or physical worlds and cannot slow down and relax. Some young children, if permitted, would continue to be drunk with running and movement until they were so exhausted they would actually "drop in their tracks." Once you sense that children have had enough activity, move them to story time, puzzles, or similar sedentary activities.

Outside Climate and Weather

To balance outside and inside activities, you must be aware of your general climate and be prepared to make daily adjustments. In tropical climates during the summer months, you might have outside time in the early mornings when it is relatively cool, and stay indoors in the afternoon. The opposite is true for cold climates or winter months, when you might plan to stay inside in the mornings and go outside in the afternoon in the warmer sun.

Motor-Rules and "Mars Day"

A 4-year-old child gets up from snack time. He stands with the back of his legs pushing out the chair, takes three steps to the waste basket, throws out his trash, and begins to walk to the playground door. He suddenly stops; it is apparent that an idea has entered his mind. He returns to his chair and pushes it in under the

FIGURE 9.2   A Typical Schedule

7:30	Arrival
	Play Activity curriculum with one table set with Thematic-Project supervised by one available teacher
8:30	Playground
	Play Activity and Thematic-Project curriculum available
9:15	Circle Time (music, hand games, book reading, or general sharing)
9:45	Toileting/handwashing
	(transitioning into snack)
	Snack
10:30	Thematic-Project curriculum
11:30	Playground
12:00	Circle Time (story reading with transition to toileting, to noon meal)
12:20	Lunch
1:00	Toileting (with transition to rest)
	Rest
3:00	Toileting
3:15	Thematic-Project curriculum
	One-third of children on screened porch or screened outside area
	Play Activity curriculum
	Two-thirds of children inside
	(Note: Children will rotate in thirds to outside porch.)
4:45	Playground
5:25	Circle Time
	Clean-up and Depart
5:45	Close

table, so that no other child will trip over it. This action is a learned "motor-rule" (Piaget, 1965). Adults as well as young children go through their days as if on automatic pilot, moving from one motor action to the next. "Collect your papers from the snack table, stand and move to the trash basket, push in your chair" are all motor-rules that this child has internalized. Once these motor-rules are learned after entering a new school, the child "understands" the structure of the school and gains a sense of security that he can master such a world. This world is predictable; but if, for example, a photographer appears unexpectedly to take group photographs, the schedule of activities is dramatically altered. The children become demanding, whining, wanting to know "why are we not going to do so and so, Mrs. James? When are we going to have snack?" This shows tension and confusion. What is important, then, is to have the children learn quickly the motor-rules for all of the materials and rooms.

Spatial location in our adult world communicates to us motor-rules and behavior, and because we are well socialized, we respond appropriately. In a movie theater, we act with certain defined motor-rules; at a football game, these rules change; at the dinner table, they change again. This is equally true for children. The motor-rules and behavior for the playground, rug-story time, toilet area, snacking, and rest time all demand changes in both child and teacher behavior, and this must be learned.

When young children enter school for the first time, teachers "teach the walls and objects." This means that the teacher starts at the front door of the school and begins to move around the walls, teaching the children the motor-rules of using the storage cupboard, blocks and block shelves, sociodramatic play area, and so on, until objects are "taught." This technique should be repeated at each change throughout the day—the movement to outdoor playground, movement to story time, and so forth. This teaching of "walls and objects" is done using the direct instruction procedure of say, show, check (Bereiter & Engelmann, 1966; Engelmann, 1980). For example:

- *Say:* "Friends, these are the blocks and block shelves. Watch as I take out these three blocks. You will see that there is a paper block shape, here on the shelf, which tells me that this size block and shape goes here."
- *Show:* "Now I am going to ask one of you to put this block back in its 'home.' Look closely—where does this one go? (Teacher holds up wooden arch.) Mike, put this block on the right shelf. (Mike does it correctly.) Friends, is Mike correct?" (Children respond yes.)
- *Check:* "Now, watch closely! I'm going to put these three blocks back one at a time. See if I do this correctly. Is this right? (Children respond yes.) Is this right? (Children respond yes.) Is this right? (places it incorrectly) (Children respond no.) Why not?" (Children explain why not.)

"Now I am going to give each of you three blocks. Let's see whether you can put them back on the shelves, where they will sleep in their homes." The teacher watches the actions of each child to see if he or she knows the concept; if not, the teacher reteaches the child who made an error, again in the three-step lesson of say, show, check. Notice in the "check" step, once the teacher felt that the children knew the concept, she used the negation (she did it "wrong") to see if the children could make the correction (Engelmann, 1980).

At the end of this orientation, the children can answer questions such as: "How are the pencil sharpeners to be used? How do I go to the toilet?" The understanding of these motor-rules gives the child a sense of security in the school world.

Once the children gain an understanding of the use of the classroom components, activities will proceed almost effortlessly. However, after a two- to three-month period, both the children and the teachers begin to neglect the motor-rules, especially if new, improperly oriented staff are added. Puzzle pieces are found scattered among the Lego storage boxes, housekeeping equipment from the sociodramatic play area is lying on the floor, trash is left on tables after snack time, and so on. These are all signs that the structure of classroom order is falling apart—an "accident waiting to happen."

The rule of thumb in open play environments, especially for visitors who are inspecting a new school, is that if teachers and children do not take care of school objects, it is likely that the children are not taken care of properly either. The results of disorder and disarray are increased whining and aggression from children, low levels of play with children simply wandering about looking for something to do, destruction of property, and teachers becoming tense and over-directive with children—wanting to impose more verbal rules. At worst, injury may occur. The solution is to call for "Mars Day."

On "Mars Day" the teacher starts the school "anew," pretending that the children have just arrived on a rocket ship from Mars. In groups of six to eight, the children go around the school with the teacher, learning walls and objects as before, as well as the changes in space and time throughout the daily schedule. The new teacher who is unsure of the motor-rules may join one of these groups and learn the motor-rules right along with the children.

Summary

Techniques have been presented for smoother handling of arrivals, snack eating, meal patterns, rest/sleeping, circle/story time, transitions, departures, schedules, and teaching motor-rules. Take the position that children can be trusted, that their inappropriate actions stem from a lack of ability to behave as you desire. Give them a secure environment where they can learn.

To accomplish this task, you must understand how to arrange a well-balanced classroom, allowing for freedom and control of error. Once a well-designed play environment is created, and the children understand the motor-rules and time schedules, the classroom runs smoothly without the need for excessive teacher control. The teacher is then free to facilitate the children's ongoing play, usually with the Teacher Behavior Continuum, to further their journey toward effectiveness, autonomy, and increased maturity.

Activities

1. Visit three classrooms and collect their schedules of activities for the day. What percentage of time is divided between the three methods of teaching: Play Activity, Thematic-Project, or Direct Instruction? Based on the age of the children in each class, are these time divisions appropriate? Consider the three spheres of relationship: (1) one to one, (2) one to group, and (3) one to all. Do the schedules permit all forms of spheres of relationship or are they heavily weighted to one to the deficit of another? Is there an appropriate division between indoor and outdoor time?

2. Observe three classrooms with young children having snacks. Analyze whether these classrooms are child centered or teacher controlled? Which form has more misbehavior by children?

3. Observe an experienced teacher doing circle time and, with the TBC, tally the types of teacher behavior used for children that might disrupt. Is this high or low profile, or appropriate? Is there a structure that gives children security (control of error) during story time? How do they arrive and depart?

4. Ask two experienced teachers for their lists of classroom rules for young children. Take each one and see how you might reorganize time, space, objects, or children to eliminate each of these rules.

5. Interview a parent who is having a 3-year-old or younger child go off to school or day care for the first time. What are her or his concerns? How does he or she view the child's protesting when the child departs? How does the child reunite? What advice can you give this parent? Observe the parent/child interaction. Can you find a strong modality of communication between the parent and child? Try to communicate with the child in that modality. Interview the teacher and get his or her view of this stressful time. Ask the teacher what actions he or she takes to help with separation.

References

Bereiter, Carl, and Siegfried Engelmann, *Teaching Disadvantaged Children in the Preschool.* Englewood Cliffs, N.J.: Prentice-Hall, 1966.

Canter, Lee, *Assertive Discipline.* Los Angeles: Canter and Associates, 1976.

Dreikurs, Rudolf, *Children: The Challenge.* New York: Hawthorne Books, 1964.

Engelmann, Siegfried, *Direct Instruction.* Englewood Cliffs, N.J.: Educational Technology Publications, 1980.

Freud, Anna, *Normality and Pathology in Childhood: Assessments of Development.* New York: International Universities Press, 1968.

Freud, Anna, *The Ego and the Mechanisms of Defense.* New York: International Universities Press, 1971.

Harris, Thomas A., *I'm OK, You're OK: A Practical Guide to Transactional Analysis.* New York: Harper and Row, 1969.

Mahler, Margaret S., *On Human Symbiosis and the Vicissitudes of Individuation,* New York: International Universities, 1970.

Mahler, Margaret S., and others, *The Psychological Birth of the Human Infant.* New York: Basic Books, 1975.

Peller, Lili E., "Libidinal Phases, Ego Development and Play," in *Psychoanalytic Study of the Child, no. 9.* New York: International Universities Press, 1959.

Phelps, Pamela, personal communication, 1984.

Piaget, Jean, *The Moral Judgment of the Child* (trans. Marjorie Gabain). New York: Free Press, 1965.

Speers, Rex W., *Variations in Separation-Individuation and Implications for Play Ability and Learning as Studied in the Three-Year-Old in Nursery School.* Pittsburgh: University of Pittsburgh Press, 1970.

Speers, Rex W., and others, "Recapitulation of Separation-Individuation Processes When the Normal Three-Year-Old Enters Nursery School," in *Separation-Individuations, Essays in Honor of Margaret Mahler,* John McDevitt, ed. New York: International Universities Press, 1970.

Toffler, Alvin, *Future Shock.* New York: Bantam Books, 1971.

10

The Child with
Special Needs

Matthew, a precocious 4-year-old, is organizing a group of children in the housekeeping area. "I'm the dad, and it's time for me to go to work. Becka, you be the mommy, Shawn is the baby, and Emily is Grandma," says Matthew. Becka replies, "It's your day to take Shawn to school. Here's your hat and briefcase."

Matthew takes the hand of Shawn, who has been rocking back and forth on the floor at the edge of the group, and leads him over to the chairs that become the car. Shawn throws himself on the floor and screams, biting at his hand and kicking his legs in the air. Mrs. Davis, the teacher, intervenes, drawing Shawn into her lap, gently rocking him and saying into his ear, "You can say no, Shawn. You can say *no* to Matthew." Shawn seems to withdraw into his inner world, shaking his head back and forth, repeating to himself, "No, no, no, no, no, no. No. No."

Shawn's speech and language development are at least two years behind his chronological age of 4 years. His typical behavior is passive and withdrawn. When any social demands are made on him, he falls apart in what looks like a temper tantrum. He has an older brother at home with autistic characteristics, some of which Shawn has picked up, such as echoing speech, head rocking, and hand shaking. The teachers wish to make a significant contribution to Shawn's developmental progress—while continuing to provide a high-quality program for the rest of the children.

About six weeks after Shawn started at preschool, his mother approached the preschool director and said, "I'm going to take Shawn out of this school. When he first came, he was a little behind in language, but at least he was well behaved. Do you know what he did last night? He got a fluorescent marker and drew scribbles all over the walls in his room. He has just gotten worse and worse since he came here." The director discussed with Shawn's mom that what she was seeing was 2-year-old aggressive behavior in a 4-year-old body. For Shawn, this was progress. What Shawn had shown earlier was aggressive behavior more commonly observed in infancy.

The director discussed how children's development moves through stages of passivity, aggression, and verbal expression—before self-control and the use of language to get needs met and to solve problems begins to emerge. Shawn's body had kept growing, but some other areas of development had slowed down or gotten off track. The mother got some tips on coping with the "terrible 2s" and channeling that aggression into acceptable forms of behavior; for example, she got some big pads of paper and gave them to Shawn for specific use with markers.

When Grandma came to visit Shawn, she brought a large, very expensive picture book. Shawn grinned with delight, took it to his room, and later proudly returned to show it to her. She called out aghast to her daughter, "Look what he's done!" Shawn's mother, after seeing that he had scribbled all through the book with marker, said, "Shawn, I am glad to see you remembered that markers are for paper." Shawn's mother had begun to understand about development and acceptable alternatives, but she had a lot of explaining to do to Grandma! Now she knew that it was time to begin to teach Shawn which paper is appropriate to write on and which is not.

During the next month, Shawn was out on the playground riding a tricycle, which had become one of his favorite activities. The wind blew his hat off, and when he got off the tricycle to retrieve it, another child got on. Shawn stood in front of the tricycle growling and grimacing at the other child; the teacher, observing, called out, "Shawn, use words." Shawn responded in his loudest voice to the child on the trike, "USE WORDS!" The teacher realized that Shawn still needed her to model for him what words should be used, so she said, "Say, 'Mine. That's my bike.'" He said, "My bike"—and he got it back through the use of words.

Gradually, Shawn became friendly with Stephen, who was a great "pretend" player. Shawn began to play and talk a little more, first with Stephen, and then with other "good players" who were encouraged by the teacher to join the "pretend" play. Everyone was pleased with Shawn's progress, and eventually he was able to attend a small individualized kindergarten class in the local public school.

Shawn's story exemplifies some of the benefits of integrating a child with exceptional needs into a child-centered program that uses the Teacher Behavior Continuum teaching strategies. Shawn can learn appropriate social behaviors through imitating the other children. Some of the social attitudes and skills Shawn can learn are sharing, cooperating, respecting the property of others, and modifying aggressive acts and impulses. The teacher can help Shawn move through the social stages from unoccupied to onlooker, to solitary play, to parallel play, to associative play, and to cooperative play. The Record of Teacher's Play Facilitation on pages 83 to 85 can help the teacher plan an intervention strategy.

Children with developmental disabilities and delays generally move along the same developmental track as children who do not have such difficulties, but at a slower pace in some areas. The teacher will probably have to start at the more structured end of the Teacher Behavior Continuum. He or she needs to provide external structures that the child does not yet have internally. With Shawn, the teacher provided the external model of the appropriate language he needed to use to get his trike back. Like a child with a broken leg who must wear a cast until the inner leg is healed and strong enough to function, the internal structures of the child with developmental delays need to be strengthened to function effectively, as in impulse control or in the use of language. The teacher must provide external support, through modeling and physical intervention, until the child has internalized the needed skills and these become strong enough to function without the teacher's direct help.

As the child makes developmental progress, the teacher can move back from modeling to directive statements, questioning, nondirective statements, and eventually simply providing the visual support of looking on. With Shawn, the teacher made the mistake of using a directive statement when what he needed was modeling. She quickly self-corrected and modeled, "That's my bike."

Inclusion

Inclusion, formerly referred to as *mainstreaming,* has become a popular approach to educating children with disabilities. *Inclusion* can be defined as placing children with disabilities into educational programs for and with nondisabled children (Odom & Karnes, 1988). This approach toward educating children who have disabilities in the least restrictive environment (i.e., in close proximity to normally developing peers) began in the 1970s with a keystone piece of legislation, PL 94-142. The benefits of this approach for the child with disabilities could include the following:

- *Improved social interactions*
- *More normal behavior*
- *Improved language development*
- *More independence*
- *Possible educational/developmental benefits, depending on the program and the teacher's intervention. (Odom & McEvoy, 1988)*

Not only does the child with special needs benefit, but the nondisabled children benefit, as well. They learn, at an early age, to live with children who are "different." The differences become less important as the children begin to play together and learn one another's individual strengths, and they learn they can truly be friends and co-players.

Public Laws 94-142 and 99-457

Until the late 1960s, children with noticeable disabilities either stayed at home or were sent to institutions to be educated. In 1975, Public Law 94-142 was passed, requiring that each state provide access to a free educational program within the public school system to all "handicapped" children between the ages of 3 and 18. This right was further expanded for children with special needs, focusing on infants and toddlers, with the later passage of Public Law 99-457, which gave parents clear rights in designing and guiding the intervention or educational program for their child with special needs. These programs are required to promote the highest degree of self-sufficiency possible and must be provided in the "least restrictive environment" or as close as possible to the same environment as non-disabled children. PL 94-142 requires school programs to have the following components: (1) identification of children who may need services, (2) evaluation of the kind and degree of need, and (3) intervention. Each eligible child within the public school services area would have an individualized education plan (IEP). This IEP would involve the parents, child, teachers, and administrators and would include an assessment of the child's present level of achievement, long- and short-term educational goals, services to be provided, and the degree of integration with the normal program.

The rationale behind PL 94-142 and the legal imperative to provide education in the least restrictive setting stems from the view that a child's civil rights are violated when he or she is segregated from normally developing children and thus presumably from a more effective program (Odom & McEvoy, 1988). A further rationale is that children with disabilities might be helped developmentally to acquire more advanced skills when they can observe and participate with children who are modeling age-appropriate behaviors.

Who Are the Children with Special Needs?

Many labels are used in trying to categorize children with special needs. Some of the terms that can be helpful to the teacher of young children in gathering information and planning for each child include *physically challenged, cerebral palsied, emotionally disturbed, mentally disabled, hearing impaired, visually impaired, learning disabled, autistic,* and *developmentally delayed.*

The following guidelines (adapted from National Easter Seal Society Guidelines) are helpful for thinking about and planning for children with disabilities:

1. Emphasize the uniqueness and worth of all children rather than differences between children.
2. Keep the individual in perspective: Avoid emphasizing the disability to the exclusion of individual achievements.
3. Think about ways the child with a disability can do something independently, or for another child.
4. Provide an environment where the child with a disability participates in activities with children without disabilities in ways that are mutually beneficial and inclusive rather than in those that foster the attitude of "one of them" vs. "one of us."

The Teacher's Role

The preschool teacher may identify a child with a learning difficulty, or may accept and integrate into the classroom a child with an already determined disability. In either case, the child with a disability should be viewed and treated first as a child, like other children. Typical patterns of child development will apply to children with disabilities, while disability-related information may provide some unique insights and techniques to add. The teacher must tap into all available sources of information—including parents, doctors, local experts, the library, and community resources and associations—to find out what to do to help that particular child.

If a child's behavior is outside the teacher's sphere of expertise, he or she will need to refer the child and family to community resources for some specialized kinds of diagnosis and treatment.

Young children generally exhibit a great variety of individual differences. Early childhood materials and activities are designed to be used at varying skill levels. For example, easel painting can be done to some extent by any child, with or without a disability, who can hold a paintbrush. The levels of skill and symbolic development are sophisticated nuances that the teacher well trained in child development can best understand, analyze, and facilitate. The Teacher Behavior Continuum provides the ideal structure for the teacher to individualize both educational and social interventions with children who have disabilities, as well as with those who do not.

At a practical level, there are two processes that can help the teacher provide for a child with special needs in the classroom: a staffing process and a written individualized education plan (IEP).

Individualized Education Plan

The staffing process would bring together specialists such as teachers of young children, administrators, and psychologists to create an individualized education plan (IEP). In doing so, much time may be spent in determining "who is in charge" or who is chairing the meeting and what are the roles of individuals around the table, as well as listening to anecdotal evidence for the correctness of certain members' "personal wisdom." For an effective working staff meeting, we suggest a preestablished structure based on the following six steps:

1. *Statement of problem(s)*
2. *Generating possible solutions*
3. *Evaluating solutions*
4. *Deciding on solutions*
5. *Implementing*
6. *Evaluation (Gordon, 1974)*

For each step, an arbitrary set of rules is established regarding who may speak, time allotted, and purposes. (*Note:* The classroom teacher chairs the meeting and, in the seating arrangement, places himself or herself at the end of the table in a power position. Administrators attending the meeting are considered the teacher's staff and assistants, not authorities.) A timekeeper should be appointed by the teacher.

- *Step 1. Statement of Problem(s):* Overview of the student's behavior (time: 15 minutes)

    Purpose: To gather all necessary information about the child *before* moving to possible solutions

    Procedures: The chair ascertains that all members are informed about data that have been collected. If formal test data are available, all members should have received and read copies before the meeting. The following information is then presented: Teacher's Statement (teacher only) regarding the behavior of the child; Teacher Background Information (teacher only, or specialist who has collected background information); and all members' contributions to background information (all staff).

    a. The teacher who is chairing the committee opens the discussion or overview of the child's needs and behavior. If the teacher has had previous experience with the child, she or he would discuss typical behaviors or incidents that have occurred, and describe what type of intervention has taken place and the results.

    b. The teacher or any other specialist who has collected any form of data reports it at this time. These data might be results on any packaged program checklist or formal test, the Adjustment Behavioral Profile, Behavioral Play Profiles (Parten's social stages, developmental level in the classification of play, use of play materials), and so on.

c. The meeting is now open for input from any other members who have information such as profile, testing, or baseline data. No solutions are to be proposed at this time.

Guideline for timekeeper: Let the group know when the 10-minute mark occurs.

- *Step 2. Generating Possible Solutions* (time: 10 minutes)

Purpose: To facilitate the entire group's "brainstorming" of possible actions to help this child, and to draw on the techniques available in the three teaching models

Procedures: Each staff member should quickly outline on paper his or her ideas for solutions, answering the questions, and the time, space, and object changes needed by this child so that his or her special needs are met. Then all members would orally present their suggestions, one at a time around the table. Criticism is not permitted during this step, as it might inhibit the creative idea exchange.

- *Step 3. Evaluating Solutions* (time: 10 minutes)

Purpose: To open critical evaluation of the range of possible actions and to gain consensus

Procedures: Staff members now discuss what their suggestions have in common. As much as possible the chair should draw on the constructs and techniques discussed in this book, asking such questions as, "Can the child's needs best be served by play-activity experiences, or through direct instruction? Can we use techniques from these models?" (*Note:* It is important in this step that the teacher and staff have progressed from "personal wisdom" and speculative thinking to designing intervention using a more scientific basis. "Personal wisdom" based speculation is where teachers try to solve and design intervention by "stabbing in the dark." The established techniques provide a framework for more scientific problem solving. Next, the five to six suggestions with the most support could be listed on a chalkboard.

- *Step 4. Deciding on solutions* (time: 20 minutes)

Purpose: To agree on, in writing, an orderly plan, including goals

Procedures: The staff comes to a written agreement on steps, procedures, goals, and a plan by using the IEP form (see Figure 10.1). Responsibilities are accepted by staff members, and the IEP signed. Also required is an agreement as to when the committee will reconvene for step 6, evaluation.

- *Step 5. Implementing* (time: preestablished in Step 4)

Purpose: To carry out the intervention responsibly

Procedures: The intervention is carried out.

- *Step 6. Evaluation* (time: 20 minutes)

Purpose: To meet to reevaluate the success of the plan

FIGURE 10.1   Individualized Education Plan

Student's Name _____

                                          Birthday   ___/___/___/

School _____   Date   ___/___/___/

Teacher _____

Staff Members   _____

                            _____

                            _____

I. Student's Behavior

a. General Concern: _____

_____

b. Developmental Level of Functioning: _____

_____

_____

c. Specific Improvement Desired: _____

II. Goals and Action(s) to be Taken:

a. _____

By Whom: _____

Teaching Strategies: _____

_____

Success Criteria: _____

_____

Date
Start ___/___/___/   Accomp. ___/___/___/

b. _____

Staffing Members (signatures):

Teacher: _____

                    _____

                    _____

                    _____

Procedure: This meeting would take place after a reasonable amount of time has gone by, permitting everyone to fulfill his or her role in the IEP—or at the end of a teaching unit, or any other reasonable break in time. Any member of the committee may call for an earlier date if it becomes obvious that the IEP is not working as intended.

Activities

1. Interview an experienced teacher for his or her suggestions for working with children with disabilities.
2. Visit an early childhood site and observe the most difficult child, and the manner of intervening with him or her. Is it possible that this child might have a developmental delay or disability and that a referral for specialized services might help?
3. Observe three young children with disabilities in a play or art setting. Plan how you would use the TBC to help them move toward the next developmental level. (Use the Record of Teacher's Play Facilitation on pages 83 to 85.)
4. What are the advantages and disadvantages of labeling children "developmentally different" at an early age?

References

Gordon, Thomas, *T.E.T.: Teacher Effectiveness Training.* New York: Peter H. Wyden, 1974.

Odom, S. L., & M. Karnes, eds., *Early Intervention for Infants and Children with Handicaps: An Empirical Base.* Baltimore: Paul H. Brooks, 1988.

Odom, S. L., & M. A. McEvoy, "Integrating of Young Children with Handicaps and Normally Developing Children," in *Intervention for Infants and Children with Handicaps: An Empirical Base.* Baltimore: Paul H. Brooks, 1988.

11

Working with Parents

COWRITTEN WITH BETH QUICK

Parent involvement has deep roots in early education. Increasingly, collaboration among home, school, and community is necessary to ensure that every child's learning potential is realized and that educational experiences are appropriate and optimal for the child's development. With the growing diversity of families and children, it becomes important that teachers know and utilize multiple strategies for dealing with all the participants in a child's education. This will include interaction with parents and may also involve special education teachers, early intervention specialists, social workers, counselors, and others.

Families continue to grow and change, and with these changes teachers face increasing challenges to build relationships to support the development of the young children they teach. The number of children living in the traditional nuclear family (parents married for the first time, living together with their biological children, and no other adults or children living in the home) continues to decline as varying and different family configurations emerge. The single parent is now one of the most common family units. Additionally, the number of children living in a blended family or stepfamily continues to grow.

Just as family units grow and change, so does the population of the United States. This is reflected in the growing diversity of languages and cultures represented in the children and families served by early childhood education. More than 30 million Americans speak a language other than English at home, and more than another 13 million "do not speak English well" (U.S. Bureau of the Census, 1991). Similarly, children of various ethnic backgrounds attend early education programs due to the increase of intercultural and interethnic marriages (Barbour & Barbour, 1997). The effects of poverty are particularly profound on young children: In 1990, one out of every five children in the United States lived in poverty (Lamison-White, 1991).

Children represent a wide array of family units, cultures, ethnicities, and religions. They and their families bring diversity to their classroom experiences and relationships. This diversity is furthered by the increasing number of children with disabilities who attend regular education or inclusion classrooms. When teaching a child with disabilities, it is not sufficient merely to understand the disability; teachers must also understand the impact of the disability on the parents and family unit.

Communicating with Families

The configuration and diversity of families continues to grow and change, but teachers must continue to meet the challenge of building relationships with all families of the children they teach. Both the family and the teacher are responsible for educating children. We will explore a variety of communication strategies, some traditional and others more innovative, that can be helpful in establishing and maintaining partnerships with parents. Additionally, strategies for dealing with difficult parents will be addressed.

Teacher Attitudes

Research on successful U.S. companies, chronicled in the bestseller *In Search of Excellence* (Peters & Waterman, 1982), points out that these companies understand how important it is to "go the extra mile" for consumers. Teachers' attitudes convey their willingness to build a similar relationship with parents. Listening to parents, and accommodating their needs when possible, communicates true concern for children and families—the "consumers," or clients, of education.

Newsletters

A weekly or monthly newsletter can provide a source of regular ongoing communication between teachers and parents. The format may be a simple handwritten photocopied letter or a more sophisticated letter created by desktop publishing software. What is important is not the format, but the information— and the effort to provide the information. Items in a newsletter might include:

Current themes or topics of study
Staff changes
Procedures from the parent handbook to serve as friendly reminders
Personal announcements ("Mrs. Walker had an 8-pound baby girl")

Arrival or departure of students ("Our newest class member is . . .")
Community activities of interest to parents and children
Decisions made by the parent/teacher board
Suggested resources for parents and children
Accomplishments or remarks of children

Parent Resource Room or Lending Library

A small bookshelf or separate room or closet can be dedicated for display and storage of books and videotapes that would be helpful to parents. With a simple system established for checking out resources, parents can take the resources home to read or view. Some schools have extended this idea to other resources, such as children's board games, puzzles, and building blocks, which parents can also check out to use at home with their children for a given period of time.

Back-to-School Night

This traditional event is often highly successful, since parents are eager to meet their child's new teacher and learn about the educational program. Teachers can use this opportunity to help parents better understand the curriculum, classroom arrangement, and expectations for children's growth and development. Time reserved for questions and answers can be quite helpful. Usually, the meeting is held on a weekday evening or a Saturday morning so working parents can attend.

Parent Workshops or Education Groups

Workshops for parents will be more successful if parents are surveyed to determine what topics are of interest to them. The workshops or meetings can range from a single three-hour session to a month-long series of meetings on a particular subject. Meetings can be offered periodically or whenever a need arises. Topics might include child development, discipline and behavior issues, budget and finance concerns, and so on. Sessions might be led by teachers or by an outside expert invited to speak.

Covered-Dish Dinners and Socials

Periodically plan an evening where parents and children can come together to meet and eat. This might be planned in conjunction with the conclusion of a unit of study, so that children can share products, songs, or skits related to the completed unit. A reservation system would be preferable to determine how many participants to expect. Occasionally, a guest speaker might be invited to speak. A similar event could be planned where all grandparents are invited to attend and see their grandchildren participate in a drama or musical presentation.

Art and Product Display

Save and label the children's paintings, books, and similar products. Ask a local appliance dealer for large upright refrigerator boxes, which stand up easily, and at the end of a unit, attach the children's products to it. Have a two-day art display in an indoor hallway, entrance area, or playground.

School/Home Activity Packs

Help parents extend topics or units of study at home by providing suggestions of supplementary books, activities, cooking projects, or experiences the parent and child might do together. This can be as simple as a printed calendar that gives suggestions for each day corresponding to the unit of study (e.g., for a unit on plants, "Go on a nature walk and look for a variety of plants") or you might provide tote bags that children can take home. Each tote bag could contain items necessary to complete an activity to support the unit of study.

Toy or Book Exchange

Children sometimes grow tired of or outgrow their toys and books. Provide a time once or twice a year for parents to bring children's unwanted toys and books (some schools include clothing, as well) so parents can exchange items or perhaps sell them for a small price.

Telephone Tutor or Message System

With a telephone answering system or call-forwarding, the school can provide assistance and information. A telephone answering system might be structured so that parents could leave messages for individual teachers after hearing a brief message about the skills and concepts the children are currently learning. Call-forwarding might allow parents a way to reach a teacher or director after hours with emergency information or pertinent questions.

Suggestion Box

A suggestion box placed in a high-traffic area, such as in an entry way or front hallway, allows parents to share comments, concerns, questions, and compliments with the school anonymously. The availability of a suggestion box reminds parents that the school values and desires parental input and participation.

Saturday Work Day

Both mothers and fathers might enjoy getting some hands-on experience building structures on your playground or assisting in remodeling or refurbishing projects. This event should be well planned, with all necessary materials and equipment available. We had one very proud child say, "My daddy built this bench!" Many evenings he would ask his father to sit with him on "their bench."

Drop In/Planned Lunch

Invite parents to drop in for lunch with their child once a month. Or, at the end of units throughout the year, invite manageable groups of parents to the classroom and allow the children to serve their parents foods they have prepared related to a unit of study. Tablecloths, a printed menu, and aprons or uniforms for the "wait staff" can complement the restaurant set-up.

Breakfasts

Plan several mornings throughout the year to have pastries or fruit, coffee, tea, or juice available so parents may stay for 10 to 15 minutes to have breakfast and carry on casual conversation with teachers and other parents.

Parent Message Book

The parent message book allows parents to write any messages they wish to give to the staff each morning, thus supporting two-way communication.

Family/Child Entertainment Day

Pick one entertainment day, such as when the circus is in town, and buy a block of seats where all the families and children from your school may be seated together.

Holiday Celebration

Organize a seasonal holiday celebration as a social event for parents, children, and families.

Toddler Morning

The school can host a toddler day where siblings from ages 1 to 3 are invited to the school along with their parents. This allows them an opportunity to experience the school, perhaps on the playground if weather permits.

Parent/Teacher Conferences

Parent/teacher conferences provide a valuable source of information and an opportunity for personal communication. These are usually scheduled at least twice a year to share development information and insights concerning the child's growth. Additional conferences may be scheduled at the parents' request or as the teacher deems necessary. Work samples, photographs, and anecdotal notes can help parents understand changes in the child's development. Here are some guidelines for the conference:

1. Be prepared for the conference. Gather all the information you have available concerning the child.
2. Begin and end the conference on a positive note. If there is a concern to be communicated, it is best done in the middle of the conference (Fuller & Olsen, 1998).
3. Allow time and encourage parents to ask questions or share information concerning their child.
4. Help parents arrive at solutions to problems that really belong to them. Read the explanation of problem ownership in Gordon's (1974) *Teacher Effectiveness Training.*
5. Conferences should be held at a convenient time for parents. Allow for privacy and, if possible, provide child care for siblings so parents can attend the conference without the responsibility of caring for children.
6. Stay on schedule so that other parents who are waiting for a conference time are not inconvenienced.
7. At the end of the conference, summarize the agreements made, write them down, and put them in the child's folder (Cherry, 1987).
8. If necessary, share information from the conference with other school personnel, support services personnel, special education personnel and so on.

Parent Handbook

A parent handbook is an excellent way to inform both teachers and parents about your classroom and school philosophy and procedures. It can include information concerning the following topics:

Teachers' education and experience
Financial costs and methods of payment
Health and safety matters
Appropriate clothing and necessary supplies
Car pool and transportation procedures
Nutrition

Policy on children bringing toys or objects from home
Sickness policy
Overview of program philosophy
Typical daily schedule

Telephone List

With parents' permission, provide each family with a class or school roster containing the names, addresses, and families of each child and family enrolled. The roster will facilitate communication among families.

Parent Bulletin Board

A strategically placed bulletin board reserved for sharing and displaying information with parents can be a valuable means of communication. The board should be in a prominent place and contain interesting, relevant information that is changed and updated regularly.

Babysitting List

Some schools provide a list of babysitters available to families on weekends or evenings. These names could be obtained from local Girl Scout troops, high schools, or older siblings of enrolled children.

Home Visits

Some teachers go to the home of each child enrolled in their class at the beginning of the school year; however, home visits can be done any time during the year. Be sensitive to parents by writing a note or making a phone call to request a specific time to visit, and allow parents to refuse a home visit. Home visits allow teachers to obtain valuable information about the child and home environment, to meet the child and family, and to learn how to support the child's transition to school.

School Gate Parent/Teacher Discussion

When a child is picked up by a parent at the end of the day, the brief teacher/parent verbal exchange presents a critical opportunity to reassure parents and share information, successes, or concerns related to the child's experiences that day. Assign one teacher (normally the lead teacher) to be available to speak with parents during the first hour in the morning and the last hour at the end of the day.

Addressing Parents' Concerns and Complaints

When Accidents Occur

In a classroom of active young children, accidents will happen. When an accident does occur, a report should be completed, detailing the nature of the accident and what the teacher did in response to it. Most parents know that bumps and scrapes are normal, but they will be upset if they find a severe mark or bruise on their child. Parents who discover such a scratch or bruise often believe the teacher was not supervising the children properly; thus, the teacher should report any marks, bruises, or injury to parents at the end of the day, as well as what was done about it. It is advisable to keep a small, fairly inexpensive ($200 for 75 children) school accident insurance policy. If a child's tooth is knocked out at school, the policy pays all medical expenses. If there is a serious accident, the head teacher or director should call the child's home that evening to find out how the child is doing.

Handling Parents' Complaints

Be sure staff and teachers understand that all parent complaints must be reported. Establish a system for recording and documenting this information. It is advisable to survey parents every six to eight months to determine their concerns and views of the classroom and school. Many times, this can offset parent complaints.

Dealing with Difficult Parents and Situations

Though most parents are cooperative, supportive, and concerned about their child and the success of his or her experiences at school, occasionally some parents or situations with parents will present difficult encounters or circumstances with which a teacher must cope. Specific strategies can be helpful when experiencing an awkward or difficult situation with parents. Let's turn our attention to those now.

Parents' Problems
The day-to-day life of the teacher is almost never free of questions or problems stemming from relationships with parents or students. Parents' statements, questions, and behaviors—sometimes seemingly destructive behaviors—are signals that alert teachers to parents' needs and those of their children. How can teachers make sense of this continuous parental input, prioritizing needs and making reasonable responses? On what basis would you make a decision to take action as a teacher in the following situations?

Situation 1: The "Hole" In the Donut
Holly's parents are full-fledged "yuppies." Her father is personable, greets you warmly, and is always ready to question you about the latest "how to parent"

book, public television program on children, or article on "how to raise your children smarter" that he has found in an "inflight" magazine. His attitude was described by one teacher, with some frustration; as: "He always sees the 'hole' in the donut!"

Holly's dad wants the school to provide him with a parallel curriculum so he and his daughter can have specific hours set aside for instruction. Holly's mother is a volunteer for a host of social actions in the city, and is first to respond when parent help is called for. She is well liked by teachers, but periodically brings questions from her husband: "Jim wants to know . . . "

There is always an urgency and intensity to their demands, though they are grateful and positive toward teacher observations and suggestions. After a school pageant, they were very displeased that their daughter did not have a more central part to play.

Situation 2: New Role Demands and Family Separation

Jason, a new student, is 3 years old and has a brother, apparently much preferred by the parents, who is age 8. His father has opened a new store located near the school, and his mother has just returned to a full-time job on the opposite side of town. Father's new responsibilities include getting the boys up, getting breakfast, making lunch, and dropping the boys off at school. He is at the school gate 15 to 30 minutes before the school opens. When teachers arrive early to make preparations, he requests that Jason be allowed to enter early so he can get to his store. Normally, Jason enters the school carrying a bag containing an Egg McMuffin and orange juice.

During the first three weeks of school, Dad forgot Jason's lunch on four occasions. On the first and second occasion, he returned at 11:45 A.M. with a pizza and cola for Jason, to the envy of all the other children. On the third occasion, he appeared after lunch was half over, carrying a fast-food hamburger and soda. The fourth time, he forgot completely. Because of father's morning haste, there is no time to talk to him, and when mother is informed at the end of the day, when she picks Jason up, her response is, "That's his responsibility. Tell him about it, not me." Jason is a personable child, greeting you with a warm smile much like that of his father, which makes you feel special; but at times, especially when he is asked to do a task, his expression becomes flat and emotionless. He usually responds to a new activity, no matter how simple, with, "No, I can't do it." During these times, when he seems to pull inside himself, he also pulls at his hair on one side of his head, until now he has a number of bald spots.

Situation 3: Aggressive Behavior

Robert is the only son of a rugged, athletic, chain-smoking father and an attractive primary school teacher mother. Because of recent moves, he has been in and out of a number of day-care centers. He is a thin-featured, pale-complexioned (to the point of looking anemic), tense child who appears as tightly coiled as a spring. He cannot look a teacher directly in the eyes, and usually turns away when invited to join activities. At lunch or snack, he seats himself with the more excitable boys, and uses bathroom talk in a whispered, covert manner, whipping the boys into a giggling frenzy that usually ends with their throwing food at each other. When the teacher approaches to stop this behavior, Robert puts his head down, smiles slightly, and acts as if he is totally innocent.

His most productive behavior is during story time, when his eyes are focused on the teacher and the book. It is rare that the teacher finds a book to read to the group that his parents have not already read to him. His answers to questions after story readings are insightful, animated, and show understanding as well as enjoyment of books (recall that his mother is a primary teacher).

During play activity curriculum, Robert is like a caged tiger, normally crouched in a protective corner in the block room, wanting to use the materials but not feeling free to do so. His attitude stems from fear that if he starts a block structure, someone will destroy it. This nearly total fearful and untrusting view of his peers causes him to lash out with sharp fingernails, sometimes directly at the other children's eyes, and to repeatedly bite peers for the most minor contact. After his aggression, he tells the teacher that the other child was hostile to him; but upon investigation, it usually turns out that the other child merely bumped him accidentally or inadvertently stepped on one of his toys. During conferences, his mother refuses to discuss the behavior, changing the topic to his performance in the more academic curriculum.

On the rare occasions when the father picks him up, the father seems impatient to get in and get out. Robert complicates this by refusing to come when called, running to the opposite side of the playground, causing his father to move after him. The frustrated father, when he feels no teacher is looking, strikes Robert sharply on the backside and departs with Robert crying and being dragged by one arm. Robert also refuses to depart with his mother. She reacts by whispering in his ear with bribes of candy or gifts that she has for him in the car. Last week, the mother and father separated, and when school closed yesterday, there was no one to pick him up. The home and emergency numbers provided by Robert's parents at registration time were called with no results. Robert was taken home by the head teacher; repeated telephone calls were made with no success, and Robert spent the night at the teacher's house.

Situation 4: Sexual Actions and Apparent Injuries

Carol's mother has a new boyfriend who brings Carol to school, normally an hour to two late each morning. She appears wearing black leotards, a tank top, and, on one occasion, a red lacy garter belt. The boyfriend does not come into the school, but leaves 4-year-old Carol at the school gate with a kiss that appears passionate and adult-like. Carol is a beautiful child with long black hair and large round eyes, but a nervous smile. She often drops her eyes when spoken to by the teacher and turns away, looking over her shoulder in a coy manner. She is not defiant but simply passive and noncompliant to teachers. For the last two weeks, she has been preoccupied with masturbation, and repeatedly attempts to enlist others to join her in parallel fashion or to masturbate her.

Female teachers first talked to Carol in a supportive manner, asking her not to "do that." This counseling escalated to outright demands that she stop inviting others to join her. She repeatedly gets the children who are more easily controlled to go behind the storage shed, where they are found with their dresses up and fingers in their panties. The behavior is so repetitive and excessive that a teacher is assigned to watch her at all times, but she is expert at concealing her lower body behind the toys, or the sand table, or the block shelves, while she signals a nearby child to watch what she is doing. She was seen having the boys place their fingers in her, as she and they giggled. One of the boys reported this to his mother, who came to school and announced: "My child is being sexually abused by this 4-year-old girl and I want something done immediately, or I will call the child abuse number." The following day, Carol came to school walking as if in pain, and was found to be bruised and bleeding in her anal area.

Most teachers will realize that some of these parent situations are clearly not serious, while others might call for consulting or legal action. However, each situation does demand a degree of teacher intervention; each situation requires the teacher to make a reasoned decision.

To respond effectively to these situations, you must determine what degree of power would be appropriately used in your intervention. Various incidents might call for simply a relationship-listening response, while others would call for a confronting-contracting response, a logical consequences response, or even a legalistic-coercive approach that goes beyond your or the school's authority. The following construct may be useful in determining appropriate teacher responses to particular parent situations.

Needs of Students

The preceding four examples involved Holly's parents (with their competitiveness and "hole-in-the-donut" questions), Jason's father (new role demands and family separations), Robert (aggressive behavior and parent difficulty in handling him), and Carol (excessive sexual actions and apparent injuries). Obviously, each of the situations is related to a need of the parent or child. Analyzing these needs by using a construct such as Maslow's hierarchy of needs can give order to what might appear to be unrelated behaviors of parents and children:

Level 4:   Self-actualization
Level 3:   Belonging
Level 2:   Security
Level 1:   Physiological

From a Maslowian position, before parents or children can gain self-fulfill-ment, their lower needs must be met: One must first meet the *physiological* needs of food, water, and basic physical health care (needs that were not met in situation 4, when Carol was physically injured).

Once these physiological needs are attained, *security* can become a focus for a parent's or student's energies. The teacher can attempt to help establish these feelings of security. (Robert, in situation 3, exemplified a child with fears of others' aggression.) The next hierarchial need is *belonging:* attaining a degree of respect from one's peers and those to whom one is related (situation 1, Holly's parent's competitiveness.) It is only after these three needs have been met that a person can experience *self-actualization,* or the feeling of self-worth.

Within the context of Maslow's theory, it is suggested that a teacher can ana-lyze the behavior of the parents and identify what need of the child is being blocked and where this would fall in the Maslowian hierarchy. The teacher is then ready to evaluate the degree of severity of these problems.

Degrees of Crisis

When looking at the human needs underlying some of the problems portrayed in the previous situations, it is apparent that the degree of seriousness of the situation may vary from life or psychologically threatening (sexual abuse, physical injury) to limited seriousness (social competitiveness of Holly's parents). Moving through Maslow's needs hierarchy, one sees a classification of crises: (1) imminent crisis (2) developing crisis, and (3) potential crisis (McMurrain, 1975).

Imminent Crisis

An imminent crisis is a situation in which the *physiological* needs (level 1) are involved, and there is a life-threatening situation. If Carol's injuries are not immediately treated with medical care, irreversible damage will occur. Time is of the utmost importance with this incident.

Developing Crisis

Developing crises are generally related to the blocked needs of *security* (level 2). The consequences are serious, but there appears to be more time to head off the event. Robert's loss of home and home stability constitutes a developing crisis. If changes do not occur, his behavior will likely continue to regress, with the potential to become an imminent crisis. In the situation of Jason and his busy parents, another blocked need is *belonging* (level 3), which also suggests a develop-ing level of crisis.

Potential Crisis

With the desire of Holly's parents for their child to be always special, the need level is *esteem* (level 4) and there is a potential crisis. The situation might be strongly felt by the parent, but the seriousness is related to a blow to self-esteem.

The Teacher's Helping Behavior

With the understanding of the two correlated constructs—Maslow's levels of need, and levels of crisis—we come to the question of what responding actions the teacher should take. The answer is found in the continuum of human relationship models, which can be classified under the headings of relationship-listening, confronting-contracting, rules and consequences, and legalistic-coercive. The degree of power of the teacher's intervention would escalate or deescalate with relation to the level of needs and the severity of the crisis (see Table 11.1).

In the case of Holly's parents, with their social competitiveness, the need level is esteem, and there is a potential level of crisis. The helping techniques for the teacher are found in the relationship-listening model. Gordon's (1974) *Teacher Effectiveness Training (TET)* discusses problem ownership and how to establish an accepting relationship to help the parents gain some emotional control and do some problem solving to meet their own needs (see Figure 11.1).

In the case of Jason's parents with their busy schedules, the blocked need is belonging, which suggests a developing crisis. The techniques of confronting-contracting seen in Glasser's (1967, 1969) and Dreikurs and Cassell's (1972) book would be most useful for the teacher in dealing with such situations. Both models place a high value on getting needs met in a social context and give clear suggestions as to how to accomplish a positive sense of belonging (see Figure 11.2).

In the case of Robert, with his aggressive behavior and the family separation, the need level is security and the level of crisis can be considered as developing. The teacher in this instance may choose techniques under rules and consequences. This means that with Robert *and his parents* the teacher would specify actions to be carried out by Robert's parents. If they carried out these actions,

TABLE 11.1   Needs, Crises, and Relationship Models

Need	Crisis	Model
Level 4 Esteem	Potential	Relationship-Listening
Level 3 Belonging	Developing	Confronting-Contracting
Level 2 Security	Developing	Rules and Consequences
Level 1 Psychological	Imminent	Coercive-Legalistic

FIGURE 11.1   Techniques for Use with Holly/Competitive Parents

Need: Level 4—Esteem
Crisis: Potential
Model: Relationship-Listening
Teacher Effectiveness Training (Gordon)
Critical listening
Acknowledgment of responses
Door-openers
Active listening
Six Steps to Problems Solving
"I"-message
TA
Respond with the adult ego state
Give strokes

FIGURE 11.2   Techniques for Use with Jason/Can't Depend on Parents

Need: Level 3—Belonging
Crisis: Developing
Model: Confronting-Contracting
Dreikurs
Confronting
Question motivation
   Attention-getting
   Power
   Revenge
   Helplessness
Make a plan based on motivation
Use encouragement
Design class activities or class meetings
Do sociogram
Glasser
Ask "what" questions
Help child develop a plan
Sign agreement
Intense counseling
Class meetings
With a lack of success,
   bring in principal,
   parent, outside agency

every effort would be made by the teacher to be positively reinforcing; if they did not, negative actions, including moving to the coercive-legalistic, might be necessary. The coercive-legalistic solution for the teacher and school might include using a social service agency to get family counseling, or turning the case over to the legal authorities (see Figure 11.3).

In the case of Carol, the injured student, the need level is physiological and the crisis is imminent. This life-threatening situation calls for very powerful intervention: coercive-legalistic. When time is of utmost importance, the teacher, with school officials, could use the assertiveness techniques as described by Alberti and Emmon's (1978) book, *Your Perfect Right,* to get immediate help and legal protection for the child (see Figure 11.4).

FIGURE 11.3   Techniques for Use with Robert/Loss of Dependable Home

Need: Level 2—Security
Crisis: Developing
Model: Rules and Consequences
Behavior Modification
   Set up contingency with parents
   Establish positive and negative reinforcers
   Set up contingency with Robert's father
   Establish positive and negative reinforcers
Behavior Modification/Punishment
Assertive Discipline
   Establish rules for parents' behavior
   Establish rules for Robert's father
   Use broken-record approach if necessary
   If necessary, Robert might be removed from school

FIGURE 11.4   Techniques for Use with Carol/An Abused Child

Need: Level 1—Psychological
Crisis: Imminent
Model: Coercive-Legalistic
Assertive Model
Establish actions by
   administrators with legal
   authority to protect this child
Assertive Nonverbal and Verbal
   action towards officials
Use broken-record approach if necessary
Follow-up on administrative actions

Usually, in serious cases, the legal steps required by the teacher are set by law. The teacher would be ethically bound, if not legally bound, to take coercive action for the student's welfare. To clarify, coercive-legalistic is not a model, but a process whereby the teacher, using assertive techniques, carries out the actions required by law. What is suggested is that the teacher, as a problem solver dealing with parent/child situations, can reexamine his or her own "personal wisdom response" in the broader perspective of the constructs described earlier. For our discussion, direct parallels were made between situations, needs, and models; in reality, this division might be less clear-cut, and actions would have to be adjusted accordingly.

Summary

Involving and working with parents is basic to an effective early childhood class-room, center, and school. We have provided a host of proactive activities to make parents feel welcome, involved, and contributing to their effectiveness with their own child. At times, life experiences place parents under great emotional pressure, affecting their behavior toward their child and to early childhood educators. When interacting with parents, especially in conflict situations, you are challenged to respond in a supportive manner that effectively supports the development of the child. We have provided some broad practical techniques for dealing with such parents in various kinds of crisis situations. The list of Associations Concerned with Teacher, Parent, and Family Relationships (page 229) will also be useful.

Activities

1. Survey three early childhood centers or schools in your area, and attempt to analyze what proactive steps these schools take in regard to parents and parent involvement. Then attend one of these parent/school functions.
2. Interview five experienced early childhood teachers and get vignettes related to the top three most difficult problems they face in working with the parents of children in their school. Select three of these "difficulties" and analyze them based on Table 11.1. What advice could you give to the teachers related to these three problems?
3. Collect 5 to 10 back copies of newsletters that have been sent to parents by your local centers or schools. Analyze them as to their subheadings and then design your own letter with subheadings as categories you would use in your own classroom.
4. Interview three to five early childhood specialists or five or more experienced teachers and ask them to list parent-oriented books they feel would be best to place in a parent lending library.

5. Design a parent survey form in cooperation with a local early childhood center or school, mail it, and tabulate the results. What actions could this school take to eliminate the negatives in such a survey?

References

Alberti, Robert, and Michael Emmon, *Your Perfect Right.* San Luis Obispo, Calif.: Impact, 1982.

Barbour, C., and Nancy Barbour, *Families, Schools, and Communities: Building Partnership for Educating Children.* Upper Saddle River, N.J.: Merrill, 1997.

Berne, Eric, *Games People Play.* New York: Ballantine Books, 1964.

Canter, Lee, *Assertive Discipline.* Los Angeles: Canter and Associates, 1979.

Cherry, Clara, *Nursery School & Day Care Center Management Guide,* 2nd ed. Belmont, Calif.: David S. Lake Publishing, 1987.

Dreikurs, Rudolf, and Pearl Cassel, *Discipline without Tears.* New York: Hawthorn Books, 1972.

Fuller, Mary Lou, and Glenn Olsen, *How School Relations Work Successfully with Parents and Family.* Boston: Allyn and Bacon, 1998.

Glasser, William, *Reality Therapy.* New York: Harper and Row, 1967.

Glasser, William, *Schools without Failure.* New York: Harper and Row, 1969.

Gordon, Thomas, *Teacher Effectiveness Training: T.E.T.* New York: Wyden Books, 1974.

Gordon, Thomas, *Leadership Effectiveness Training: L.E.T.* New York: Wyden Books, 1977.

Harris, Thomas, *I'm OK, You're OK: A Practical Guide to Transactional Analysis.* New York: Harper and Row, 1969.

Hommes, Loyd, *How to Use Contingency Contracting in the Classroom.* Champaign, Ill.: Research Press, 1970.

Lamison-White, Lawrence, *Income, Poverty, and Wealth in the United States: A Chart Book.* Current Population Reports: Consumer Income Series (P-60, No. 179), Washington, D.C.: Bureau of the Census, 1991.

McMurrain, Thomas, *Intervention in Human Crisis.* Atlanta, Ga.: Humanics Press, 1975.

Muriel, James, *The OK Boss.* Millbrae, Calif.: Celestial Arts, 1979.

Peters, Thomas, and Jame Waterman, *In Search of Excellence: Lessons from America's Best-Run Companies.* New York: Harper and Row, 1982.

Simon, Sidney, Leland Howe, and Howard Kirschenbaum, *Value Clarification.* New York: Hart, 1972.

Smith, Manuel, *When I Say "No" I Feel Guilty.* New York: Dial, 1975.

U.S. Bureau of the Census, *Census of Population and Housing Data.* CPH-L-80. Washington, D.C.: U.S. Government Printing Office, 1991.

Wolfgang, Charles H., *Solving Discipline Problems: Strategies for Classroom Teachers.* Boston: Allyn and Bacon, 1995.

Suggested Teacher Resources

Berger, E. H., *Parents as Partners in Education: Families and Schools Working Together* (4th ed.). Upper Saddle River, N.J.: Merrill, 1995.

Getswicki, C., *Home, School, and Community Relations* (3rd ed.). New York: Delmar, 1996.

Gomby, S. S., S. L. Larson, E. M. Lewit, & R. E. Berhman, "Home Visiting: Analysis and Recommendations," *The Future of Children, 3* (3) (1993).

Gonzalez-Mena, J., *Multicultural Issues in Child Care.* Mountain View, Calif.: Mayfield, 1992.

Powell, D., *Families and Early Childhood Programs.* Washington, D.C.: National Association for the Education of Young Children, 1989.

Swap, S. M., *Developing Home-School Partnerships: From Concepts to Practice.* New York: Teachers College Press, 1993.

Weiss, H. B., "Home Visits: Necessary But Not Sufficient," *The Future of Children, 3* (3) (1993).

Associations Concerned with Teacher, Parent, and Family Relationships

Association for Childhood Education International
11501 Georgia Avenue, Suite 315
Wheaton, MD 20902

Center on Families, Communities, Schools and Children's Learning
The Johns Hopkins University
Joyce Epstein and Don Davies, Co-Directors
3505 North Charles Street
Baltimore, MD 21218

Children's Defense Fund
122 C. Street NW, Suite 400
Washington, D.C. 20001

Council for Exceptional Children
1920 Association Drive
Reston, VA 22091

Family Resource Coalition
200 South Michigan Avenue, Suite 1520
Chicago, IL 60604

The Home and School Institute (founded by Dorothy Rich)
1201 16th Street NW
Washington, DC 20036

International Reading Association
800 Barksdale Road, P.O. Box 8139
Newark, DE 19714-8139

National Association for the Education of Young Children
1509 16th Street, NW
Washington, DC 20036-1426
1-800-424-2460

National Association of Partners in Education
209 Madison Street, Suite 401
Alexandria, VA 22314

National Parent Network on Disabilities
1600 Prince Street
Alexandria, VA 22314
703-684-NPND

12

Assessment and Evaluation of Learning

The classroom teacher is faced with the task of demonstrating that students have grown developmentally, or that they have learned skills. When child-centered teaching methods are used, assessment and evaluation are made through direct observation of the child's self-initiated actions in the regular classroom setting. In contrast, the teacher-directed models use criterion-referenced tests, which focus on the child's attainment of one key skill that can be related to a scope-and-sequence chart. The child-centered methods (open) and teacher-directed methods (closed) would be at the extremes of a continuum illustrating methods of gathering data for assessment. Figure 12.1 shows the various methods of data gathering that will be discussed in this chapter.

Child-Centered Assessment

The primary assessment tool of the play activity (child-centered) curriculum is the direct observation of children, or the specimen record. The teacher becomes a "potted plant"; that is, the teacher withdraws from classroom activity and finds a corner where the children can be clearly observed and he or she takes observational notes. Usually, the teacher focuses on one child for a period of 20 minutes, recording all of his or her actions in longhand or with the use of a tape recorder. The observational recording is placed into the format shown in Figure 12.2.

After filling in the top several blanks on the observation form, the introduction is completed, much as if it were a program for a Broadway play:

Figure 12.1   Methods of Data Gathering

Open	Closed
No Selectivity	High Degree of Selectivity
No Inference Required	High Degree of Inference

Specimen Records (observations)
Diary
Anecdotal Records
Time Sampling
Rating Scales
Criterion-Referenced Test

Introduction:

This is the monthly observation of James Kent (age 3-8) at 10:12 A.M. on Friday. We find James in the block corner with Bill Womack, Paul Henly, and Sara Weiner. He is dressed in blue jeans, flannel shirt, and sneakers. This is the second day he has been back after missing school for seven days with chickenpox.

A simple map is drawn of the classroom or the corner area where the observation takes place. Furniture and play materials are labeled, as well as names of peers or adults.

MAP

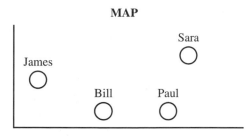

The page is divided down the middle with a line that separates the observation side and the theory/comment side. On the observation side, the teacher records the actions of the target child for a period of 20 minutes, putting time references every 4 to 6 minutes whenever there is a natural break in the activities. If the child makes products, such as painting a bird or building a block structure, the teacher sketches them in on the observation side so that the reader can see the shape or form. Detailed descriptions of the child's gross and fine movements and, as much as possible, his or her visual and verbal actions should be noted. The

FIGURE 12.2   Child Observation Form

Child's Name _____   Date _____ Time _____

Observer's Name _____

Other People in General Area (list) _____

_____

Location _____

_____

Introduction _____

_____

_____

Map

Observations	**Theory/Comments**

Summary

_____

_____

_____

Educational Recommendations _____

_____

_____

_____

teacher should leave out interpretations and comments or, if necessary, put the comments or explanations in brackets to set them apart. General words ("He played with the toy truck") should be avoided. The reader wants to know exactly what the child did with the truck. A form of shorthand can be used during the actual recording and later transcribed into more understandable written form. (See Carbonara, 1982, for examples and suggestions for recording.)

Observations:

10:05: James reaches out with his right hand and grabs the red tow-truck, as he crawls across the floor on hands and knees. He makes roaring noises with his mouth (like a truck motor) pushing the truck up to a toy gas station and says to Paul, "Fill it up with unleaded gas."

Getting no response, he takes off the toy gas hose, places it to the back of his truck, and makes hissing noises. The pump hose is "hung up" and he pushes the truck across the room, moving on hands and knees until he stops in front of the rocking chair.

Puts finger in his mouth and looks around the classroom at each child's activity (appears to be thinking). His face lights up with a smile and he crawls quickly to the block shelves.

James takes from the shelf six 1-unit blocks, building two parallel walls; using four 1/2-units, he makes a roof between the two parallels, and closes one open end with two more 1/2-unit blocks.

10:10: With "motor" sounds, he backs the tow-truck into the open end of the block structure, selecting two more 1/2-units and placing them before the open end to close in the truck.

He stands, walks quickly to the shelf, takes down the woven basket with two hands and brings it to his block structure. Sara is now kneeling before the structure, looking intently. James shouts firmly at Sara, "No, no!" Sara smiles and responds, "I have a flat tire." James says, "What?" Sara replies, "I have a flat tire." James asks, "Where?" Sara points to a small car at the opposite end of the room that is missing a tire. James looks at Sara and smiles. James quickly removes the two blocks from the structure's entrance, drives out the truck with motor noises, selects a male doll from the basket, places it on top of the cab of the truck, and both children crawl across the floor with great speed and giggles, with James pushing the truck before him, stopping before Sara's car. James states, "Which tire is flat?" Sara says and points, "Here." James says, "That's not flat. There's no tire, where is it?" Sara shrugs her shoulders.

10:15: James mumbles, takes male doll from top of truck, "walks" doll to Sara's car, directs doll's hands at the missing tire area, and makes clicking noises with tongue. James drops male doll, runs to opposite side of room and returns with a similar size car, pushes Sara's car aside, and replaces it with a new one with the wheel intact. James states, "It is fixed now." Sara replies, "Thanks." Sara makes motor noises, pushes her car across the room toward James's block structure with James following, pushing his truck. . . .

On the right side of the paper, the theory/comments section is used to explain in developmental terms what is occurring on the observations side.

Theory/Comments:
James is symbolically representing a truck, and is beginning to elaborate dramatic play. He attempts to engage Paul in the activity without success; as a result, his play can be classified initially as isolated social play.

He now builds a "garage" with blocks (structured-construction). When approached by Sara, his first response is a verbally aggressive *no,* but Sara responds with role-playing and their play progresses into the beginnings of sociodramatic play (beginning of associative).

These observations and theory/comments are, of course, based on the 20-minute observation period. Once these are written, a line is drawn, separating the main data from the summary section. In the summary, the observer-teacher looks back over the entire 20-minute period, attempts to label predominant activities, and perhaps comments on age-appropriateness. Also, comments based on the teacher's knowledge and experience can now be added to give greater meaning to the summary.

Summary:
The observation this morning shows James, age 3 years and 8 months, primarily enjoying wheel toys such as cars and trucks. His first building is a detailed and elaborate block structure of a garage, house, and gas station, and with the wheeled vehicles and miniature mother, father, and sister, he has played out dramatic themes of getting a car repaired, going shopping at the mall, and being chased by a police officer. This dramatic play was isolated, with James making seven overtures to Paul to join him, without success. For the first time, he was able to pick up the role and cues of Sara and they were able to play an elaborate theme of cars, trucks, and domestic home life. This was his first attempt at associative/cooperative play with another child. Sara has made repeated attempts in the last two weeks to befriend him by showing him where to store his painting, sitting near him at circle time, and running freely with him in large motor play on the playground.

James was enrolled one month ago and has been ill seven of these days.

The last section on the observation form, Educational Recommendations, allows the teacher to make specific recommendations, such as formal testing, or raise questions she feels need to be discussed with other staff members:

Educational Recommendations:
This morning it appears that James is able to accept Sara's overture of friendship and can be a co-player in sociodramatic play. I will make this known to other staff members and we will take actions to help this friendship continue, possibly: (1) put James into Sara's group for projects, (2) move Sara's and James's storage lockers together, (3) tell James's mother, who has been asking if he has made friends with Sara, and she might be invited over on the weekend.

Understanding Specimen Observations

The evaluation of all the instruments that follow can be understood with relationship to their openness versus closedness, degrees of selectivity, degrees of inference required, advantages, and disadvantages (Bentzen, 1985).

Open versus Closed

The specimen observation is considered the most open data-gathering instrument because it attempts to capture a slice out of the child's daily life as fully as possible without initial interpretation, allowing the data to be read and interpreted—and reinterpreted. The setting and context in which the behavior occurred is also recorded. Videotaping could be an even more complete form of data gathering.

Degree of Selectivity

The observation is not selective; all actions and behaviors are recorded, to the fullest extent possible.

Degree of Inference Required

At the time the recording is being done, no inferences are made. These may come later.

Advantages

Child-centered advocates see behavior as a holistic process; that is, it cannot easily be directed into small pieces, and all domains—social, cognitive, and so on—are important. The specimen observation captures the whole child at a point in time, and can be revisited for reinterpretation.

Disadvantages

Specimen observations are very time consuming, and great skill is needed to "get on paper" all the child actions. Videotaping could be helpful, but equipment and a person with technical skill would be needed. Also, the specimen observation is not quantifiable and can't be used for summary comparisons. Thus, it might not meet specifications for certain funding sources that require number-based data as demonstrations of effectiveness.

Diary

In a diary, the teacher makes daily written summaries of a child's behavior, focusing on a selected aspect (e.g., use of materials), hence the name *topical diary*. This permits a long-term overview of the child's actions and requires that the writer-observer-teacher be in daily contact with the child over many weeks or months.

September 5
This is John's first day at school. He cried and demanded that his mother not leave him. Mother remained until mid-morning, and when she did depart, he cried for 3 to 4 minutes, and cuddled on the teacher's lap. After the initial cry, he used the paint easel and puzzles for the remainder of the morning. Ate well at snack, but was demanding at lunch, refusing to eat anything. He cried again at cot-time, but was able to get comfortable by using his "blankie" and teacher's cuddling. He fell asleep and slept deeply for the entire period. He wandered aimlessly after rest, and did not play. He was flat and expressionless with his mother when she picked him up.

September 6
Refused to get out of the car this morning, causing great concern for mother, who had to depart for work immediately. He cried at the gate as she departed, refused affection from the teacher, but went to the paint easel and puzzles, which he used age-appropriately for the entire morning. At snack, he seemed very hungry and ate all of his lunch. He went immediately to his cot at rest, using his blankie for comfort. After rest, he attached to Mark, and followed him around doing large motor activity with laughter and joy. When mother arrived, he ran to the gate, smiled, and called her name. They hugged affectionately, but he insisted on carrying his artwork to the car, and refused to give it to mother.

(The diary would continue for many more days in a similar manner.)

Open versus Closed

The diary is considered open because it contains a wide range of data and general observations, notes behavioral changes over time and in context, and preserves data for later comparison and interpretation.

Degree of Selectivity

The diary is unselective in that it is not restricted to one narrow, predefined behavior. It is not as selectively open as a specimen observation, however, because it specifies a "topic," such as initial school adjustment.

Degree of Inference Required

A moderate amount of inference is required because the teacher must decide what is related to the topic; this is not as limiting as the more restrictive instruments.

Advantages

The advantage of the diary is that behavioral information can be collected over a very long period of weeks or months without the great expenditure of time required for the specimen observation. The behavior is placed in context, is permanently recorded, and can document the nature of the child's growth and behavior.

Disadvantages

The major limitation to the diary is that it can be kept only by teachers or parents who are in daily contact with the child over a long period of time. For the teacher with 15 to 20 children, this would require a defined focus on one particular child, and might be prohibitive.

Anecdotal Records

Anecdotal records of unusual events are written by the teacher after the fact. They are done sporadically throughout the year and can be continued the next year. The records are made by the teacher from direct observation and written with as much detail as possible, including context and setting.

October 13 (4:35 P.M.)
Carol was climbing the large tower on the playground in a game of "run and

chase" with Allen. As Allen climbed the steps toward her, she began to flee, running to the fireman's pole. Her flimsy "jelly" shoes caught in the space between the platform boards, causing her to fall face forward off the climber platform into the sandpit. She cried intensely, was picked up by Mrs. Barker, had sand wiped from her face, and her face and body were physically inspected by this teacher. She was taken to the shaded bench and an ice pack was brought and applied to her face. Mrs. Barker talked to her softly, attempting to comfort her, and stayed on the bench with her until her mother arrived at 5:25. Mother was told what occurred, and instructed not to permit Carol to fall asleep when she got home and to watch for indications of a head injury, such as rolling eyes, throwing up, cramps, and other discomfort. The parent was asked to take Carol to a doctor if any symptoms occurred and the school would pay any medical expenses (school has an accident policy). The mother's response was that "these things occur as part of life experiences," and she indicated that she was capable of watching Carol at home over the next few hours. The teacher called Carol's home at 8:00 and talked to the father, who indicated that all was well with Carol. Carol returned the next day with a 2-inch bruise under her left eye. No other negative reaction was seen from Carol as the result of this fall. (Note: "Jelly" shoes were declared not approved for school wear in the next school newsletter and the rule put into the parent handbook.)

Open versus Closed

The anecdotal record is considered open because the data can be saved for reinspection.

Degree of Selectivity

The anecdotal record is highly selective because the teacher records only unusual events.

Degree of Inference Required

The written anecdotal record calls for a high degree of inference, but the recording itself, especially if the teacher adheres to factual description, can be viewed as requiring minimal inferring.

Advantages

The anecdotal record is a running record of unusual events, in context, that occur in a child's life over a long time period. Compared to other forms of data, it is easy to gather with a limited time commitment.

Disadvantages

Because the recorded incidents are unusual, they may be emotionally loaded for the teacher, and the records may therefore be written with bias. Unreliability is therefore a major disadvantage.

Time Sampling

Certain categories of behavior are preselected in the time sampling procedure, such as Parten's social stages or play classifications. A time sequence is pre-established, and then every five minutes, for example, the teacher-observer will record what is being seen. This time procedure must be followed consistently over a fairly long period of time, so that the behaviors may be considered typical. The observer-teacher will make tally marks in each of the well-defined categories at each of the times established; thus, the name *time sampling.*

The Social Observation System (Figure 12.3) is a time-sampling instrument requiring the teacher to record a slash mark on a chart that scores the child on Parten's social stages (see also Figure 12.4). After a sufficient period of recording, totals and percentages can be obtained for the subcategories above. These percentages can be graphed for a visual display of the child's behavior.

Open versus Closed

The time sampling system is considered closed because at the time the observation is done, only one category or a few categories are accounted for, and all of the other behavior is lost.

Degree of Selectivity

The time sample is highly selective because only one predetermined behavior is recorded.

Degree of Inference Required

Time sampling with an instrument such as the Social Observation System requires an immediate inference by the teacher: a decision as to what behavior is being seen, and in what category it should be scored. It is therefore important that the categories be clearly defined. To make the time sampling instrument reliable, two or three teachers could score the same children at the same time, and their scores be compared. If there is a 90 percent or higher agreement, there is inter-observer reliability.

FIGURE 12.3   Social Observation System

Directions:

It is suggested that the classroom teacher mount the Social Observation System form on the back of a solid supply cupboard door at eye level in a central room where most children would be playing. At the same time period each day for a two-week period, the teacher would take a few minutes to score his or her way down the list of children on the left side of the form. First, he or she observes the child's activities and then puts one tally mark in the space under the substage of the social development in which the child is performing.

After a two-week period (longer if the teacher decides), totals for each child are obtained by adding down the columns under each category. A grand total is obtained by adding all totals left to right. The total number of each social category is then divided by the Grand Total to get a percentage for that social level. The percentages can now be graphed on the Individual Social Graph for each child.

The information permits you to know where each child is functioning socially, and could call for intervention if the results are not age-expected.

Observer's Name _____

Dates: Began _____   Ended _____

Child's Name	Unoccupied	Solitary	Onlooker	Parallel	Associative	Cooperative
1.						
2.						
3.						
4.						
5.						
6.						
7.						
8.						
9.						
10.						
Total ÷ No. of Recordings						
Percentage						

FIGURE 12.4   Individual Social Graph

Child's Name _____

Date: Began _____   Ended _____

	Unoccupied	Solitary	Onlooker	Parallel	Associative	Cooperative
100 90 80 70 60 50 40 30 20 10 0						
Observe	1 2 3 4 5	1 2 3 4 5	1 2 3 4 5	1 2 3 4 5	1 2 3 4 5	1 2 3 4 5
%						

Advantages

The advantage of time sampling is that the teacher may choose beforehand the type of behavior on which to focus (incidents of aggression, friendship patterns, use of equipment, etc.). This method can be done with much less time and effort than specimen observations. The teacher can compare his or her recording to another teacher's to check reliability. The score, a total number of marks in each category, can be used to make group comparisons or be displayed on graphs.

Disadvantages

Time sampling requires categorizing schemes, which means the loss of context and other behaviors. For example, if you were making a comparison of a child's usage of different types of play materials (symbolic, fluid-construction, structured-construction, etc.), and for a few days the water table was broken and the paint pots empty, the category of fluid-construction would show a depressed usage.

Rating Scales

At times, you might wish to have a colleague act as an "expert witness" if this teacher has had a great deal of experience working with a certain child. Rating scales—such as the Child-Play Behavioral Rating Scale (Figure 12.5), the Child-Play Behavioral Rating Scale Profile (Figure 12.6), the Adjustment Behavioral Profile (Figure 12.7), and the Adjustment Behavioral Profile Score Sheet (Figure 12.8)—indicate at what level in a certain category a child might be functioning. A number scale from 1 to 5 is used. Rating can be done after directly observing a child, such as setting up a testing situation where you ask the child to walk a balance beam, but it is usually done from recall. To make the rating more reliable, two or three teachers could discuss each item and come to a group agreement.

An example of a rating scale item might be:

Never   Always
1   2   3   4   5   a. Can use language to express basic needs
(example: toileting)

FIGURE 12.5   Child-Play Behavioral (CPB) Rating Scale

Date Scored	Rating			
	1st	2nd	3rd	4th
Starting	____	____	____	____
Ending	____	____	____	____
Color Used	____	____	____	____

Birthdate ____

Age: Yrs ____ Mos ____

Child's Name   _____

Teacher(s)   1st   _____

2nd   _____

3rd   _____

4th   _____

Directions
1. Observe child in wide variety of play situations for six to eight weeks, before rating.
2. Make rating on most recent behavior.
3. Some items will require setting up a test situation in the classroom context, and requesting performance by the child.
4. Base rating on your experience only.
5. Consider each item separately from all others.
6. Use extreme high and low rates when warranted.
7. Rate every question.

Profile Scoring Sheet
1. Move number score from each item to the item number found under the heading FACTOR ITEM RAW SCORES on the scoring sheet (Figure 12.6).

FIGURE 12.5   *(Continued)*

2. Add all numbers in that row and put total in space under the heading TOTAL RAW SCORE. Circle the raw score number on the scale to the right under the heading APPROX. AGE. The numbers under approx. age—2, 3, 4, 5, and 6—represent the score most children at this age would score in the row for sociodramatic play, dramatic play, fluid construction, etc.
3. Children who score one and one-half ages below their approximate age might require play facilitation by the teacher.

Creative Use of Materials and Activities

Score the following based on:
(a) the degree to which the child uses the materials or uses action in an appropriate manner, showing an understanding of symbolic growth and development.
(b) the extent to which the child does not limit himself to the obvious use of the materials itself, but uses it in a creative manner.

Score each item on a five-point scale in regard to the following:
___ 1. The material is used without regard to its physical or representational properties in a manner recalling the play of infants.
      e.g.   Examines the material superficially. Picks up a toy and bangs it on the ground or on his own body. Stirs the sand with his finger.
___ 2. The material is used with some regard for its properties, but these are not exploited to the fullest. There is an element of lack of vision in the handling.
      e.g.   Shovels or rakes at the sand without making anything. Clicks a toy pistol in an aimless kind of way. Hammers a piece of wood without inserting a nail. Dabs paint on paper or wood.
___ 3. The material is used with regard to its properties (symbolic use), but in an obvious way. There is no coherent play theme that transcends the given materials and within which their appropriate use figures (symbols) as meaningful behavior.
      e.g.   Fills the bucket, or makes a sand-pile without naming it. Paints waste wood with the intention of coloring it, but without any further imaginative or constructive intent. Puts the doll to bed in the cot provided, without extending the imaginative theme to other aspects of the domestic situation. Hammers a nail in wood.
___ 4. The material is used in a manner transcending its merely obvious properties.
      e.g.   Builds an elaborate block structure. Makes a recognizable human figure of plasticine. Makes or attempts to make a sword or an airplane of waste wood.
           or
           The material is used appropriately within the meaningful context of a larger imaginative whole.
      e.g.   Uses the doll tea-set in the context of a fairly well-organized tea party. Plays with the sand, giving a representation of a store or shop.
___ 5. The material is used in a highly insightful manner, adapted to a context that clearly transcends it.
      e.g.   Builds a "ship" on the sandbox, inverting a table on it and wedging this with a blanket, using the clothes horse as the ship's ladder, and so on. Plays at a "tea-party" using sand as a birthday cake, which he decorates, perhaps using small pieces of wood as candles, or perhaps wrapping small bits of plasticine in paper to make candies, and so on.

(Continued)

FIGURE 12.5 *(Continued)*

Child-Play Behavioral Rating Scale

Sociodramatic Play (Macro)

1	2	3	4	5	(1)	Imitative role-play
1	2	3	4	5	(2)	Make-believe with objects
1	2	3	4	5	(3)	Persistence in role play
1	2	3	4	5	(4)	Interaction
1	2	3	4	5	(5)	Verbal communication

Dramatic Play (Micro)

1	2	3	4	5	(1)	Imitative role-play
1	2	3	4	5	(2)	Make-believe with objects
1	2	3	4	5	(3)	Persistence in role play
1	2	3	4	5	(4)	Interaction
1	2	3	4	5	(5)	Verbal communication

Fluid Materials

1	2	3	4	5	(6)	Water play
1	2	3	4	5	(7)	Sand play (dry)
1	2	3	4	5	(8)	Finger-painting
1	2	3	4	5	(9)	Easel painting
1	2	3	4	5	(10)	Sand play (wet)
1	2	3	4	5	(11)	Clay
1	2	3	4	5	(12)	Drawing (crayon)
1	2	3	4	5	(13)	Drawing (pencil)
1	2	3	4	5	(14)	Drawing (markers)
1	2	3	4	5	(15)	Drawing (chalk)

Materials Requiring Restructuring

1	2	3	4	5	(16)	Carpentry
1	2	3	4	5	(17)	Box/Cardboard construction
1	2	3	4	5	(18)	Paper/Cut & Paste
1	2	3	4	5	(19)	Other _____

Structured Materials

1	2	3	4	5	(20)	Pratt blocks
1	2	3	4	5	(21)	Interlocking cubes
1	2	3	4	5	(22)	Legos
1	2	3	4	5	(23)	Octons
1	2	3	4	5	(24)	_____
1	2	3	4	5	(25)	_____
1	2	3	4	5	(26)	_____

1					(27)	Puzzle (four pieces)
	2					Puzzle (six pieces)
		3				Puzzle (eight pieces)
			4			Puzzle (ten pieces)
				5		Puzzle (more than ten pieces)

Representational Ability Symbolic

					(28)	Best flat (two dimensional)
1						Random/Controlled scribbling (circle)
	2					Circle/Face (circle)
		3				Arms-Legs/Body appears (circle)
			4			Floating house (or substitute)/Bottom line (circle)
				5		Base line supports/Two-dimensional (circle)

FIGURE 12.5   *(Continued)*

Sensorimotor Abilities

Fine Motor
Draw-a-design
1   ( )   Vertical line (4")
  2   ( )   Horizontal line (4")
    3   ( )   Circle
      4   ( )   Backwards L
        5   ( )   3 line asterisk

Barrage Catch Game (three attempts)
1   ( )   Catch with both hands
  2   ( )   Catch with one preferred hand
    3   ( )   Catch with one other hand
      4   ( )   Toss in air (3' plus), catch with both hands
        5   ( )   Toss in air (3' plus), catch with one hand

Barrage Throw (three attempts)
1   ( )   Hits 15" target hole (10' distance)
  2   ( )   Hits 10" target hole (10' distance)
    3   ( )   Hits 5" target hole (10' distance)
      4   ( )   Hits 10" target hole (20' distance)
        5   ( )   Hits 5" target hole (20' distance)

Large Ball Bounce
1   ( )   Large ball, 2 bounces (preferred hand)
  2   ( )   Large ball, 5 bounces (preferred hand)
    3   ( )   Large ball, 2 bounces (other hand)
      4   ( )   Large ball, 5 bounces (other hand)
        5   ( )   Large ball, dribbles forward 7 feet

Gross Motor
Walking
1   ( )   Walking on tiptoe
  2   ( )   Walking a straight line
    3   ( )   Standing on one foot
      4   ( )   Standing on the other foot
        5   ( )   Skipping

Climbing
1   ( )   Climbs rope ladder
  2   ( )   Climbs pole
    3   ( )   Fixed Rope Climb, 6' knots
      4   ( )   Fixed Rope Climb, 12' knots
        5   ( )   Unfixed Rope Climb

Balance
1   ( )   Walks balance beam
  2   ( )   Walks balance beam holding 5 lb. object
    3   ( )   Walks backward on beam
      4   ( )   Walks backward on beam holding 5 lb. object
        5   ( )   Walks beam, bending under barrier at child shoulder
                                     height

FIGURE 12.6   Child-Play Behavioral Rating Scale Profile

Child's Name _____

Age _____

Birthday _____

Sex _____

Rater's Name _____

Rater's Relationship to Child _____

Date of Rating _____

Play Form
    Factor Item

				Approx. Age				
Raw Scores				2	3	4	5	6
			Total Raw Score					

1. Sociodramatic
    role   1___   2___objects
    persist   3___   4___interact   _____   4 6 8 10 12 14 16 18 20
    verbal   5___

2. Dramatic play
    role   6___   7___objects
    persist   8___   9___interact   _____   4 6 8 10 12 14 16 18 20

3. Fluid-Construction
    water   11___   12___sand (dry)
    finger   13___   14___easel pt   _____   4 10 16 22 28 34 40 46 50
    wet sand 15___   16___clay
    crayon 17___   18___pencil
    marker 19___   20___chalk

4. Restructuring-Construction
    carpet 21___   22___cardboard
    paper/ 23___   _____ 3 4 5 6 7 8 9 10 11 12 13 14
    paste

5. Structured-Construction
    block   24___   25___cubes
    Legos   26___   27___Octons   _____ 4 6 8 10 12 14 16 18 20

6. Puzzles (item 27)   _____ 1   2   3   4

7. Symbolic/flat construction (item 28) _____ 1   2   3   4

8. Fine motor
    draw   30___   31___catch
    throw   32___   33___bounce _____ 4 6 8 10 12 14 16 18 20

9. Gross motor
    walk   34___   35___climb
    balance 36___   _____ 3 4 5 6 7 8 9 10 11 12 13 14

FIGURE 12.7   Adjustment Behavioral Profile

Directions:
1. Observe the child in a wide variety of play situations for six to eight weeks before rating.
2. Make a rating on the most recent behavior.
3. Base rating on your experience only.
4. Consider each item separately from all others.
5. Use extreme high or low rating when warranted.
6. Rate every question.

Profile Scoring Sheet
1. Move each score from the question statements on the Profile to the Scoring Sheet under the heading FACTOR ITEM RAW SCORE (Figure 12.8).
2. Add all numbers in that category and put a total in the space under the heading TOTAL RAW SCORE. Circle the raw score number to the right on the scale and heading ADJUSTMENT. NEEDS INTERV suggests that an intervention is needed, and WELL ADJUSTED indicates good adjustment.

Adjustment Behavioral Profile

Child's Name _____

Rater's Name _____ Date of Rating _____

Based on your recent knowledge of this child, rate him or her on the five-point scale to follow, based on what is considered normal for this age child.

Rating Levels:
Never 1, 2, 3, 4, 5 Always   Compared to normal children, how often does the child . . .

Self-Control
1 2 3 4 5   1   Carries an art assignment to completion

Detachment
1 2 3 4 5   2   Cuddles with teacher responsively after moments of positive affection
1 2 3 4 5   3   Allows cuddling and comforting by teacher after being accidentally hurt

Language
1 2 3 4 5   4   Uses language to express needs
1 2 3 4 5   5   Engages teachers in conversation
1 2 3 4 5   6   Engages peers in conversation

Social Isolation
1 2 3 4 5   7   Hides in corner or takes steps to avoid peers
1 2 3 4 5   8   Exhibits an expression that is flat and lifeless

Social Aggression
1 2 3 4 5   9   Swears, name-calls, and uses bathroom talk toward peers

(Continued)

FIGURE 12.7   *(Continued)*

1 2 3 4 5	10	Swears, name-calls, and uses bathroom talk toward teacher
1 2 3 4 5	11	Bites, strikes, or attacks other children in a free-play situation with peers, without apparent cause

Conflict over Possessions

1 2 3 4 5	12	Acts passively when others take his or her toys
1 2 3 4 5	13	Acts physically aggressive when others take his or her toys
1 2 3 4 5	14	Acts verbally aggressive when others take his or her toys
1 2 3 4 5	15	Has temper tantrums when others take his or her toys

Critical Times

1 2 3 4 5	16	Shows fear of loss of parent when he or she departs, but recovers with teacher's help
1 2 3 4 5	17	Refuses most food during snack
1 2 3 4 5	18	Fights for and hoards food at snack
1 2 3 4 5	19	Does not rest or sleep fully after a period of settling
1 2 3 4 5	20	Wets cot at rest time
1 2 3 4 5	21	Stays at circle for more than 10 minutes
1 2 3 4 5	22	Reunites without conflict with parents

Open versus Closed

The rating scale is considered closed because the categories are determined or preselected by the authors of the scale.

Degree of Selectivity

The rating scale is highly selective because only a narrow selection of behaviors is observed.

Degree of Inference Required

The degree of inference required is extremely high because usually the judgment is made from memory. Thus, the reliability of the teacher's response may not be consistent. Interobserver reliability would need to be established on any such instruments.

Advantages

The major advantage is that the teacher can complete the rating scale in a matter of minutes if done by memory. Also, the data can be reduced to numbers to make statistical comparisons, so that you may obtain answers to questions such as,

FIGURE 12.8 Adjustment Behavioral Profile Score Sheet

Child's Name _____

Age _____   Birthday _____   Sex _____

Rater's Name _____

Rater's Relationship to Child _____

Date of Rating _____

Behavioral Category	Factor Item	Raw Score	Total	Adjustment				
				Needs Interv				*Well Adjusted*
1. Self-Control	Completion	1. __	__	1	2	3	4	5
2. Detachment	Cuddling positive Cuddling negative	2. __ 3. __	__	2	4	6	8	10
3. Language	Language needs Teacher conversat. Peer conversation	4. __ 5. __ 6. __	__	3	6	9	12	15
4. Social Isolation	Hides Flat expression	7. __ 8. __	__	10	8	6	4	2
5. Social Aggression	Swears at peers Swears at teacher Attacks	9. __ 10. __ 11. __	__	15	12	9	6	3
6. Conflict over Possessions	Passive Aggressive Verbal aggressive Tantrum	12. __ 13. __ 14. __ 15. __	__	20	16	12	8	4
7. Critical Times	Departure Food Hoard Rest Wets Circle Reunites	16. __ 17. __ 18. __ 19. __ 20. __ 21. __ 22. __	__	35	28	21	14	7

"What is the average age at which a child can do this and how early or late is this particular child?"

Disadvantages

A disadvantage would be that the rating could be influenced by a teacher's feelings; if a parent was critical of a teacher, for example, and threatened to "go to the director," and it was time that very afternoon to rate this parent's child, the teacher might have difficulty making objective judgments.

Criterion-Referenced Test (Checklist)

The following are criterion-referenced tests widely used in early childhood programs. Notice that many of these tests have been designed for identifying special needs of children with developmental delays.

Alpern-Boll Developmental Profile, Dr. Gerald Alpern, PO Box 3198, Aspen, CO 81611

Assessment Programming Guide for Infants and Preschoolers, Developmental Services, Inc., PO Box 1023, Columbus, IN 47201

Bayley Scales of Infant Development, Psychological Corporation, 304 East 45th Street, New York, NY 10017

Beginning Milestones, DLM Teaching Resources, One DLM Park, Allen, TX 75002

Behavioral Developmental Profile, Marshalltown Project, 507 East Anson, Marshalltown, IA 50158

Behavior Maturity Checklist II, Psychology, Research and Evaluation Section, O'Berry Center, Goldsboro, NC 27530

BKR Development and Trainability Assessment Scale, BKR Educational Projects, PO Box 16986, Plantation, FL 33317

Brekken-Drouin Developmental Spotcheck, Children's Developmental Services, Casa Colina Hospital, 255 East Bonita Avenue, Pomona, CA 91767

Carolina Developmental Profile, Kaplan School Supply, 600 Jonestown Road, Winston-Salem, NC 27103

Cassel Developmental Record, Psychologists and Educators, Inc., 211 West State, Jacksonville, IL 62650

Cattell Infant Intelligence Scale, Psychological Corporation, 304 East 45th Street, New York, NY 10017

Classroom Behavior Inventory, Earl S. Schaefer, Frank Porter Graham Child Development Center, University of North Carolina, Chapel Hill, NC 27514

Denver Developmental Screening Test, Ladoca Project and Publishing Foundation, East 51st Avenue and Lincoln, Denver, CO 80216

Distar Instructional System (includes assessment instruments), Science Research Associated, Inc., 2590 East Erie Street, Chicago, IL 60611

Early Independence, Edmark Associates, PO Box 3903, Bellevue, WA 98009

Early Learning Accomplishment Profile for Developmentally Young Children, Kaplan Press, 600 Jonestown Road, Winston-Salem, NC 27103

HICOMP Preschool Curriculum and Test, Charles E. Merrill Publishing Co., Columbus, OH 43216

Kahn Intelligence Test, Psychological Test Specialists, PO Box 1441, Missoula, MT 59801

Koontz Child Developmental Program, Western Psychological Services, 12031 Wilshire Boulevard, Los Angeles, CA 90025

Peabody Developmental Motor Scales, IMRD Publications, Box 154, George Peabody College, Nashville, TN 37203

Portage Guide to Early Education, Portage Project, Cooperative Educational Service Agency 12, 412 Past Slifer Street, Portage, WI 53901

Preschool Developmental Profile, 839 Greene Street, PO Box 1104, Ann Arbor, MI 48106

Prescriptive Learning Accomplishment Profile, Kaplan School Supply, 600 Jonestown Road, Winston-Salem, NC 27103

Slosson Intelligence Test for Children and Adults, Slosson Educational Publications, Inc., PO Box 280, East Aurora, NY 14052

Vineland Social Maturity Scales, American Guidance Service, Publishers Building, Circle Pines, MN 55014

Criterion-referenced tests nearly always come with the direct-instruction programs. These tests contain a series of behavioral items—such as "child counts to 5" or "can use under/over when told to place a block in position"— that are answered by the teacher with a *yes* or *no* response after directly testing the child.

Open versus Closed

The criterion-referenced checklist is closed, because only one very narrow behavior is being observed, and the context and all other behaviors are lost.

Degree of Selectivity

The degree of selectivity is high because a judgment has been made that a particular behavior is important for every child to learn, as in the direct instruction curriculum. An instrument is needed to document that the teaching has been effective, so the test items are deliberately selected to cover the preselected behaviors.

Degree of Inference Required

The criterion-referenced test requires a high level of inference on the teacher-observer's part, but many of the packaged tests have gone through rigorous processes to ensure that each item is related to a behavioral objective. Since the behavior is very narrow, there is little question about whether the child can perform the skill.

Here is an example of a criteria-referenced item:

Yes   No

( )   ( )   1. Matches 2 colors

Materials: eight 2-inch paper squares
(2 red, 2 blue, 2 yellow, 2 green)

Procedure: Place 1 square of each color in front of child. Give child stack of matching colored squares arranged in random order. Demonstrate matching response with red card and return it to stack. Say, "Put each piece of paper on the one that is just like it." Credit if child matches at least 2 colors. Spontaneous corrections of errors are acceptable. Allow 1 trial. If child matches all 4 colors, credit item. (Learning Accomplishment Profile, Chapel Hill Training-Outreach Project, Cognitive Skill 36 (item 12), page 47.)

Advantages

This system requires little recording skill. The items are directly related to the teaching curriculum and the results provide a guide for reteaching. Number comparisons can be made, permitting a statistical evaluation of the children and program.

Disadvantages

Only narrow behaviors are considered, usually cognitive skills, with all other aspects of the child's growth being lost or ignored.

Summary: A Wider Point of View

We have looked at commonly used forms of assessment and evaluation, from "open" observation to "closed" criterion-referenced tests (checklists). All of these can and should be used in the classroom. At times, direct observation of one child or a group of children is needed—perhaps to enlighten you as to sources of a continuing intragroup conflict or for a similar purpose. At other times, diaries recording behaviors centered on certain topics might be the most useful tools, or anecdotal records might best serve a certain purpose.

If you want to know how many of the children in the class are using certain play materials, or at what social level they are functioning, time sampling would give you the answers. Criterion-referenced tests might be used to assess the results of teaching.

It is necessary to ask good questions about children's growth and learning, and to then make judgments about what assessment instruments might best be used to find answers.

Activities

1. Attempt to carry out each of the methods of data gathering found in this chapter. Which was the most time consuming? Which gave you the widest variety of data or the narrowest?
2. Find, evaluate, and contrast three criterion-referenced tests. What justification would you give for selecting each? Give one of these tests to three young children. What have you learned after the application? What other information, not provided by the test, would you like to have about these children?

References

Bentzen, W. R., *Seeing Young Children: A Guide to Observing and Recording Behavior.* Albany, N.Y.: Delmar Publishers, 1985.

Carbonara, N. T., *Techniques for Observing Normal Child Behavior.* Pittsburgh: University of Pittsburgh Press, 1982.

Sanford, A. R., & J. G. Zelman, *LAP: The Learning Accomplishment Profile* (rev. ed.). Winston-Salem, N.C.: Kaplan Press, 1981.

Spivack, G., & J. Spotts, *Devereux Child Behavior (DCB) Rating Scale.* Devon, Pa.: Devereux Foundation, 1966.

Willoughby-Herb, S. J., & J. T. Neisworth, *HICOMP Preschool Curriculum.* Columbus, Ohio: Charles E. Merrill, 1983.

Index

Acting or physical intervention, as behavior
   on TBC, 167
Adams, M. J., 126, 140
Adcock, D., 18, 27
Adjustment Behavioral Profile, 247–249
Aggression, 169–171
   channeling, 170
   verbal, 176
Alberti, R. E., 178, 225, 227
Anecdotal records, 237–239
Anti-bias environments, 35
Arrivals, 180
Assessment of learning, 230–253
   anecdotal records, 237–239
   criterion-referenced tests, 250–252
   diaries, 236–237
   rating scales, 241–250
   specimen observations, 235–236
   student learning, 134
   time samplings, 239–241
Associative, social stage, 65
Associative play, 23

Babysitting list, 217
Bank Street Model, 1–2, 62
Barbour, C., 211, 227
Barbour, N., 211, 227
Bathroom talk, 176
Beams, balance, 148–149
Behavior, emitted, 115
Behavior analysis, 115
Behavior Analysis Model, 2–4

Behavior rehearsal, 127–130
Beliefs about Teaching Inventory, 8–10
Bentzen, W. R., 235, 253
Bereiter, C., 24, 27, 198, 200
Bereriter-Englemann Model, 2–4
Berne, E., 227
Biber, B., 1, 7, 24, 62–63, 82
Biting, 170
Block area and microsymbolic play, 58–59
Blocks, large, 150–151
Bloom, B., 119, 125, 140
Book exchange, 214
Brainerd, C. J., 24, 27
Breakfasts for parents, 215
Brearley, M., 32, 61, 91, 113
Bredekamp, S., 7, 140
Briggs, C., 113
British Informal Model, 2–3
Brody, J., 24, 28
Burns, S. M., 24, 27

Canter, L., 178, 190, 200, 227
Canter, M., 178, 200
Carbonara, N. T., 233, 253
Carnine, D., 7, 126, 141
Cassel, P., 165, 179, 223, 227
Catching, motor patterns of, 15–16
Cazden, C. B., 113
Centeredness, 31
Chall, J., 2–3, 126, 141
Chard, S. C., 2–3, 7
Cherry, C., 216, 227